Tenerife
& La Gomera

DIRECTIONS

WRITTEN AND RESEARCHED BY
Christian Williams

D0388292

ROUGH GUIDES

NEW YORK • LONDON • DELHI
www.roughguides.com

When to visit

The climate across the Canary Islands is mild year-round, with relatively minimal seasonal change. High season is during the European winter, and places get especially busy from mid-December to February, when temperatures hover around 20°C. The islands are also popular at Easter and during summer holidays (June–Sept) when temperatures can get up to 30°C. A low season of sorts exists between these times, with the notable exception of the carnival period (Feb or March), when Santa Cruz is at its busiest.

Tenerife first became a holiday destination over a century ago when the fashionable European aristocracy began to winter here. Since then, and particularly since the birth of **mass-tourism** in the 1960s, holidaymaker numbers have shot up. Traditionally most of these visits were based around low-budget, sun-sea-sand package deals; but in recent years, there's been a local drive to re-brand the island – by promoting watersports, rural tourism and golf – to improve the island's niche appeal and attract smaller numbers of higher-spending visitors.

It is away from the coast that Tenerife is at its most surprising and a quick foray inland unveils a beautiful and fascinating natural world which makes the island a hiker's delight. For its size, the island has a startling range and number of distinct ecological zones that arise from its mountainous topography – which includes the gigantic and barren volcano Mount Teide at its centre. These upland areas

▲ Hiking, Tenerife

block prevailing winds making northern Tenerife damper and greener, while the southern side of the island is left to bake in the sun. Consequently, most of Tenerife's population lives and works in the north, while the bulk of the island's sun-seeking holiday industry is in the south. Undeterred by the near-desert conditions and encouraged by the presence of holidaymakers, it's in the south where most of the island's golf courses are scattered: verdant oases in parched brown lands to which golfers flock year-round.

Aside from providing a backdrop for all sorts of outdoor activities, Tenerife is a worthwhile destination for a spot of sightseeing due to its unique history and culture.

◀ Harbour, Vueltas

Identity and society today

After years of Spanish colonial rule, the Canaries became an **autono-mous region** in 1982. Since then the islands have fostered an introverted nationalist politics and a culture of resistance to intervention from the greater political entity; many islanders push for still greater **indepen-dence** from Madrid.

Yet while the rift between the Spanish mainland and the Canaries might be widening, the islands' links with the rest of Europe are strengthening. This is partly due to the fact that their economy is dependent on European tourists, and partly related to the rapid increase in the number of northern Europeans settling here. Since the Canary Islands **joined the EU** in 1992 the numbers of permanent European residents have steadily increased. Today, around 30,000 or four percent of Tenerife's total population are expatriate foreigners. The numbers in La Gomera are much smaller, but the proportions much the same.

On both islands these patterns, together with the booming tourist trade, have significantly changed the cultural milieu, adding new dimensions to an already diverse society.

The island's original inhabitants, the Guanche, left pyramids and mummies as an enduring legacy. Later, as a stop on the American and African shipping routes, it developed a cosmopolitan culture of fusion still apparent in the Genoese merchant villas, which incorporate North African carvings on their ornate balconies.

While Tenerife has many peaceful areas, those wanting to really get away from it all should head to the strikingly precipitous and thinly populated island of La Gomera a 28km ferry-ride away. A hippy retreat since the 1960s, the island's lack of major beaches and resorts has preserved a sense of remoteness and left the laid-back rural tranquillity fully intact. The likeable and very manageable island capital San Sebastián offers the chance to briefly integrate yourself into what is still a tightly-knit community; the main resort town Valle Gran Rey has a snazzy selection of bars and restaurants; and a day's car hire enables exploration of the lush laurel jungle at the centre of the island.

▼ Mount Teide

Tenerife & La Gomera
AT A GLANCE

SANTA CRUZ, LA LAGUNA AND THE ANAGA

Tenerife's present and former capitals offer the chance to experience traditional architecture, local cuisine, fine beaches, lively nightlife and one of the world's biggest carnivals. This dense urban area's backyard is the remote and wildly rugged Anaga region – perfect for day-trips and hiking.

▲ The Teno massif

◀ Old town, La Laguna

THE WEST COAST AND THE TENO

Tenerife's West Coast boasts a string of tourists resorts. Most remain a modest size and all have good access to the Teno massif, an area known for its giant sea-cliffs Los Gigantes. This area is packed with great hiking.

PUERTO DE LA CRUZ AND LA OROTAVA

Puerto offers a more genteel alternative to the southern resorts. Close by, in the island's most fertile valley, La Orotava's former wealth as an agricultural centre is evidenced by its grand houses.

▲ Lago de Martiánez, Puerto de la Cruz

PLAYA DE LAS AMÉRICAS, LOS CRISTIANOS AND THE COSTA ADEJE

A gigantic holiday city built on the sunniest part of Tenerife, with the island's major beaches. This is where you'll find the hedonistic playgrounds the island is famed for.

▲ Canarian Pine Forest

▲ Strolling the promenade, Los Cristianos

MOUNT TEIDE AND THE INTERIOR

The 3718-metre-high volcano Mount Teide is the symbol of Tenerife. Standing in a national park at the centre of a vast, treeless volcanic wasteland, it's encircled by damp and often misty Canarian pine forest. This otherworldly national park was used as a backdrop in *Star Wars*.

SOUTHERN TENERIFE

The resorts of Southern Tenerife are similar to the Las Américas area, but with far less going on – unless you are a golfer or windsurfer: it's the Golf Del Sur and El Médano respectively that attract members of the two groups in their hundreds.

▲ Costa Silencio, Southern Tenerife

SAN SEBASTIÁN AND VALLE GRAN REY

La Gomera's two most notable settlements offer attractive bases for a low-key holiday. While the beaches are modest, the quality and variety of restaurants, particularly in Valle Gran Rey, is very good.

▲ San Sebastián, La Gomera

NORTHERN LA GOMERA

Cool and damp northern La Gomera is better suited to banana plantations than tourist resorts, with slow-paced rural villages remaining relatively untouched. The area's highlight is the Parque Nacional de Garajonay, a UNESCO World Heritage Site containing the world's premier laurel forest.

◄ Laurel Forest, Garajonay

Ideas

The big six

With their dependably warm, sunny climate no stay on Tenerife or La Gomera would be complete without a day on the beach, followed by an evening eating freshly caught fish by the sea. But it's also well worth seeking out the interiors of the islands. A foray into the national parks will reveal extraordinary landscapes, spanning primeval forest to desolate volcanic moonscape. The cultural heritage of the islands is no less intriguing. Back on the coast, boat trips to see whales and dolphins are a real highlight.

▲ Tan on a beach

Unwind, soak up some rays, read a book and go for a paddle.

P.110 ▶ LOS CRISTIANOS, LAS AMÉRICAS AND COSTA ADEJE

▲ Whale and dolphin watching

The channel between Tenerife and La Gomera is populated by several species – pilot whales being the most common.

P.114 ▶ LOS CRISTIANOS, LAS AMÉRICAS AND COSTA ADEJE

▶ Pirámides de Güímar

The pyramids present an enigmatic snapshot of ancient history and are the most significant relic of the indigenous Guanche society.

P.75 ▸ CANDELARIA AND GÜÍMAR

◀ Laurel Forest, Garajonay

Enter an ancient, overgrown ecosystem where laurels and mosses thrive.

P.163 ▸ NORTHERN LA GOMERA

▼ Visit Parque Nacional del Teide

Dramatic lunar landscapes and Spain's highest peak make a visit to this national park a must.

P.133 ▸ MOUNT TEIDE AND THE INTERIOR

▼ Eat seafood

Pick whichever freshly-caught fish takes your fancy in the restaurants of the south coast, an area famous for its excellent seafood.

P.125 ▸ THE SOUTH COAST

Cafés and bars

Tenerife and La Gomera have a lively café and bar culture. Food and alcohol are served in both; though generally cafés specialize in cakes and sandwiches, while bars – also called *tascas*, *bodegas*, *cervecerías* and *tabernas* – have a greater range of alcoholic drinks and tapas. *Areperas* serve South American *arepas* – deep-fried pockets of cornmeal dough stuffed with chicken, cheese or ham.

▲ Cacatua

An institution in Valle Gran Rey, this airy bar has a tropical feel and great cocktails.

P.162 ▸ VALLE GRAN REY

▼ Harry's Bar

Laid-back bar, with live music and a luxuriant African theme.

P.123 ▸ LOS CRISTIANOS, LAS AMÉRICAS AND COSTA ADEJE

▼ Natural Burguer

Popular with students, this burger bar has a wide range of tasty options at budget prices.

P.67 ▸ LA LAGUNA

▼ Mojos y Mojitos

Trendy bar in relaxed La Noria, Santa Cruz's most fashionable strip of tapas bars, eateries and late-night bars.

P.61 ▸ SANTA CRUZ

▲ La Casa Vieja

Basic tapas in a no-frills bar on one of the backstreets of La Gomera's capital.

P.152 ▸ SAN SEBASTIÁN

▶ Flashpoint

Favoured by windsurfers, this place has a patio overlooking the beach and a laid-back atmosphere.

P.131 ▸ THE SOUTH COAST

Views

Great **views** are easy to come by on Tenerife and La Gomera. The natural diversity of the islands makes for stunning panoramas, from towering **sea cliffs** rising hundreds of metres above the waves, to **leafy valleys** containing the last remnants of ancient forests. The human settlement of the land, meanwhile, has left a number of well-preserved, **picturesque towns** and villages, providing visitors with plenty of photo opportunities.

▲ Parque Nacional de Garajonay

Occasionally the canopy of this soothingly damp primeval forest parts to reveal views of La Gomera's craggy interior and Mount Teide.

P.163 ▶ NORTHERN LA GOMERA

▼ San Sebastián

A steep climb up to the Parador, or a drive up the road to Playa Santiago is rewarded with views over the town with its long sandy beach and sparkling marina.

P.144 ▶ SAN SEBASTIÁN

▼ Teide from Guajara

The trek to Tenerife's second highest point is rewarded with the best possible views of Mount Teide, as well as sweeping vistas over the southern coast.

P.133 ▸ MOUNT TEIDE AND THE INTERIOR

◀ Acantilados de Los Gigantes

Best appreciated from the ocean, these lava-formed cliffs stand hundreds of metres above the water.

P.104 ▸ THE WEST COAST

▲ La Orotava's rooftops

La Orotava's steep slopes allow wonderful views across the town's sixteenth-century rooftops.

P.89 ▸ LA OROTAVA

◀ Garachico

Head up to the Mirador de Garachico viewpoint for a perfect view of this attractive old town.

P.93 ▸ GARACHICO

Nightlife

Only after midnight does Tenerife's **nightlife** really start. Playa Las Américas is the obvious place to go for a night out, but many of the best places are a little off the beaten track where you'll find more local colour and a cheerful, relaxed atmosphere. Some bars even offer a show or live music to kick start the night. The **student scene** in La Laguna is particularly welcoming and even in sleepy La Gomera you can sometimes party all night.

▼ Bobby's

If you can't beat them join them – premier club to round off a late night with hundreds of other holidaymakers on the Las Veronicas strip.

P.123 ▶ LOS CRISTIANOS, LAS AMÉRICAS AND COSTA ADEJE

▲ El Buho

One of La Laguna's premier live music venues, which attracts a studenty crowd to its rock gigs.

P.68 ▶ LA LAGUNA

▼ Castillo del Mar

Check your lunar calendar, the unmissable full-moon parties here go on until dawn; there's also live music every weekend.

P.169, 171 ▶ NORTHERN LA GOMERA

▲ Tropicana

Cuban dance show followed by Latin-style partying into the early hours.

P.124 ▶ LOS CRISTIANOS, LAS AMÉRICAS AND COSTA ADEJE

▶ Casino Taoro

Try your luck at the slots and tables of the island's oldest hotel.

P.82 ▶ PUERTO DE LA CRUZ

▼ Jazzissimo

Slick club with great live blues, soul and jazz nightly.

P.123 ▶ LOS CRISTIANOS, LAS AMÉRICAS AND COSTA ADEJE

Beaches

Tenerife and La Gomera have few natural beaches along their **rocky coastlines**, but to satisfy the tourist appetite, a few have been made on Tenerife using **imported sand** from the Sahara. The beaches of the popular **southern resorts**, Las Américas and Los Cristianos, tend to be crowded affairs offering various watersports, though quieter, more secluded options are easy to find across both islands. Where offered, hiring a sun-lounger and parasol costs around €9 per day, but you're always welcome to bring your own.

▼ Playa de las Vistas

This huge sweep of sand between Los Cristianos and Las Américas is the best in the area and rarely overcrowded.

P.110 ▸ LOS CRISTIANOS, LAS AMÉRICAS AND COSTA ADEJE

▼ Playa de las Teresitas

Northeast of Santa Cruz, this is the best sand beach on the island – and surprisingly quiet outside summer weekends.

P.69 ▸ THE ANAGA

▲ Playa Bollullo

Idyllic beach at the base of some cliffs, an enjoyable half-day hike from Puerto de la Cruz.

P.84 ▶ PUERTO DE LA CRUZ

◀ Playa Jardin

Puerto's main beach is rarely crowded and the promenade running alongside is lined with cafés and bars.

P.82 ▶ PUERTO DE LA CRUZ

▶ Playa Fañabé

Touristy but decent beach, with plenty of bars and restaurants nearby.

P.116 ▶ LOS CRISTIANOS, LAS AMÉRICAS AND COSTA ADEJE

▼ El Médano

Easily the best natural beach on Tenerife, though strong winds sometimes make a windbreak a necessity.

P.128 ▶ THE SOUTH COAST

Restaurants

Most traditional Canarian restaurants serve simple meals at moderate prices and are broadly divided into those by the coast offering mainly **fish** and **seafood**, and inland establishments that tend to specialize in **meat** dishes. Alongside these, good-quality Italian food is ubiquitous, and you can also find Lebanese, French, Swiss, German and South American restaurants. **Opening hours** are generally 1–4pm & 8pm–midnight. In reviews we've listed opening hours only for establishments with unusual hours.

▲ **La Rosa di Bari**

Highly recommended place with wonderful Italian food, elegant surroundings and cheerfully attentive service.

P.88 ▶ PUERTO DE LA CRUZ

▲ **Pizzería Rugantino**

Simple restaurant, fabulous pizzas.

P.98 ▶ GARACHICO

▶ Restaurante Pirámide

Lively opera nights, superb food and unobtrusive service make this a great place for a splurge.

P.122 ▶ LOS CRISTIANOS, LAS AMÉRICAS AND COSTA ADEJE

▶ Sangré de Toro

Iberian food and culture is faithfully reproduced here, right down to the bull-fighting theme and nightly flamenco shows.

P.122 ▶ LOS CRISTIANOS, LAS AMÉRICAS AND COSTA ADEJE

▲ Slow boat Teppanyaki

Trendy Asian-fusion cookery, minimalist decor and impeccable service.

P.122 ▶ LOS CRISTIANOS, LAS AMÉRICAS AND COSTA ADEJE

▶ Mirador de Palmaerjo

Unless you're a vertigo sufferer the views that crash down from this gourmet restaurant might just outdo its exquisite food.

P.161 ▶ VALLE GRAN REY

Crafts and souvenirs

In town centres and villages, **handicraft** stores and small-time retailers dominate proceedings and **craftsmanship** and personal **service** is still as important as ever. Here you'll find **traditional souvenirs** like wooden carvings, basketware, pottery, embroidery and lacework, cigars and novelty liqueurs. Also worth looking out for is honey taken from hives around Teide, the islands' goats cheeses and *mojo* (see p.28), the favourite local dip.

▲ Lace

Two traditions of fine lace-making are practised in Tenerife – techniques in La Orotava use a wooden frame while elsewhere small rosettes are sewn together to form larger pieces.

P.91 ▸ LA OROTAVA

▼ Pot making, Las Hayas, La Gomera

Traditional hardwearing pots, produced by hand in La Gomera's uplands from a single lump of clay as they have been since Pre-Hispanic times.

P.169 ▸ NORTHERN LA GOMERA

CASA LOS BALCONES LA OROTAVA TENERIFE

▶ Zapatería Taller de Artesanía

Treat yourself to a pair of hand- and tailor-made sandals or shoes crafted in a time-honoured fashion.

`P.160` ▶ VALLE GRAN REY

▲ Wines

Tenerife has a decent range of dry white wines. Look out for *Viña Norte*, characterised by its fruity flavour, and wines from El Sauzal such as the *Viñatigo*, known for their crisp freshness.

`P.78` ▶ PUERTO DE LA CRUZ

▶ Tabacos Arturo

Handmade Cuban quality cigars at less expensive prices, making it easy to see why Canarian cigars were Winston Churchill's favourites.

`P.97` ▶ GARACHICO

◀ Religious Curios

Quench even the most insatiable thirst for kitsch in Candelaria where every imaginable saint and idol is available for purchase: large or small and made from gaudy plastic.

`P.74` ▶ CANDELARIA AND GÜIMAR

Watersports

Watersports are a favourite pastime for both locals and holidaymakers alike on Tenerife. As you'd expect from an island with reliably good weather, there are plenty of options to suit every pocket and interest. Reliable offshore winds fuel a vibrant sailing, windsurfing and surfing scene, while the calmer waters of sheltered bays encourage divers and snorkellers to explore the impressive underwater geology. Bear in mind though that water temperatures tend to be cool year-round, so wetsuits are the norm.

▲ **Sailing**

Follow in the wake of Colombus, with a sailing trip in the La Gomeran Channel.

P.179 ▸ ESSENTIALS

▲ **Jetskiing**

For a bit of high-speed water fun, the Costa Adeje is the place to try your hand at jetskiing.

P.115 ▸ LOS CRISTIANOS, LAS AMÉRICAS AND COSTA ADEJE

◀ Surfing

Tenerife attracts surfers and bodyboarders keen to test their skills against the large Atlantic rollers. Beginners are best starting out in Las Américas.

P.178 ▸
ESSENTIALS

▲ Snorkelling

Sheltered bays suitable for snorkelling can be found in many places on both Tenerife and La Gomera.

P.178 ▸ ESSENTIALS

▲ Windsurfing and kitesurfing

The coast around El Médano is internationally renowned for its excellent conditions, bringing international competitions here regularly.

P.125 ▸ THE SOUTH COAST

▼ Diving

Good visibility, plenty of fish and a few wrecks make the coastal waters of Tenerife and La Gomera an excellent choice for experienced divers. Novices can take courses.

P.178 ▸ ESSENTIALS

Art and architecture

Tenerife's capital is a cultured place. The **performing arts** thrive, streets and parks are dotted with sculptures and its **contemporary architecture** – particularly the opera house – is truly arresting. For **traditional architecture** stop by the old towns of La Laguna, La Orotava and Garachico, where the trademark carved balconies are at their most exquisite. But if it's modern, outlandish architectural landmarks you're after, head to the resort areas for the likes of Mare Nostrum in Las Américas.

▼ Teatro Guimerá

Traditional performing arts venue with a good, mixed programme.

P.63 ▸ SANTA CRUZ

▼ Modern art sculptures

Modern art fans can blaze a sculpture trail along the Rambla General Franco and adjacent parks.

P.57 ▸ SANTA CRUZ

▲ Doce Casas

View the beautiful mansions of the merchants who grew rich trading the bountiful harvests of La Orotava valley in the seventeenth and eighteenth centuries.

P.89 ▸ LA OROTAVA

▼ Mare Nostrum

This huge holiday complex's extravagant architecture makes it Las Américas' most eye-catching sight.

P.110 ▸ LOS CRISTIANOS, LAS AMÉRICAS AND COSTA ADEJE

◀ Museo de Bellas Artes

Tenerife's main art gallery has a small permanent collection of coins and sculptures and also attracts an interesting range of temporary exhibitions.

P.53 ▸ SANTA CRUZ

▼ Auditorio Tenerife

Santa Cruz's opera house and most elegant landmark has equally impressive acoustics, making it a great venue for all kinds of performances.

P.58 ▸ SANTA CRUZ

Food and drink

Fresh fish and seafood provide one of the culinary highlights of a visit to Tenerife and La Gomera. **Paellas** using the local catch are common on the islands, as is the traditional Canarian **fish stew**, *zarzuela*. Specialities of the interior include the rich *conejo en salmorejo* – marinated rabbit in a garlicky sauce.

Both fish and meat are generally grilled and served with **papas arrugadas**, a typical Canarian potato dish, and the presence of **mojo** can be virtually guaranteed. To wash it all down, there's a good range of Canarian wines and beers.

▲ **Liqueurs**
Island liqueurs based on local produce like bananas or honey are served in bars and restaurants everywhere – often lacing a coffee.
P.78 ▸ PUERTO DE LA CRUZ

▲ **Mojo**
This garlic dip comes in two varieties: spicy *rojo* (red), made with chillies; or milder *verde* (green), made with coriander. To many Canarians the quality of its *mojo* is the measure of a restaurant.
P.170 ▸ LA LAGUNA GRANDE

▶ Gofio and potaje de berros

A finely ground mixture of roasted wheat, maize or barley, this Canarian staple is regularly offered alongside soups such as *potaje de berros* (watercress soup).

▼ Dorada

Refreshing and ubiquitous Tenerife lager, downed by the gallon in Las Américas.

▼ Papas arrugadas

A speciality of the Canary Islands, these unpeeled new potatoes, boiled dry in salt water, are a delicious accompaniment to fresh seafood.

▼ Casa del Vino La Baranda

For an introduction to Tenerife's long-standing wine industry head to this informative museum, where there's the chance for a bit of sampling too.

Sports and activities

Both Tenerife and La Gomera have a wide range of options for an **active holiday**. On land golf and cycling are popular, as is hiking (see p.38); while the coast sees fishing and swimming occur alongside the many possible watersports (see p.24). Happily all activities are possible year-round and after a few days of any of them it's worth taking time out to visit one of the islands' good **spas**.

▲ Cycling

With roads and tracks crisscrossing Tenerife, there's plenty of scope for exploring the island by bike. The steep climbs on La Gomera make them the preserve of the very fit.

P.180 ▸ ESSENTIALS

▲ Fishing

You don't need a permit to join the locals in one of their favourite pastimes.

P.179 ▸ ESSENTIALS

▶ Swimming in seawater pools

On the frequent occasions that the sea is too blustery, seawater pools are a dependable and attractive bathing choice.

P.167 ▶ NORTHERN LA GOMERA

◀ Golf

Tenerife is ideal for a winter golf fix with more than half a dozen established and well-maintained courses.

P.180 ▶ ESSENTIALS

▲ A spa treatment at the Mare Nostrum

Indulge yourself with a range of beauty treatments; a day of pampering costs €90, including use of pool, saunas and gym.

P.118 ▶ LOS CRISTIANOS, LAS AMÉRICAS AND COSTA ADEJE

▼ Karting

Budding Schumachers can test their road skills at this Karting centre.

P.181 ▶ ESSENTIALS

Churches

The churches of Tenerife and La Gomera are generally simple affairs. Their most distinctive touch is the blending of eastern and western styles, with traditional Early Modern Spanish church architecture complemented by Islamic-influenced *Mudéjar* ceilings. Churches with no fixed opening times generally open an hour before the generally well-attended masses when you're welcome to have a look inside as long as you're discreet. Church interiors are relatively stark, though in almost all the altar is a feast of kitsch adornment, often with a locally important relic at their centre.

▲ Iglesia de Nuestra Señora de la Peña Francia, Puerto de la Cruz

Puerto de la Cruz's seventeenth-century church is beside pretty gardens with a good-sized dragon tree.

P.79 ▸ PUERTO DE LA CRUZ

▲ Santa Iglesia Catedral

Imposing Baroque and Gothic cathedral, situated in Tenerife's original capital.

P.64 ▸ LA LAGUNA

▼ Iglesia de Nuestra Señora de la Concepción

Santa Cruz's main church displays pieces of the cross planted by Tenerife's Spanish conquerors.

P.53 ▸ SANTA CRUZ

▲ Iglesia de la Virgin de la Candelaria, Chipude

Simple church with many Moorish touches, in the shadow of Mount Fortaleza.

P.168 ▸ NORTHERN LA GOMERA

▶ Iglesia de la Concepción

Tenerife's oldest church has a fine coffered ceiling and historic baptism font.

P.66 ▸ LA LAGUNA

Natural wonders

A turbulent geological history and unique evolutionary paths have furnished both Tenerife and La Gomera with a multitude of unique and eye-catching natural wonders. The ancient **Dragon Tree** is among the oldest living things in the world; no less spectacular are the **plants** in Tenerife's national park, particularly the *Tajinaste rojo*. In geological terms, the volcanic **landscape** of the park is jaw-dropping, and the effects reach all the way down to the coast. **Wind** is another major force of nature on the island as windfarms on Tenerife's southern coast attest.

▲ Garachico's rock pools

Swim and snorkel amid the tongues of lava that closed off Garachico's port in a series of seawater pools.

P.93 ▸ GARACHICO

▼ Paisaje Lunar

This extraordinary lunar landscape in the midst of majestic Canarian pine forest has some great trails running through it.

P.136 ▸ MOUNT TEIDE AND THE INTERIOR

▲ Tajinaste rojo

These gigantic endemic plants add a blaze of colour to the otherwise brown and beige footslopes of Mount Teide.

P.133 ▸ MOUNT TEIDE AND THE INTERIOR

◀ Parque Eólico, El Médano

A windfarm-cum-visitor centre that dominates the south coast and offers an insight into renewable energy.

P.129 ▸ THE SOUTH COAST

▼ Los Roques de García and Mount Teide

A mesmerizing outcrop of warped rock, rising up from an otherwise flat plain in the shadow of Mount Teide.

P.137 ▸ MOUNT TEIDE AND THE INTERIOR

▲ Dragon Tree, Icod de Los Viños

Guanche elders once held meetings under this proud old tree – the largest of its kind – but now it's visitors who flock here.

P.96 ▸ GARACHICO

Kids' Tenerife

A family holiday destination for over fifty years, Tenerife has risen to the challenge of catering for kids. All the **resorts** are child-friendly and many **commercial ventures** offer entertainment.

Aside from the man-made attractions, there are also many natural ones – rock pools, beaches, mountains and forests – which can be just as much fun, if not more.

▲ Parques Exóticas

Children love being able to get into the enclosures with the birds and animals at this hands-on zoo.

P.116 ▸ LOS CRISTIANOS, LAS AMÉRICAS AND COSTA ADEJE

▶ Aqualand

Big, lively water park with slides and dolphin shows.

P.114 ▸ LOS CRISTIANOS, LAS AMÉRICAS AND COSTA ADEJE

◀ Pueblo Chico

Tenerife as a miniature toy town is sure to delight kids who've already done some sight-seeing around the island.

P.83 ▸ PUERTO DE LA CRUZ

▲ Loro Parque

The shows involving parrots, seals and dolphins at this Puerto de la Cruz zoo are guaranteed to entertain.

P.82 ▸ PUERTO DE LA CRUZ

▶ Parque Las Águilas

Top southern Tenerife attraction where if the kids get bored of the zoo and its lush vegetation, they can tire themselves out on the assault course.

P.117 ▸ LOS CRISTIANOS, LAS AMÉRICAS AND COSTA ADEJE

Hiking

With incredibly varied terrain, impressive landscapes and unique ecologies, Tenerife and La Gomera make great year-round **hiking** destinations. On **Tenerife**, the Parque Nacional del Teide is the obvious place to head, though well-marked hikes also include the rugged Anaga and Teno regions and the densely forested Orotava Valley. **La Gomera's** most enticing areas are among the ancient laurel forest of the Parque Nacional de Garajonay but, again, you can find first-class hiking along almost any of the island's steep-sided gorges. The times given for hikes indicate the difficulty of terrain that distances can't convey.

▲ Anaga

Rugged and undeveloped, the Anaga region is the serious hiker's idea of heaven.

P.69 ▸ THE ANAGA

▲ Guajara

Tenerife's best day hike for the fit; the climb up the island's second highest peak delivers some of the best views of the national park and the south.

P.138 ▸ MOUNT TEIDE AND THE INTERIOR

▲ La Catedral

A hike around Los Roques de García allows a closer look at the weird rock formations in this area, including La Catedral.

P.138 ▶ MOUNT TEIDE AND THE INTERIOR

▲ Hermigua

La Gomera's most verdant valley, Hermigua is an ideal day hike from deep forests of the island's national park.

P.165 ▶ NORTHERN LA GOMERA

▼ Barranco de Masca

Hiking and scrambling down this gorge is a unique and awe-inspiring experience – but strictly for the fit.

P.101 ▶ THE TENO

◀ Garajonay

Hiking up La Gomera's highest mountain takes you through ancient laurel trees and offers views over four neighbouring islands.

P.163 ▶ NORTHERN LA GOMERA

Festivals

A look at the islands' **festival calendar**, with over three hundred annual entries, shows that Canarians are more than partial to a party. Most festivals are of **Catholic** origin and the biggest shindig is undoubtedly the **Carnival**, in February or March. But you can take your pick from the many major and minor festivities throughout the year as most are worth planning your holiday around. Often, festivals see locals, particularly performers, donning **folk costumes** – women in striped skirts, embroidered lace tops and headscarves; men in linen shirts, red vests and knee-length trousers wrapped with a cummerbund.

▲ Fiesta del Vino

Rowdy and extraordinarily noisy celebration of the wine harvest, in which daredevil sled riders take to the steep streets of Icod.

P.93 ▸ GARACHICO

▼ Carnival

Europe's biggest and liveliest carnival celebrations begin in Santa Cruz before continuing across Tenerife.

P.183 ▸ SANTA CRUZ

◀ Fiesta de San Juan

Odd and good-humoured festival in which unwilling livestock is ceremonially dunked in the sea in the harbour of Puerto de la Cruz.

P.78 ▶ PUERTO DE LA CRUZ

▼ Romería

Several towns organize a late summer harvest festival or *romería*, Garachico's is the most extravagant.

P.93 ▶ GARACHICO

▼ Corpus Christi

This religious festival has become famous for the extraordinarily intricate floral carpets that cover the old town streets of La Orotava.

P.89 ▶ LA OROTAVA

▲ Fiesta Virgen de la Candelaria

A day of pilgrimage to Tenerife's holiest spot; the most die-hard pilgrims walk here from all around the island.

P.74 ▶ CANDELARIA AND GÜÍMAR

Shopping

Low sales tax makes Tenerife and La Gomera something of a **shopper's paradise** with hundreds of small outlets in the resorts selling everything from jewellery and perfume to electrical gadgetry, not to mention the huge **malls** stationed at the edge of the main towns. These malls attract Canarian shopaholics in their droves, so are often where the largest and best-value selections of designer clothing are found. **Opening hours** in the resorts and larger towns are typically daily 8am to 8pm; the rest of the islands keep more restricted hours (usually Mon–Sat 9am–1pm & 4–8pm).

▲ Los Cristianos

The pedestrian core of Los Cristianos has an array of outlets selling the kind of luxury goods that airport shops usually specialise in.

P.110 › LOS CRISTIANOS, LAS AMÉRICAS AND COSTA ADEJE

▼ Calle del Castillo

Tenerife's Oxford Street is pedestrianized and packed with clothing boutiques and electrical shops.

P.53 › SANTA CRUZ

▲ El Corte Inglés

Tenerife's biggest department store has more than enough to give shopaholics their fix.

P.60 ▸ SANTA CRUZ

◄ Flea Market, Santa Cruz

For unusual souvenirs, head for the flea market held outside Santa Cruz's Mercado de Nuestra Señora de África on Sunday mornings.

P.60 ▸ SANTA CRUZ

▼ Mercado de Nuestra Señora de África

Santa Cruz's bustling, Moorish-style covered market sells mostly groceries and is a great place to pick up inexpensive local produce, particularly cheeses.

P.60 ▸ SANTA CRUZ

History and culture

Developing in the shadow of mainland Spain and as a vital transatlantic crossroads, **Canarian culture** has been shaped by various European and Latin American influences and its history has been interesting and varied.

Furthermore, evidence of the islands' pre-Hispanic history also remains, providing a window into the **native Guanche culture**. A trip to the pyramids (see p.75), and the statues of native kings in the town of Candelaria is more than worthwhile, and Guanche history figures largely in Tenerife's museums – Santa Cruz's Museo de la Naturaleza y el Hombre shouldn't be missed.

▲ Basilica de Nuestra Señora de Candelaria

Grand church housing a statue of the Virgin Mary that was once a Guanche idol and is now the holiest relic in the Canaries.

P.74 ▸ CANDELARIA AND GÜÍMAR

▲ Museo de la Naturaleza y el Hombre

The place to head for an overview of Tenerife's natural and aboriginal history. The Guanches are well covered and there's the chance to view some of their mummified remains.

P.56 ▸ SANTA CRUZ

MUSEO
DE HISTORIA
DE TENERIFE

▲ Museo de la Historia de Tenerife

The place to head for an overview of Tenerife's history, with well presented displays on the Guanches particularly worth a look.

P.64 ▸ LA LAGUNA

▶ Guanches

The line of statues on Candelaria's main plaza give a vivid artist's impression of the various Guanche kings that ignites the imagination.

P.75 ▸ CANDELARIA AND GÜÍMAR

▼ Museo Militar

Hundreds of military exhibits, enlivened by interesting insights into Nelson's failed attack on Santa Cruz.

P.56 ▸ SANTA CRUZ

Rural bliss

An island best known for package tours might seem an odd choice for a **rural getaway**, but Tenerife has many hidden-away spots, well off the beaten track, where it's easy to find peace and quiet and enjoy modest natural treasures such as wild flowers and the sight of scampering lizards. And with sun, sea, warm temperatures and few insects it's easy to relax undisturbed. The forests at the centre of both Tenerife and La Gomera are particularly atmospheric destinations which, thanks to the presence of some *Casas Rurales* – or rural holiday cottages – and a campsite, are ideal places for an extended stay, not just a pleasant hike.

▲ Camping

The best of Tenerife and La Gomera's very few campsites is set amid the lush greenery of Garajonay's National Park.

P.163 ▶ NORTHERN LA GOMERA

▲ Wildlife

While big beasts are notably absent from the islands' wild areas there's a multitude of different lizards and birds for the attentive to spot.

P.133 ▶ MOUNT TEIDE AND THE INTERIOR

▶ Canarian Pine forest

Suck in the cool, fresh air and marvel at the unique Canarian pine trees in this atmospheric forest.

▼ Wild flowers

May and June are excellent months to visit, when wildflowers, including orchids, add a splash of colour to many hillsides, particularly in the damper areas of La Gomera.

▼ Casas Rurales

These "rural houses" in isolated locations are the perfect hideaway for those seeking solitude amid natural beauty.

▼ Hermigua

The pace is slow in this verdant Gomeran valley, and banana trees far outnumber houses or people.

Hotels and pensions

Surprisingly, for an island that traditionally caters to package tourists, Tenerife has a good stock of **luxurious hotels** and **quirky pensions** for the independent traveller. These are generally outside the modern resort complexes, and often their location in less heavily trodden parts of the island is a boon in itself. But even if you'd rather have the practical convenience of a location within one of the larger resorts you are not without good choices; you may not find much historic charm, but there's plenty of interesting flamboyance, particularly among the themed places like the Mare Nostrum.

▲ Hotel San Roque

Quiet luxury hotel with understated flair tucked away on a backstreet of this stylish old town.

P.96 ▸ GARACHICO

▼ Hotel Mencey

Stylish, elegant accommodation in Tenerife's capital with everything you'd expect from one of the island's best hotels.

P.58 ▸ SANTA CRUZ

▶ Mare Nostrum

If you want to embrace the practical simplicity of an accommodation package, the vast number of choices, facilities, services and location make the Mare Nostrum resort hard to beat.

P.118 ▶ LOS CRISTIANOS, LAS AMÉRICAS AND COSTA ADEJE

◀ Los Geranios, Puerto de la Cruz

Spotless and friendly family-run pension in the quiet pedestrianized old fishing quarter close to the centre of town.

P.86 ▶ PUERTO DEL LA CRUZ

▼ Pension Alcala

Off-beat pension run by South American owners which helps foster a real travellers' vibe in its much-graffitied bar.

P.107 ▶ THE WEST COAST

◀ Parador Nacionál de Cañadas del Teide

Treat yourself and your beloved to this luxury hotel, with its stunning backdrop of the national park and Mount Teide.

P.142 ▶ MOUNT TEIDE AND THE INTERIOR

Places

Santa Cruz

The dynamic city of **Santa Cruz** is where the Spanish conquest of Tenerife began – it was here that Alfonso de Lugo planted his holy cross in 1494 before heading inland to found the island's first town, **La Laguna**. The government moved from La Laguna to the flourishing port of Santa Cruz in 1723 where it has remained since, and though the city is no aesthete's delight, its uniquely Canarian urban vibrance is worth experiencing. The seafront Plaza de España – and its controversial memorial to the 39 soldiers from the island who fought for Franco and the fascists in the civil war – forms the central focus for the city and adjoins Plaza de Candelaria which is lined with cafés and shops. The main pedestrian drag, Calle del Castillo, extends west from here and Santa Cruz's few sights are scattered in the streets either side of here and along the seafront.

Museo de Bellas Artes

C/José Murphy 4 ☎ 922 53 32 72. Mon–Fri 9am–2pm & 5–9pm, Sat 10am–2pm. Free. Though it also holds an eclectic mix of weapons, coins and sculptures – including a Rodin – the Museo de Bellas Artes concentrates mainly on paintings. There's a good selection of Canarian artists on display, plus nineteenth-century landscapes along with some battlefields and religious depictions by old masters such as van Loo and Brueghel.

Centro de Arte la Recova and the Centro de Fotografía

Plaza Isla de la Madera ☎ 922 29 07 35. Mon–Fri 11am–1pm & 6–9pm. Free. Modern art and photography museum with frequently changing, often experimental and generally engaging exhibitions of little-known artists and photographers.

Iglesia de Nuestra Señora de la Concepción

Plaza Concepción. Mass Mon–Sat 9am & 7.30pm; Sun & church holidays 9am, 11am, noon, 1pm, 6pm & 8pm with entry 30min before. Begun

▼ CALLE DEL CASTILLO

PLACES

Santa Cruz

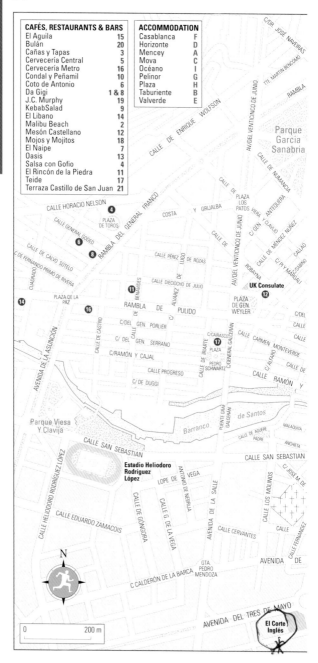

CAFÉS, RESTAURANTS & BARS
El Aguila	15
Bulán	20
Cañas y Tapas	3
Cervecería Central	5
Cervecería Metro	16
Condal y Peñamil	10
Coto de Antonio	6
Da Gigi	1 & 8
J.C. Murphy	19
KebabSalad	9
El Libano	14
Malibu Beach	2
Mesón Castellano	12
Mojos y Mojitos	18
El Naipe	7
Oasis	13
Salsa con Gofio	4
El Rincón de la Piedra	11
Teide	17
Terraza Castillo de San Juan	21

ACCOMMODATION
Casablanca	F
Horizonte	D
Mencey	A
Mova	C
Océano	I
Pelinor	G
Plaza	H
Taburiente	B
Valverde	E

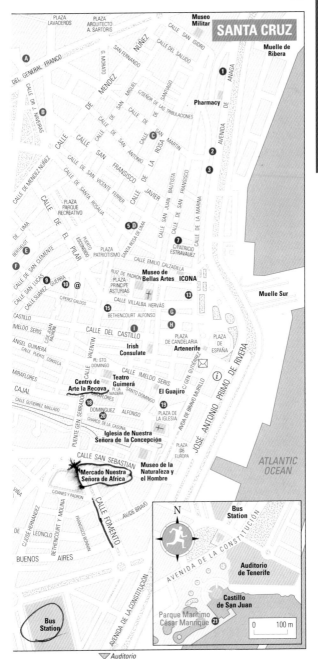

SANTA CRUZ

Auditorio

in 1502 and taking over two centuries to complete, the Iglesia de Nuestra Señora de la Concepción is Santa Cruz's oldest and most important church and a handy landmark thanks to its tall belltower. The building has been gutted by fire several times, meaning that what remains today dates mostly from the seventeenth and eighteenth centuries. Relics and articles of historic significance kept here include part of the *Santa Cruz de la Conquista* (Holy Cross of the Conquest), which dominates the silver Baroque main altar and gave the city its name. The church also holds the remains of one General Gutierrez, the military commander who successfully repulsed Nelson's attack on the town.

La Noria

Dominguez Alfonso. Ask most Santa Cruzers where the street of Dominguez Alfonso is and you'll likely get a blank look, but call it La Noria and most will know you are referring to the street that stretches west from the Iglesia de Nuestra Señora de la Concepción and forms the heart of one of the oldest, best-preserved and most colourful parts of the city. Though renamed in 1917, the street's history stretches back much further – Nelson's troops were documented running down the street in confusion

and disarray (see opposite). Now pedestrianized the road has become home to several easy-going pavement cafés and restaurants. It's pleasant for a stroll, and you'll often hear the songs and dances of the *murgas*, *comparsas* and *rondallas* (groups of singers, musicians and dancers) who practise their carnival routines in several houses along the street – indeed, carnival headquarters is at number seven.

Museo de la Naturaleza y el Hombre

C/Fuente Morales ☎ 922 535 58 16, ⊛ www.museosdetenerife.org. Tues–Fri & Sun 10am–8pm; Sat 10am–3pm. €3. Housed in an eighteenth-century, former hospital building, the city's premier museum, the Museo de la Naturaleza y el Hombre (Museum of Nature and Man) contains informative and well-constructed displays on Canarian natural history and archeology. The most fascinating exhibits relate to the Guanches with examples of their pottery, tools and rock art all displayed here, though most memorable are the gruesome mummified bodies and collection of skeletons.

Museo Militar

C/San Isidro 2 ☎ 922 84 35 00. Tues–Sun 10am–2pm. Free. Official photo ID necessary for admission. Santa Cruz's Museo Militar (Military

Museum) has exhibitions on the evolution of weaponry through the ages, but largely focuses on the town's finest military hour – its repulse of the attack by Lord Nelson in 1797 in which the seafaring hero lost not only many of his men, but, more famously, his right arm. The cannon "El Tigre", that allegedly blew off the limb, is on display, as are captured flags.

Parque Garcia Sanabria and Rambla del General Franco

The city's two most popular places to stroll away a weekend evening are the grand boulevard Rambla del General Franco and the tidy urban park at its northern end, the Parque Garcia Sanabria. Both are worth a visit at any time to see their collection of open-air modern art sculptures.

Information on the sculptures and park events can be picked up in the park's small visitor centre (Mon–Sun 10am–9pm). Two pieces of particular note are *La Fecundidat*, a voluptuous female nude by Frances Borges Salas and *Monumento al Gato* by Oscar Dominguez, a local artist.

While the sculptures in the park are recent arrivals in town, those along the Rambla have been here since Santa Cruz's 1974 hosting of the First International Street Sculpture Exhibition. Many are now time-worn, though the Henry Moore is as magnificent as ever. Walking along the Rambla, plan for a detour down to the Plaza

Nelson's attack on Santa Cruz

In 1797 Admiral Nelson, commanding a fleet of eight men o' war, launched a bungling, unsuccessful and ultimately embarrassing attack on Santa Cruz, that cost the lives of many of his men and, more famously, the admiral's right arm.

The assault on Santa Cruz was carried out after four years of war against Spain, with the intention of capturing New World gold from the galleon *San José* that was sheltering in the town's harbour. The battle plan involved the British encircling then invading the town, and Nelson,

▲ NELSON'S BUST, MUSEO MILITAR

never one to shirk from the action, was among the second wave of landing craft. He was about to land when he was struck by grapeshot on his right arm, shattering the bone and severing a major artery. By all accounts, Nelson bore this stoically, his first action being to switch his sword to his good hand before returning to his ship and telling the ship's surgeon that the arm had to go, and the sooner the better. Within half an hour of the amputation, the admiral was up, giving orders and practising his left-handed signature for an ultimatum demanding the town give up the galleon. The letter would never be sent, however, since by daylight all seven hundred British on shore decided to surrender. Nelson left the scene thoroughly frustrated at his misjudgment – though this would be his only military defeat – and depressed that his disablement might spell the end of his naval days.

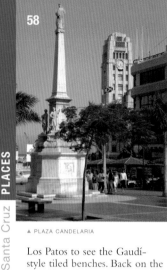

▲ PLAZA CANDELARIA

Los Patos to see the Gaudí-style tiled benches. Back on the Rambla and near the town's football stadium is the most eye-catching of the boulevard's sculptures: Francisco Sobrino's vibrant red, twelve-metre-high *Movil*. A bronze by Joan Míro is in the adjacent Parque Viera y Clavijo.

Auditorio de Tenerife

Avda. de la Constitución ⓦwww
.auditoriodetenerife.com. Looking like a huge wave, the new, immense and head-turning Auditorio provides Santa Cruz with a first-class venue for the arts. The building cleverly plays on a nautical theme, with many of its windows shaped like portholes and the tiny tiles on its bright white exterior shimmering like fish scales. For a glimpse inside you'll have to attend a performance (see p.63).

Castillo de San Juan

Avda. de la Constitución. The Castillo de San Juan makes a striking contrast with its neighbour, the Auditorio. This dark, stout little seventeenth-century portside fort once guarded the town's harbour and was also the site of a bustling trade in African slaves.

Unfortunately it's not open to visitors.

Parque Marítimo

Avda. de la Constitución ⓣ922 20 32 44. Daily 10am–7pm. €1.50. In the absence of a city beach, the Parque Marítimo is where Santa Cruz's inhabitants come to take a dip in one of the seawater pools or soak up the sun and the views along the coast. The complex was designed by Canarian artist César Manrique – in the same style as the more famous lido in Puerto de la Cruz (see p.82) – and includes, apart from the pools, shops, fountains, a restaurant and a sauna. If you'd rather be at a beach, hop on one of the frequent buses (#910) to Playa de las Teresitas (see p.69).

Hotels

Horizonte

C/Santa Rosa de Lima 11 ⓣ & ⓕ922 27 19 36. Inexpensive hotel on the edge of the central pedestrian area with worn and dated decor, but large en-suite rooms and some good-value singles. €45.

Mencey

C/Doctor José Naveiras 38 ⓣ922 60 99 00, ⓦwww.sheraton.com. Swanky, 286-room pile whose architecture is inspired by 1920s casino hotels. Rooms have plush antique furnishings and facilities include a pool and tennis courts in the palm garden, plus a ritzy casino open to non-residents (ⓣ922 29 07 40, daily 9pm–5am). €120.

Océano

C/Castillo 6 ⓣ922 27 08 00. Good-value hotel, above the shops of the town's main pedestrian street. The functional rooms are cramped, but rather grandly appointed with a surfeit of marble. Room rates include breakfast. €57.

Pelinor

C/Béthencourt Alfonso 8 ☎922 24 68 75, ☎922 28 05 20. Large, airy rooms in a labyrinthine hotel complex right in the centre. Though the straightforward rooms are in a good state of repair, the hotel as a whole has a slightly run-down feel – but it's clean throughout and prices include breakfast. €57.

Plaza

Plaza Candelaria 10 ☎922 27 24 53 ⓦwww.hotelplazastil.com. Well-run hotel with plain but comfortable rooms. At weekends there are good-value two-night offers, and its singles are the best value in town. Price includes a breakfast buffet. €74.

Taburiente

C/Dr José Naveiras 24A ☎922 27 60 00, ⓦwww.hoteltaburiente.com. Grand, modern hotel with reasonable prices. All rooms are en suite and have TV and fridge, and many overlook the Parque García Sanabria. Communal facilities include a roof terrace with small pool, a jacuzzi and a sauna. €85.

Pensions

Casablanca

C/Viera y Clavijo 15 ☎922 27 85 99. None-too-clean pension with mostly windowless rooms and shared bathrooms, whose redeeming feature is its excellent downtown location and small roof terrace that creates a sociable vibe lacking elsewhere. Some smarter rooms and singles are available. €20.

Mova

C/San Martin 33 ☎922 28 32 61. The pick of the low-budget pensions, with clean singles and doubles available (with or without private baths) in a slightly run-down part of town that's nevertheless handy for the nightlife along Avenida Anaga. The owners speak some English. €36.

▼ MENCEY HOTEL, SANTA CRUZ

Valverde

C/Sabino Berthelot 46 ☎922 27 40 63.
Well-turned-out but not very
friendly pension above a bar on
a centrally located pedestrian
street. Some rooms have private
bathrooms. €24.

Shops

Artenerife

Plaza de España ☎922 29 15 23.
Mon–Fri 10am–1.30pm & 4–7pm,
Sat 10am–1pm. One of a chain
of small shops in all the major
towns of the island, selling
high-quality handicrafts made in
Tenerife – mostly pottery, lace
and woodwork.

El Corte Inglés

Avda. Tres de Mayo 7. Mon–Sat
10am–10pm. Comprehensive
department store where the
emphasis is on high-quality
products and first-class service.
The café at the top has great
views of the harbour and
makes an ideal break from
shopping.

▼ MERCADO NUESTRA SEÑORA DE AFRICA

El Guajiro

C/Imeldo Seris 15. Mon–Fri 9am–1pm
& 5–8pm; Sat 9am–1pm. Small,
old-fashioned tobacconist
where cigars are packed by
hand and a good range of
smoking paraphernalia is on sale.
A similar shop is on the same
street at no. 23.

Mercado Nuestra Señora de Africa

C/San Sebastián. Daily early to 1pm.
Large multi-level covered
market in simple but elegant
Moorish buildings. Great for
groceries and deli items at
reasonable prices – look out for
local cheeses like the salty and
deliciously light *queso fresco*. Just
outside, the Sunday-morning
flea market is a great place for
unusual souvenirs.

Cafés

El Aguila

Plaza Alféreces Provisionales ☎922
27 31 56. Mon–Sat until 11pm. With
lots of outdoor seating beside an
elegant dragon tree and the lush
Plaza Príncipe de Asturias,
this café is a popular
meeting place and a better
bet than the more obvious
but bland and relatively
pricey choices lining Plaza
Candelaria.

Condal y Peñamil

Callejon del Combate 9 ☎922
24 49 76. Mon–Sat 9am–
midnight. The selection of
newspapers and extensive
range of coffees and cigars
encourage lingering in
this gloriously old-world
café with polished brass,
dark wood, maroon drapes
and suave service. Seating
is either inside or in a
small pedestrian alley.

Oasis

C/de la Marina 19b. Closed Wed. Basic little strip-lit café with a range of excellent but inexpensive Italian ice creams and sinful cakes. For a unique kick try the *gofio* flavour ice cream.

Mojos y Mojitos

C/Antonio Dominguez Alfonso 40 ☎922 24 10 28. Tues–Sat 1–4pm & 8.30–midnight. Trendy café and bar with pleasant outdoor seating along the strip of eateries on pedestrianized La Noria (see p.56). A good range of tapas and other light fare is served – the menu of the day is a very reasonable €8.50 – and unusually there are always decent veggie options.

Restaurants

Cañas y Tapas

Avda. Anaga 15. Branch of the moderately expensive restaurant chain with dark wood and tile decor and some outside seating. A large selection of tapas includes blood sausage, a salami platter and octopus. Vegetarians will find quite a few options too.

Cervecería Central

C/Santa Rosalia 47. Mon–Thurs 8.30am–1am, Fri–Sun 8.30am–2am. With a pleasant plaza-side location, this large restaurant is a good option for lunch, offering a fair selection of reasonably priced tapas, sandwiches, omelettes and *revueltos* (scrambled-egg dishes) plus an acceptable gazpacho. More substantial meals are provided by a predictable range of local fish and meat dishes.

Coto de Antonio

C/General Goded 13 ☎922 27 21 05. Closed Sun & Aug. Elegant, simply decorated place, consistently popular with locals and visitors alike. The excellent menu is based around Basque and Canarian cuisine, with superb and varied – though pricey – daily dishes as well as regular favourites including roast kid.

Da Gigi

Avda. Anaga 43 ☎922 24 20 17 and Rambla del General Franco 27 ☎ 922 27 43 26. Daily 5–11pm. Italian restaurant, with two outlets, each with stylish brick interiors and located in the city's most popular dining areas. The menu features a good selection of antipasti, an excellent range of fresh pastas and a large selection of fantastic thin-crust pizzas – all moderately priced. Also offers takeaway.

KebabSalad

C/Suárez Guerra 31. Daily 11am–11pm. Bright little self-service place that's the best budget option in town. Here €6 gets you a kebab, a trip to the great salad bar and a canned drink.

El Libano

C/Santiago Cuadrado 36 ☎922 28 59 14. Daily 8pm–late. Simple Lebanese restaurant tucked in a side-street and offering old favourites such as kebabs and stuffed vine leaves at reasonable prices, along with more unusual dishes such as *beme* – a traditional vegetable dish – and a superb selection of vegetarian options.

Mesón Castellano

C/Lima 4 ☎922 27 10 74. Mon–Sat 1–4pm & 8pm–midnight. Atmospheric basement restaurant serving expensive fish and meat dishes and specializing in a range of sausage-based dishes. The rustic little bar on the ground floor above the restaurant is a pleasant place for a quiet drink.

El Rincón de la Piedra

C/Benavides 32 ☎ 922 24 97 78. Closed Thurs. Cavernous and beautiful old house with restored woodwork, beamed ceilings and a friendly atmosphere. The expensive food includes a good range of salads and some fish, but the restaurant is best known for its meat dishes, including a superb *solomillo*.

Teide

C/Cairasco 13. No-nonsense strip-lit bar with plastic tables, football on TV and a selection of four daily menus of reasonable quality for €5.40 including a drink.

Bars

Bulán

C/Antonio Dominguez Alfonso 35 ☎ 922 27 41 16. Mon–Fri 1.30pm– 1.30am, Sat & Sun 1.30pm–3.30am. One of several pavement cafés, restaurants and bars on relaxed pedestrianized La Noria (see p.56). Great for the menu of the day: for €8.50 you get a three-course meal which often includes a great gazpacho. Inside, the rooms all have atmospheric themes (including Moorish and Indian) which help make this a chic nightspot; it's legendary for its wild full-moon parties.

Cervecería Metro

Rambla de Pubido 89. Dingy pub-style place with a huge range of European beers and a varied crowd, close to the Plaza de la Paz in an area that's something

▼ NIGHTLIFE, SANTA CRUZ

Santa Cruz **PLACES**

of a focus for bars. For alternative watering holes check out the unnamed street opposite.

J.C. Murphy

Plaza de la Concepción ☎ 922 28 48 64. Mon–Thurs 5pm–2.30am, Fri & Sat 7pm–3.30am, Sun 6.30pm–2.30am. Classy Irish pub that's great for a quiet drink among thirty-somethings in an upcoming area of bars and restaurants around the Iglesia de la Concepción.

Terraza Castillo de San Juan

Avda. de la Constitución. June–Sept generally Thurs–Sun 10pm–5am. Outdoor bar with spectacular setting beside the Auditorio and Castillo de San Juan. During the summer months this and other *terrazas* largely eclipse local indoor venues.

Clubs

Salsa con Gofio

C/Horacio Nelson 11. Open until 5am. Though some distance from other nightspots, this enjoyable club, with fabulous gardens and two dance floors – one with Latin music, the other hip-hop or chart – is worth the trek.

Malibu Beach

Avda. Anaga 31. Thurs–Sun 11pm–3.30am. Lively, surfing-theme club that's a popular option among the many trendy bars and clubs that line the town's main nightlife strip Avenida de Anaga. None get going until midnight, but most pump out chart music until around 5am.

El Naipe

C/Patricio Estevanez 6. 10pm–3am. Simple little salsa bar with a great Latin vibe, where everyone's having a good time and novices on the dance floor are happily tolerated.

Live music

Auditorio de Tenerife

Avda. de la Constitución 1 ☎ 922 31 73 27, ⊛ www.auditoriodetenerife. com; ticket office Mon–Fri 10am–2pm & 5–7pm; Sat 10am–2pm. This eye-catching venue for the performing arts (see p.58) has great acoustics and is home to Tenerife's well-respected symphony orchestra though its programme of events is much wider, including jazz, classical guitar and folk. The Festival de Música de Canarias in February is the highlight of the annual calendar.

Teatro Guimerá

Plaza Isla de la Madera 2 ☎ 922 60 62 65, tickets 902 36 46 03, ⊛ www.teatroguimera.es. Imposing Classical building with elaborate stuccowork that's Tenerife's longest-standing performing arts venue. Its programme includes classical music, ballet, opera and theatre performances.

La Laguna

A good deal higher than Santa Cruz and considerably cooler and rainier, the lively university town of **La Laguna** was Tenerife's first major settlement and, for over two hundred years, its capital. The government may have moved and the town's bland suburbs now blur into Santa Cruz, yet La Laguna remains the cultural, religious and academic centre of Tenerife and its well-preserved historic centre provides a showpiece of Canarian architecture. South of here, it's the university district that is the busiest area of town, its streets buzzing with bars, cafés and bookshops.

Plaza del Adelantado

Leafy Plaza del Adelantado is at the heart of the historic centre and contains the *ayuntamiento* (town hall) and the Convento Santa Catalina, built in 1611, whose wooden grille on the upper floor allowed the nuns to watch events in the square below without being seen. The focal point of the plaza is a statue of Friar Anchieta, who was born in the town and later

▼ SANTA IGLESIA CATEDRAL, LA LAGUNA

emigrated to South America, where he is said to have converted over two million local people to Christianity.

Museo de la Historia de Tenerife

C/San Agustín ☎ 922 82 59 49. Tues–Sun 9am–7pm. €3. In a line of sixteenth-century houses, the Museo de la Historia de Tenerife occupies the beautifully restored former home of the wealthy Lecaro family – Genoese merchants, moneylenders and speculators, who, having made their fortune running mercantile operations on spice routes through Asia, became one of Tenerife's most powerful families. The house is worth a look in its own right but there are also exhibits containing numerous documents, maps and artefacts relating to the town's history and that of the Lecaro family.

Santa Iglesia Catedral

Plaza de la Catedral. Mon–Sat 10.30am–1.30pm & 5.30–7pm. The town's largest church and technically the religious centre of Tenerife, the Santa Iglesia Catedral was only consecrated in 1913. Its exterior is rather

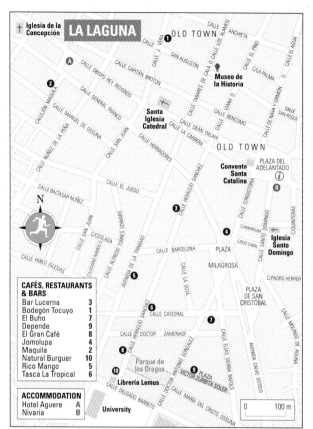

† Iglesia de la Concepción

LA LAGUNA

OLD TOWN

Museo de la Historia

Santa Iglesia Catedral

OLD TOWN

Convento Santa Catalina

PLAZA DEL ADELANTADO ⓘ

Iglesia Santo Domingo

PLAZA MILAGROSA

PLAZA DE SAN CRISTÓBAL

CAFÉS, RESTAURANTS & BARS

Bar Lucerna	3
Bodegón Tocuyo	1
El Buho	7
Depende	9
El Gran Café	8
Jomolupa	4
Maquila	2
Natural Burguer	10
Rico Mango	5
Tasca La Tropical	6

ACCOMMODATION

Hotel Aguere	A
Nivaria	B

Parque de los Dragos

PLAZA ZURBITA SOLER

Librería Lemus

University

0   100 m

drab, while the interior is a more impressive mixture of Baroque and Gothic, the latter seen clearly in the pointed arches of the presbytery and in the decorated windows of the east end. The cathedral treasury contains the figures that head the Christmas, Easter and Corpus Christi processions and behind the ornate altar is the tomb of Alonso de Lugo, conqueror of the islands, who died in 1525.

Arrival and information

Buses #14 and #15 from Santa Cruz (very frequent, 25–40min) run to La Laguna's **bus station**, a ten-minute walk west of the centre: head along Calle Manuel Hernandez Martín. If arriving by car, park on the outskirts and walk in as it's difficult to find a space in the centre.

A small **tourist information** kiosk (☏922 63 11 94. Mon–Fri 8.30am–5pm, Sat & Sun 8.30am–2pm) on Plaza del Adelantado provides a list of accommodation, town maps and a couple of glossy brochures on local architecture (in Spanish).

Iglesia de la Concepción

Plaza de la Concepción. Daily 10.30am–12.30pm. As the island's first major town and religious centre, La Laguna has several grand and impressive churches reflecting its former status. The oldest of these, and in fact the island's first, is the Iglesia de la Concepción, northwest of the cathedral, which has evolved over the years in a number of different styles of which Gothic is most evident. The green-glazed baptism pool, an original fitting in the church, was once the scene of many Guanche christenings. The church's impressive ceiling collapsed in 1972, but its replacement – a coffered *Mudéjar* affair with a complex geometric design – is, if anything, even more splendid.

Hotels

Aguere

C/Obispo Rey Redondo 57 ☏922 25 94 90, ⊛922 63 16 33. Stylish old hotel whose uncluttered rooms surround a pretty central courtyard. Singles are available and prices include breakfast. €67.

Nivaria

Plaza del Adelantado 11 ☏922 26 42 98, ⊛922 25 96 34. A restored eighteenth-century house, overlooking the town's main plaza, with small, simply decorated apartments. The complex also contains a squash court and a bar. €75.

▼ PLAZA DEL ADELANTADO

Shops

Librería Lemus

C/Heraclio Sánchez 64 ☎ 922 25 11 45.
Easily Tenerife's best bookshop,
this place has an extensive range
of titles – including a useful local
travel section – though most are
in Spanish.

Cafés

El Gran Café

C/Heraclio Sánchez 50. Trendy,
inexpensive café, aimed at
students, offering snacks and
tapas. In the evenings it becomes
an unpretentious and sociable
place to sit, drink and smoke.

Restaurants

Bar Lucerna

C/Heraclio Sánchez 10. Inexpensive,
brightly lit bar with predictable
bar food but a great selection
of fish and meat dishes. Good-
value menu of the day, delicious
potato and lentil soup and a
fine range of fruit juices too.

Maquila

Callejón Maquila ☎ 922 25 70 20.
Closed Tues & Aug. In business
for over a hundred years, this
is the best restaurant in town.
The decor is rustic and simple,
as are many of the dishes,
such as rabbit and goat in
spicy sauces and oven-baked
lamb. The stuffed squid is the
house speciality. In light of
the quality, prices are very
reasonable – with most mains
around €8.

Natural Burguer

C/Heraclio Sánchez 58. One of many
bars and bistros on this street,
this hip burger joint courts
students with a varied, cheap
and surprisingly healthy menu
that includes veggie options.

Rico Mango

Avda. de la Trinidad 47. Mon–Sat
1–4pm & 7.30–11.30pm. Vegetarian
restaurant with great, reasonably
priced South American cooking
and somewhat Bohemian decor
– customers visit Mars or Venus
toilets.

Tasca La Tropical

Corner of C/Heraclio Sánchez &
C/Catedral. This place has a
good selection of snacks and
moderately priced meals
including a huge range of
excellent *revuelto* (scrambled-
egg) dishes.

Bars

Bodegón Tocuyo

C/Juan de Vera 16. Daily noon–3pm
& 7pm–2am. A dingy, darkwood
pub, covered in graffiti and with
barrels for tables, this is easily
the town's most atmospheric bar
for a quiet drink. The cheese
and meat platter is a good
accompaniment.

Depende

Plaza Victor Zurbita Soler local 11–12
☎ 922 25 44 42. One of the more
stylish of a number of studenty
bars lining Calle del Doctor
Antonio González and the
adjacent Plaza Victor Zurbita
Soler. This place also has a
variety of board games to play.

Clubs

Jomolupa

Plaza Milagrosa. Thurs–Sun 11pm–late.
Late-night basement club that's
reliably busy once everywhere
else has shut; music can vary

▲ OLD TOWN, LA LAGUNA

between hip-hop and salsa. No cover charge.

Live Music

El Buho

C/Catedral 3. Daily 6pm–late. One of La Laguna's few dependable live-music venues which calls itself a chill-out jazz bar, though you're more likely to hear rock. For gig details look out for posters along Calle del Doctor Antonio.

The Anaga

Geologically the oldest part of the island, the volcanic **Anaga** range is a rugged jumble of knife-edge ridges and deep valleys that offers some of Tenerife's most spectacular hiking. One sinuous main road runs along the length of the range, following its central ridge through upland areas smothered in the last remnant of a forest that dominated the Mediterranean until ice ages restricted it to the Canary Islands. To the north of the road, the coastline is dotted with small pebble beaches, while to the south lie two fine stretches of sand – Playa de las Teresitas and the quieter Playa de las Gaviotas. Small communities have survived in isolated hamlets in this remote region but there's little in the way of services, meaning the area is best explored on long day-trips from Santa Cruz.

Playa de las Teresitas and Playa de las Gaviotas

Buses #910, #245 & #246 from Santa Cruz, frequent, 20min. Below the leafy hillside village of San Andrés, the large artificial Playa de las Teresitas was built to provide Santa Cruz with a beach escape beside the towering Anaga mountains. A large man-made breakwater eliminates waves and currents around the palm-studded sand, and good facilities make it a pleasant place for a day of sunbathing.

Playa de las Gaviotas (bus #245 only), the next cove east after Las Teresitas, is named after the seagulls that frequent it and is a much quieter stretch, popular with

▲ PLAYA DE LAS TERESITAS

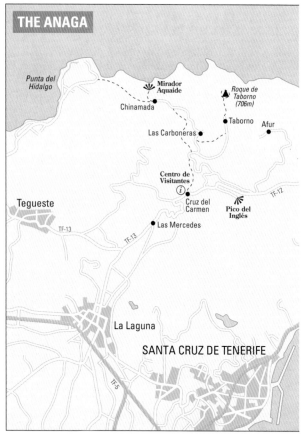

THE ANAGA

Punta del Hidalgo

Mirador Aquaide

Chinamada

Roque de Taborno (706m)

Taborno

Afur

Las Carboneras

Centro de Visitantes ⓘ

Cruz del Carmen

Pico del Inglés

TF-12

Tegueste

TF-13

TF-13

Las Mercedes

La Laguna

SANTA CRUZ DE TENERIFE

TF-5

nudists. A bar on the front serves snacks.

Taganana

Bus #246 from Santa Cruz, 6–8 daily, 45min. Though by far the largest settlement in the Anaga, Taganana is a tiny town that began as a sugar cane centre before moving into wine production. Precariously sprawled over several ridges and steep hillsides, it was long remote from the rest of Tenerife and is worth a quick stroll for its narrow streets lined with simple old Canarian houses.

Almáciga

Bus #246 from Santa Cruz, 6–8 daily, 50min. Almáciga – terminus of the bus from Santa Cruz – is a useful point of access for Playa de San Roque and Playa de Benijo, both of which are popular with local surfers – high winds along this coast can make for awe-inspiring breakers – and have a few bars and restaurants.

Benijo and El Draguillo hike

The sealed road from Almáciga ends at the tiny village of Benijo. From here a dirt road continues 2km east along

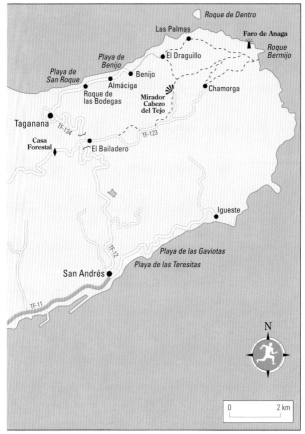

the coast to the village of El Draguillo – so called for its dragon tree – where the path splits. The coastal trail (a 6km return hike) heads east to the Faro de Anaga lighthouse via the scenic village of Las Palmas and within sight of the bird reserve Roque de Dentro, while the route heading inland climbs steeply to Chamorga (see p.73). The two can be made into an 11-kilometre loop; if you do this, it's best to head in an anti-clockwise direction first to get all the climbing out of the way early on.

Cruz del Carmen hike

Buses #73, #75, #76 or #77 from La Laguna, 10–15 daily, 25min. Cruz del Carmen is a good gateway to the region as it's easily accessed by bus, though there's not much here save a viewpoint, a basic restaurant and a visitors' centre (daily 9.30am–3pm; ☎922 63 35 76), which can supply a hiking map.

A good walk from here (2hr one way), with excellent views from the outset, leads 3km north, past the village of Las Carboneras, to the hamlet of Chinamada. If you do this as a

▲ TAGANANA

loop, consider hiking back along the quiet road from Chinamada to Las Carboneras before either heading back to Cruz del Carmen the way you came, or extending the hike to Taborno, the village on the opposite side of the valley, where you can walk around the imposing volcanic rock monolith, the Roque de Taborno. This adds another two or three hours to the hike.

Chinamada

Known for its houses built in natural caves in the rock, the hamlet of Chinamada has some of the most spectacular views in the region. The panorama from the Mirador Aguaide just beyond the village (accessed via an obvious track beside the town plaza) is particularly dizzying. From here you can head down to the unattractive and sleepy town of Punta del Hidalgo (approx. 3hr) to catch buses back to Santa Cruz (#105;

36 daily, 1hr 10min). This route can also be done in reverse – though it's all climbing – to Cruz del Carmen (around 5hr).

El Bailadero and Mirador Cabezo del Tejo hike

Bus #77 from La Laguna, 2 daily, 50min; and #246 or #247 from Santa Cruz, 9 daily, 45min. For a long hike with stunning views across the rugged northern coast, get off bus #77 or #247 – or park the car – at the viewpoint of El Bailadero. On bus #246, get off at Cruce El Bailadero and follow a path opposite up to the viewpoint. From here, you can walk in a loop to Almáciga (approx 10km; 4–5hr, see p.70) and catch the bus back to Santa Cruz. The walk heads east from the viewpoint along the road to Chamorga for just over a kilometre before turning onto a track signposted El Pijara. This passes through prime laurel forest and joins then leaves the road before you eventually come to the Mirador Cabezo del Tejo with superb views across the whole north side of the Anaga range. A little further along from the viewpoint, the path comes to a crossroads where you turn left to head down to El Draguillo and from there to Almáciga (see p.70), right to Chamorga (6km/3hr hike from El Bailadero; see opposite), or straight on to Roque Bermijo (4km/2hr; see below).

Chamorga

Bus #247 from Santa Cruz, 3 daily, 1hr 10min. Chamorga is a small, well-kept village spread across a valley that's studded with palms and dotted with neat terraces. The village is an easy day-trip from Santa Cruz and gives access to some of the best walks in the region. One good hike (7km/3hr) follows a loop from Chamorga east down the valley to a small cluster of houses near Roque Bermijo, a sharp spit of land in the sea. From here you climb back to Chamorga by way of a well-graded ridge walk that starts near the Faro de Anaga lighthouse. For a longer loop (14km/7hr) hike north to El Draguillo and then east along the remote coastal path to the lighthouse (see p.71) before completing the loop to Chamorga via either the valley or ridge.

Restaurants

Bar La Caseta de Pastora El Frontón

Benijo ☎ 922 59 01 07. Closed Mon. Great place for simple, moderately priced Canarian food, at the end of the tarmac road in Benijo. The views over the coast are tremendous.

Bar El Petón

Behind Castillo de San Andrés, San Andrés. Tucked away behind the old fort, this excellent, inexpensive seafood place stays open until the day's catch has been served. Inferior local fish and seafood places line the seafront.

La Gran Paella

C/Pedro Schwartz 15, San Andrés. Closed Tues. Simple but elegant restaurant behind the ruined Castillo de San Andrés. The paella is fantastic and, unusually, there are a large number of sauces to accompany the seafood.

José Cañón

Afúr ☎ 922 69 01 41. Closed Mon. Rustic place in the centre of tiny Afúr, with basic food cooked in vast pots and served with minimum fuss. Best place on the island for upland food such as goat or rabbit and chickpeas.

Candelaria and Güímar

Though easily bypassed on the main TF-1 motorway from Santa Cruz to the southern resorts, the barren landscape of Tenerife's east coast does contain two outstanding attractions – the **Basilica at Candelaria**, considered the holiest site in the Canary Islands, and **the Pirámides of Güímar**, which predate the Spanish conquest and are of global archeological importance. Both are easy day-trips from all the main resorts – but particularly accessible from Santa Cruz – and are offered on some bus tours. As Tenerife's Lourdes, Candelaria is well set up for day-trippers, Güímar rather less so, though the Puertito de Güímar – its coastal outpost – has a couple of good seafood restaurants.

Basilica de Nuestra Señora de Candelaria

Mon–Fri 7.30am–1pm & 3–6.30pm, Sat & Sun 8am–7pm. Buses #122 or #131 from Santa Cruz, 21 daily, 30min. Signposted from the motorway. West of Santa Cruz stretches a string of dormitory settlements that peter out around Candelaria, a largely avoidable town were it not for the Basilica de Nuestra Señora de Candelaria. Housing a famous statue of the Virgin Mary, the patron saint of the Canary Islands, this is the

▲ BASILICA DE NUESTRA SEÑORA DE CANDELARIA

The Guanches

Tenerife's native islanders, the **Guanches**, were tall, powerfully built Scandinavian-looking people. They lived in caves and were primarily **hunter-gatheres** with little more than Stone Age technology and no knowledge of weaving. They domesticated goats and sheep and wore a *tamarco*, a large goatskin fastened with fish bones and thorns – fashioned to cover a woman's chest and feet. Similarities in ceramics, language and culture suggest that the Guanches were overwhelmingly of **Berber origin**, probably related to cultures from the High Atlas Mountains in today's Morocco.

In contrast to their primitive technology, the ancient Canarians had a complex **society**. Both Tenerife and La Gomera were divided into several *meneceyatos* (kingdoms) – the names of which survive as modern place-names, including Anaga, Tegueste, Tacaronte, Taoro, Icod, Adeje, Abona, Güímar – which often warred with one another. Each tribe had three classes of society: the monarchy, a nobility and the remaining population: mainly peasants, craftsmen and goatherds. The rank of nobility – which bestowed the right to grow long hair – was attained not through birth but as a result of personal qualities or actions.

The Guanche were a **religious** and deeply superstitious people, who worshipped a single God, Achaman, to whom animal sacrifices and libations were made and whose physical manifestation was thought to be the sun. His opposite number was Guayota, a devil that dwelt in hell, Echeyde, within the crater of Mount Teide – and who punished misdeeds through volcanic eruptions. Other than building flat-topped **pyramids** (see below), the most significant Guanche religious practice was the **mummification** of their nobility, to be buried in caves with their possessions, particularly their *pintadera*, a person's unique wooden seal worn on a leather thong necklace and thought to be useful in the afterlife.

The role of **women** in Guanche society was strong, for the most part due to a hereditary practice in which monarchic titles – as well as possessions among the rest of the populace – would transfer through the female line. Women could also take all kinds of jobs, and are known to have been priests, doctors, potters and even warriors. And, since there were fewer women than men on the islands (probably the work of slave raiders), many took several husbands. At the same time it was customary for household guests to be offered use of the wife – a facet of local culture particularly popular with the conquistadors.

archipelago's most important religious site.

The foundation of the church was inspired by the arrival of a wooden sculpture of the Virgin (probably from the prow of a wrecked ship) washed up here in the 1390s. Initially kept in a cave and worshipped by the local Guanches, it passed into Spanish hands after the conquest. Though the original was swept out to sea by a tidal wave in 1826, a replica, draped in silk cloth, adorned with gold and jewels and holding a baby Jesus in her arms, now forms the centrepiece of this splendid late nineteenth-century colonial-style basilica. For the Feast of the Assumption (August 15), the parading of the statue around the town attracts pilgrims from across the Canary Islands and further afield. Outside the church, the waterfront plaza is guarded by ten statues of Guanches, the work of local sculptor José Abad.

Pirámides de Güímar

☎922 51 45 10, ⊕www
.piramidesdeguimar.net. Daily 9.30am–
6pm. €10. Bus #121 or #124 from

PLACES

Candelaria and Güímar

CANDELARIA & GÜÍMAR

N

Candelaria

Basílica de
Nuestra Señora
de Candelaria

TF-28

Pirámides

Güímar

TF-1

TF-61

Finca Salamanca

Puertito de
Güímar

0   2 km

Santa Cruz to Güímar, 15–23 daily,
45–50min. Signposted "pirámides".
The once thriving agricultural
town of Güímar is best known
as the location of the Pirámides
de Güímar. Built by the native
Guanches, they were long
dismissed as piles of stones
heaped by farmers clearing the
land. However, close inspection
by archeologists revealed three
pyramidal constructions, each at
least 100 metres long and made
of carefully squared stones laid
out with considerable geometric
exactitude. The structures point
to the location of the sun
during the winter and summer
solstices and the stairs up each
flat-topped pyramid face the
rising sun. Now carefully rebuilt
to what is thought to be their
original form, a platform and
series of walkways allow visitors
to inspect the pyramids – there's
no climbing allowed. The
importance of these structures
goes far beyond an intriguing
insight into indigenous culture
and is generally considered as
evidence of a stepping-stone
in the migration of an ancient
African culture to South
America. The site museum
focuses on this, its displays –
largely petroglyphs and pottery
– suggesting the Canaries are
a missing link between these
ancient cultures.

Hotels

Finca Salamanca
Carretera Güímar, El Puertito km1.5,
Güímar ☎922 51 45 30, ⊛www.
hotel-fincasalamanca.com. Tranquil
and stylish country hotel, whose
collection of adobe buildings
huddles around a small pool and

▲ PIRÁMIDES DE GÜÍMAR

is surrounded by lush gardens and orchards. There's a stylish restaurant too (see opposite) where guests eat breakfast – included in rates. €68.

Shops

La Casa de las Imágenes

Obispo Pérez Cáceres 17, Candelaria ☎922 50 21 01. Daily 10am–2pm & 4.30–8pm. One of the largest of a series of shops selling religious paraphernalia along the pedestrian road that leads to the Basilica. Choose from a bewildering array of almost invariably kitsch images, trinkets and figurines, with something for every budget.

Cafés

Alexia's

C/Juan P. Rodriguez Cruz 2, Puertito de Güímar. Tues–Sun 11.30am–midnight. Cheerful harbourside Venezuelan café-bar, with excellent *arepas* (maize-bread sandwiches) and *cachapas* (wheat pancakes) at around €3 each.

Carlo's

Obispo Pérez Cáceres 46, Candelaria. Tues–Sun 9.30am–9pm. Indoor café, serving a delectable assortment of ice creams. If you're not interested in sitting down, then

visit the patisserie at no. 50, which has even better cakes and pastries, but no seating.

Restaurants

Cofrádia de Pescadores

C/Almirante Gravina 28, Puertito de Güímar. Daily May–Oct, Nov–April no fixed hours; closed Thurs. Run by the local fishermen's co-op, this is the best choice in town for fresh fish at low prices in non-fussy surroundings. If this place is closed, there are a number of other reliable options close by.

Finca Salamanca

Carretera Güímar, El Puertito km1.5, Güímar ☎922 51 45 30. Daily 1.30–4pm & 7–10.30pm; closed Tues. Smart hotel restaurant in an old tobacco drying room with superb and reasonably priced steaks and a phenomenal paella that requires 24 hours' notice. The lobster salad is a good lunchtime choice and can be enjoyed on the shaded outdoor patio.

Casa Sindo

Obispo Pérez Cáceres 10, Candelaria ☎922 50 06 09. Daily 11am–12.30pm. Overlooking the sea, this simple restaurant has some great fresh fish – the tuna is particularly recommended – at reasonable prices.

Puerto de la Cruz and around

With over a hundred years' pedigree in the field, **Puerto de la Cruz** does resort tourism well. The bustling, former harbour was historically much favoured by British traders who made the town a fashionable spa in the 1890s, and it soon became the preferred haunt for wintering European royalty and dignitaries such as Winston Churchill and Bertrand Russell. In more recent years mass tourism has created a jumble of high-rise hotels, bars and discos, yet Puerto retains some of its cosmopolitan style and flair and still has the feel of a small, friendly and busy Spanish town. Particularly popular with a more mature holidaying clientele, it boasts the highest rate of return visits of any resort in the world. The town's focal point is the café-filled **Plaza del Charco** – named after the shrimp pools that once formed here at high tide – and most of Puerto's historic buildings are found nearby. From here the pedestrian area spreads west into Ranilla, a quaint old fishing quarter, and east along the seafront and through the shopping district. There are few real sights – Puerto's main attractions are its beaches, lido and the nearby Loro Parque zoo, or coastal walks to quiet beaches and the preserved *hacienda* of Rambla de Castro.

Casa de la Aduana

C/Las Lonjas ☎ 922 57 81 03. Tues–Sat 11am–1pm & 6–9pm, Sun 4–8pm. Free. Though large-scale trade is now absent from Puerto's port, a handful of small fishing boats still put in here beside the town's oldest building, the timber and plaster Casa de la Aduana. This, the former customs house, was built in 1620 and now houses the town's tourist office and hosts photographic exhibitions, sometimes focused on island themes.

▲ CASA DE LA ADUANA AND HARBOUR

Arrival and information

Buses arrive at the station on C/del Pozo, on the western side of the town centre. The **tourist office** (Mon–Fri 9am–7pm, Sat 9am–noon; ☎922 38 60 00) is in the Casa de la Aduana – see opposite.

Iglesia de Nuestra Señora de la Peña Francia

Plaza de la Iglesia. Mass daily 8.30am, 6.30pm & 7pm. Dominating the square named after it, the seventeenth-century Iglesia de Nuestra Señora de la Peña Francia is Puerto's main church. The imposing, grey-stone building is only open to the public for mass, when it's worth sneaking in for a look at the simple interior, the fine *Mudéjar* ceiling and the Baroque retable.

Casa Iriarte

C/Iriarte. Mon–Sat 10am–7pm. This eighteenth-century house was once home to various over-achievers from the Iriarte family, including politicians, diplomats and writers. Today, its courtyard is given over to the peddling of handicrafts, with an abundance of embroidery and lace for sale. A room on the first floor calls

itself the town museum (free) and holds a rag-tag collection of photographs. The rest of the first floor is devoted to a scrappy naval museum (€1.20), which displays a range of painstakingly recreated model boats from the sixteenth century onwards. Other nautical odds and ends include a copy of the last letter Nelson wrote with his right arm and the first he scrawled with his left. But the most (unintentionally) entertaining display of all here is a diorama depicting the island's conquest – dreadful life-size models of a conquistador, a priest and a Guanche with an Afro prostrating himself before them.

Museo Arqueológico

C/del Lomo 9a ☎922 37 14 65. Sept–July Tues–Sat 10am–1pm & 5–9pm, Sun 10am–1pm. €1. The former fishermen's quarter of

Spanish Conquest

At the dawn of the great age of discovery and conquest of sophisticated civilizations around the world by European powers, it surprised Spain to find a Stone Age culture on its doorstep. Even more of a shock was the struggle conquistadors had to control Tenerife and La Gomera; the native islanders, the Guanches (see p.75), fought only with sticks and stones, yet it took the vast majority of the fifteenth century for Spain's crusaders to conquer all of the Canary Islands. Tenerife was the last to fall, and even when Columbus sailed past on his famed 1492 voyage it was still in Guanche hands.

Only the following year would the process of conquest begin, and the final defeat of the Guanches didn't come until Christmas Day 1495, at a location now marked by the town La Victoria. At this time Spanish victory was virtually assured since the Guanches had suffered a gigantic epidemic of a flu against which they lacked immunity. Of the six hundred Guanche that remained, most forcibly entered into domestic service or were sold as slaves; only a handful, known as Guanches alzados – rebellious Guanches – continued their traditional ways in remote, mountainous areas.

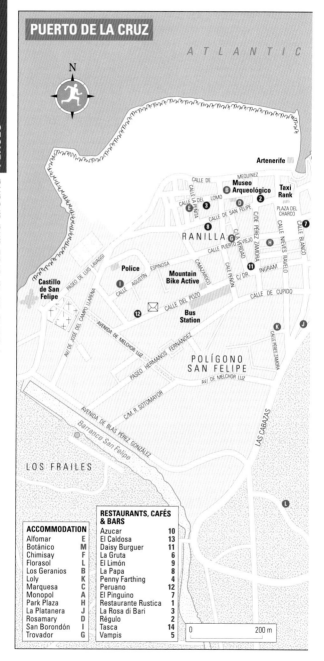

PUERTO DE LA CRUZ

ATLANTIC

N

Artenerife

CALLE DE
MEQUINEZ
Museo
Arqueológico **2**

Taxi
Rank

PLAZA DEL
CHARCO

CALLE DEL
LOMO

CALLE LA PEÑITA

CALLE DE SAN FELIPE

7

CALLE NIEVES RAVELO

CALLE BLANCO

C/DE PÉREZ ZAMORA

E

B

D

3

8

A

C/LA VERDAD

CALLE PUERTO VIEJO

INGRAM

H

11

RANILLA

C/ DR.

CALLE PENÍN

C/MAZARICO

CALLE AGUSTÍN ESPINOSA

PASEO DE LUIS LAVAGGI

Police

I

Mountain
Bike Active

CALLE DE CUPIDO

Castillo
de San
Felipe

CALLE DEL POZO

12

Bus
Station

K

J

AV. DE JOSE DE CAMPO LLARENA

AVENIDA DE MELCHOR LUZ

POLÍGONO
SAN FELIPE

CALLE PÉREZ ZAMORA

PASEO HERMANOS FERNÁNDEZ

AV. DE MELCHOR LUZ

C/M. R. SOTOMAYOR

AVENIDA DE BLAS PÉREZ GONZÁLEZ

LAS CABAZAS

Barranco San Felipe

L

LOS FRAILES

0   200 m

ACCOMMODATION

Alfomar	**E**
Botánico	**M**
Chimisay	**F**
Florasol	**L**
Los Geranios	**B**
Loly	**K**
Marquesa	**C**
Monopol	**A**
Park Plaza	**H**
La Platanera	**J**
Rosamary	**D**
San Borondón	**I**
Trovador	**G**

**RESTAURANTS, CAFÉS
& BARS**

Azucar	**10**
El Caldosa	**13**
Daisy Burguer	**11**
La Gruta	**6**
El Limón	**9**
La Papa	**8**
Penny Farthing	**4**
Peruano	**12**
El Pinguino	**7**
Restaurante Rustica	**1**
La Rosa di Bari	**3**
Régulo	**2**
Tasca	**14**
Vampis	**5**

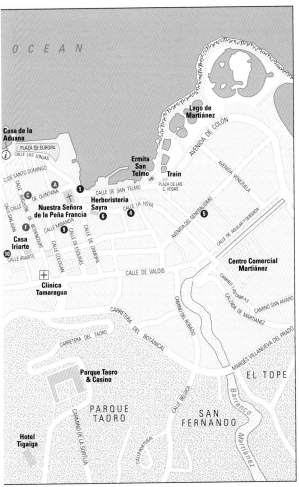

Ranilla is an area of squat, old houses and narrow roads, with the Archeological Museum on a quaint pedestrian street at its heart. The museum contains a modest collection of Guanche pottery and replicas of some mummified body parts: a collection best appreciated by specialists or on a rainy day.

Hotel and Parque Taoro

Hotel Taoro, a Puerto landmark, was the island's first large, purpose-built hotel and something of a milestone in the development of tourism. Originally constructed by an English company as a sanatorium in 1889, it was rebuilt after a fire in 1929. These days it no longer provides accommodation; instead a casino (☎ 922 38 05 50, daily 8pm–3am; €5) and restaurant attract visitors, and there are great views over the town from its elevated position. Parque Taoro, the neat grounds surrounding

▼ LAGO DE MARTIÁNEZ

the casino, contains some newer hotels, including the *Tigaiga*, a venue for folklore shows (Sun 11am; €2.50) that are actually more fun than they sound, including traditional dancing and singing as well as a display of Canarian wrestling.

Lago de Martiánez

Avda. Colón. Daily 10am–7pm. €3.30. Sun beds and parasols extra. Although there are several good beaches in and around Puerto, large waves and strong currents mean that it's often impossible to bathe safely. A vast, beautifully designed open-air saltwater lido, Lago de Martiánez was built to compensate for this and successfully attracts over a million visitors a year. The complex contains a predictable array of facilities – pools, sunbathing decks, bars, cafés and changing areas. However, it is chiefly known for its unusual design, the work of Canarian artist César Manrique (1920–92), who added soft curves and quirky surrealist touches like the upside-down trees.

Playa Jardín

Running for almost a kilometre on the western edge of town, sandy Playa Jardín is the town's premier beach and is invariably busy. It provides all the usual facilities and the sea is sometimes calm enough for swimming, but often the waters here are best left to experienced surfers.

Loro Parque

Punta Brava ☎ 922 37 38 41, ⓦ www .loroparque.com. Daily 8.30am–6.45pm (last entry 5pm). €24, under-12s €12. Free mini-train from Plaza de las C. Vegas. Loro Parque (Parrot Park) is Tenerife's best-publicized tourist attraction. Opened

▲ LORO PARQUE

in 1978, the zoo originally contained only 150 parrots, a few of which performed in a show that is still put on several times a day, and while the parrot collection now tops 1400, it's overshadowed by several more high-profile attractions. These include performances by seals and dolphins (check the timetable on entering if you plan to catch them all), some impressive aquariums (including a shark tunnel) plus gorilla and chimp enclosures. The most impressive addition, however, is the remarkable Planet Penguin, a high-tech enclosure powered by the equivalent of two thousand fridges to keep its Antarctic penguins happy. The latest addition to the menagerie is OrcaOcean, a series of pools in which four orcas from Florida's Sea World perform exceptional tricks.

Jardines Botánicos

Avda. Marqués Villanueva, La Paz. Daily 9am–6pm. €1.50. The subtropical Jardines Botánicos (Botanical Gardens) were originally created in 1788 by King Carlos III, who had an ambition to display species from all the Spanish colonies in his palace gardens back in Spain.

He hoped Tenerife would be a good place to acclimatize the plants and he was right – but unfortunately few of the species could withstand the cooler Spanish winters leading to the ultimate failure of his tropical-garden project. With some three thousand species from around the world on display here, the variety of plants is certainly impressive, with everything from Californian palms to Brazilian shrubs growing alongside one another.

Pueblo Chico

Camino Cruz de Los Martillos 62, Exit 35, Autop. del Norte. ☎922 33 40 60 ⓦwww.pueblochico.com. Daily 9am–7pm. €12, free bus from the Avda. Venezuela in Puerto de la Cruz. Presenting Tenerife in miniature, Pueblo Chico is a fun attraction to either whet your appetite to explore the island or as a neat way to round off a week of sightseeing. Here parts of the island's scenery, history and architecture are recreated, using scale models measuring one twenty-fifth of life size. Not only buildings, but whole plazas, airports and landscapes are recreated, often with a touch of humour. A recreation of the Paisaje Lunar (see p.136) provides the entrance gate, while a model of Teide lies at the centre of the park. Its painstaking construction, based on National Park service survey data, took 630 working days and thousands of kilos of material to accurately execute. Don't bother paying an extra €1.50 for an audio guide, all the information is more or less duplicated in the leaflet provided with your ticket.

Hike to Playa Bollullo

4km/1hr 30min one-way hike.
Pleasant, sandy Playa Bollullo is one of the area's best beaches – though frequently enormous waves mean that swimming is not usually an option. It's a good four-kilometre clifftop hike from Puerto, starting with a steep climb up Camino Las Cabras – beside the Centro Comercial Martiánez – following the steps leading onto Camino San Amaro. Excellent views over Puerto soon open up, and the Mirador de la Paz viewpoint is a good place from which to enjoy them. From here you can head east along the clifftop promenade and a rougher coastal path to Playa Bollullo, on the edge of town. A flight of steps leads down the cliff to the beach, while the path continues east to several smaller beaches where both nudism and wild camping are tolerated.

Casa del Vino La Baranda

El Sauzal ☎922 57 25 35 ⓦwww
.cabtfe.es/casa-vino. Tues 11am–
7.30pm, Wed–Sat 10am–9.30pm,
Sun 11am–6pm. Free. Bus #101
from Puerto de la Cruz, 21–30 daily,
40min; or Santa Cruz, 1hr to "Cruz
El Sauzal" motorway junction. Casa del Vino La Baranda, Tenerife's wine museum, is housed in a beautifully restored seventeenth-century *hacienda* in a major agricultural region, known for its fine grapes and excellent wines. Informative displays give details on the region and there's the opportunity for tastings too. If you'd like something to wash down, head to the museum's tapas bar which has excellent views over the coast, or visit its classy restaurant (see p.88).

Rambla de Castro

Buses #107, #108 & #363 from
Puerto de la Cruz, 36–38 daily,
25min; or Santa Cruz, 15–17 daily,
1hr 15min to Mirador San Pedro.
Occupying a picturesque headland on a stretch of coastline named after it, the

▲ PLAYA BOLLULLO

▲ RAMBLA DE CASTRO

Rambla de Castro estate includes a restored manor house and some fortifications at the heart of a large banana plantation. A path heads here from Puerto – follow the coastal route from the *Hotel Maritim* which lies on the coast just west of Loro Parque (you can get here using the free mini-train – see p.82) – and makes an excellent walk (2–3hr return), passing a ruined but grand pumphouse that once provided the *hacienda* with water from a spring. The house and fortifications can also be accessed from the main coastal road at the Mirador San Pedro.

Playa Socorro

Buses #107, #108 & #363 from Puerto de la Cruz, 36–38 daily, 30min; or Santa Cruz, 15–17 daily, 1hr 15min. This, the island's most popular natural beach, is a pleasant black-sand strip stretching a kilometre along the coast to Punta Brava and Loro Parque. It's usually overrun on summer weekends while on August evenings it attracts crowds to

watch the movies projected onto massive screens – for details check at the tourist office or in *El Día* newspaper. In winter the sea is generally too rough for bathing, and is given over to surfers.

Hotels

Alfomar

C/Peñita 6 ☎ & ℗ 922 38 06 82 ⓔ hotelalfomar@terra.es. A small hotel housed in a 1970s building with what's now retro-chic decor. Most of the en-suite double rooms come with a balcony overlooking a quiet pedestrian street. €26.

Botánico

Urbanización El Botánico ☎ 922 38 14 00, ⓦ www.hotelbotanico.com. A large five-star hotel, within immaculately maintained gardens to the east of town. For the price, the rooms are nothing special, though most have balconies with fine views. Facilities include three restaurants, swimming pools, tennis courts, a spa for massage and beauty treatments and an eighteeen-hole putting green. €190.

Chimisay

C/Agustín de Bethencourt 14 ☎922 38 35 52, ⓦwww.hotel-chimisay.com. Though it has an uninviting exterior and faded interiors, the 67 large, clean rooms here are well kept and overlook a quiet pedestrian street. There's also a small pool on the roof. €56.

Marquesa

C/Quintana 11 ☎922 38 31 51, ⓦwww.hotelmarquesa.com. A well-established hotel in an early eighteenth-century Canarian building. Behind the ornate balconies are good modern facilities, including a reliable restaurant and a small pool. Breakfast is included in the rate. Singles available. €70.

Monopol

C/Quintana 15 ☎922 38 46 11, ⓔmonopol@interbook.net. Elegant building from 1742, with wooden balconies overlooking a courtyard. The rooms are exquisitely presented, though some of the less expensive ones a bit cramped. With pool and rooftop sun deck. Prices include breakfast. €79.

San Borondón

C/Agustín Espinosa 2 ☎922 38 33 13, ☏922 37 13 65. A group of Colonial-style buildings, just 200m from the beach and offering over a hundred rooms, a good-sized seawater pool, tennis courts and restaurant. Prices include breakfast and dinner. €84.

Trovador

C/Puerto Viejo 38 ☎922 38 45 12, ⓦwww.hoteltrovador.com. Pleasant place in a central location where rooms are en suite and have balconies, TV and minibar. There's also a small pool on the roof with great sea views. Rates include a decent breakfast buffet. €70.

Pensions

Los Geranios

C/del Lomo 14 ☎922 38 28 10. Spotlessly clean and well-kept hotel-quality rooms (all en suite) in a friendly pension in the old fishing quarter. A basic continental breakfast is offered for a small extra charge. €29.

Loly

C/de la Sala 4 ☎922 38 36 93. A friendly, simple and clean pension, just outside the old town, offering double rooms with shared bath. €20.

La Platanera

C/Blanco 29 ☎922 38 41 57. Both single and double rooms are available in this modern house. All are en suite, and some have balconies overlooking a charming little garden. €26.

Rosamary

C/San Felipe 14 ☎922 38 32 53. A small, friendly and immaculately kept place, where all rooms are en suite – those with a balcony overlook a busy road and so are noisier than those without. €30.

Apartments

Florasol

Camino del Coche 7 ☎922 38 98 48, ⓦwww.aparthotelflorasol.com. Small complex in quiet surroundings outside the centre offering well-equipped, tastefully decorated and generously sized apartments, many with views towards Teide. Facilities include a pool, tennis courts and a restaurant. €68.

Park Plaza

C/José Arroyo 2 ☎922 38 41 12, ©cipriang@teleline.es. A modern block of well-equipped apartments, each with a kitchen, TV and a balcony. Though tired-looking, the central location and small rooftop pool compensate. €52.

Shops

Artenerife

Muelle Pesquera. Pottery, lace and carvings are some of the genuine Tenerife souvenirs available at this branch of the island-wide chain.

Herboristeria Sayra

C/La Hoya 20. Small deli specializing in local produce and so a good place to pick up miniatures of novelty liqueurs and *mojo* – also offered in powdered form for you to make at home.

Cafés

El Pinguino

Plaza del Charco. Daily 10am–10pm. A great spot to people-watch on the town's main square while enjoying one of the numerous flavours of inexpensive, home-made Italian ice creams. Sit down and gorge on extravagant sundaes or pick up a cone to take away.

Restaurants

Azúcar

C/Iriarte 1 ☎922 38 70 14. Tues–Sun 8.30pm–1am. Moderately priced Cuban food – rice-based dishes,

black bean stews, fried green bananas, croquettes and tapas-like snacks – plus lively Latin American music, in a restored house in the centre of the old town.

El Caldosa

Playa Chica, Punta Brava ☎922 38 90 18. Sat–Thurs noon–10pm. Good little restaurant off the end of Playa Jardín in Punta Brava. Superb fish and seafood at reasonable prices served in cheerful, stylish surroundings with large windows that swing open so you can hear the waves crashing on the tiny beach.

Daisy Burguer

C/Doctor Ingram 18. Cheap and bustling burger bar, popular with the locals, and also offering omelettes and a few tapas along with its great-value set meals. The "daisy burger especial" (€2.30) contains just about every ingredient in the place – including a fried egg and tuna. Open all day and well into the small hours.

El Limón

C/Esquivel and C/B.Miranda. Closed Sun lunch. Vegetarian place serving great meat-free burgers, soups, salads, sandwiches and one main dish for dinner, plus lots of fresh shakes and juices at moderate prices.

La Papa

C/San Felipe 33. Cosy restaurant with a range of Canarian food – including good thick hearty Canarian stew called *puchero* and goat dishes as well as a couple of veggie options, all reasonably priced.

Peruano

C/del Pozo 18. Closed Wed & May. Decorated and named to make its Peruvian credentials quite clear, the cuisine here follows suit. Many of the inexpensive dishes are the usual local meat and seafood options with a Peruvian spin. Dried lamb sirloin is the house speciality.

Restaurante Rustica

Punta Viento. Daily noon–11pm. Not a gourmet choice, though the Italian food is tasty and inexpensive – pizzas from €5 – and the views over the coast from its cliffside location are beautiful.

La Rosa Di Bari

C/del Lomo 23 ☎ 922 36 85 23. Suave Italian restaurant with oodles of panache and great – though expensive – food. The house salad with apple and parmesan is a good way to start, while the portions of the various home-made pastas are small enough to leave room for dessert. Not so the generously sized and delicious pizzas. The wine list includes a number of good Tenerife vintages.

Régulo

C/Pérez Zamora 16 ☎ 922 38 45 06. Closed Sun & July. One of the classiest restaurants in town – with prices to match – located in a restored town house, with much of the seating in the courtyard. There's a good spread of Canarian cuisine on offer, but the place is particularly known for its seafood.

Tasca

Casa del Vino La Baranda, El Sauzal ☎ 922 56 33 88. Closed Mon. Canarian fine dining option, in a restored seventeenth-century *hacienda* (see p.84) out of town, with cheerful service and an exhaustive local wine list. Main courses around €10.

▲ CASA DEL VINO

Bars

La Gruta

C/La Hoya 24. Grotto-themed bar that's worth a try if you'd rather settle down to some chat or live music than trawl the clubs.

Penny Farthing

C/La Hoya 32. Rather nondescript bar and disco, but nonetheless a dependable favourite along pedestrian Calle La Hoya that tends to get going a bit earlier than its neighbours.

Clubs

Vampis

Edificio Drafo, Avda. del Generalísimo ☎ 922 38 65 37. The best-known club in town – popular with transvestites – sits along the main strip of basement clubs and discos on the Avenida del Generalísimo. If you don't fancy this, there are plenty of other options nearby including, unusually for Tenerife, a few gay clubs.

La Orotava

Not only the name **La Orotava** but also the bulk of the town's original wealth comes from the prosperous, fertile green valley surrounding it. Since pre-Spanish times, this has been one of the island's most densely populated areas, and its main town blossomed as the centre of cash crop industries which still include vineyards and banana groves. Plaza de la Constitución is the busiest square in La Orotava's well-preserved old town, whose network of steep, cobbled streets is particularly known for the Doce Casas, twelve striking Canarian-style mansions that were former residences of the area's leading families. Some of these are open to the public as well-stocked handicraft shops and can, along with the town's other attractions, easily be explored on a day-trip from Puerto de la Cruz, 6km away. The best time to visit the town is during the celebrations of Corpus Christi in May or June, when the streets are decorated with murals made from flower petals, baked leaves and volcanic sand, a tradition dating back to 1847.

Jardín Marquesado de la Quinta Roja and the Jardínes Botánicos

Daily 9am–2pm. €2.50. The Jardín Marquesado de la Quinta Roja is the nineteenth-century-style garden of the Ponte family. The immaculately kept and tightly regimented layout may not be to everyone's taste, but

▼ JARDIN MARQUESADO DE LA QUINTA ROJA

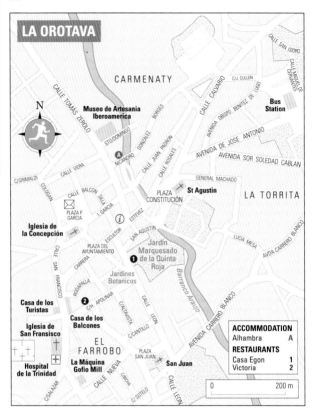

the garden does offer great views over the coast. Just west of here are La Orotava's own tiny Jardínes Botánicos (Botanic Gardens; same hours; free entrance), which include a good-sized dragon tree amid a small collection of exotic plants.

Iglesia de la Concepción

Plaza Casanas. Mass: Wed, Thurs & Fri 10am, 1pm, 5pm & 7pm; Mon 10am, 1pm, 4pm & 6pm; Sun 9am, 10am, 11.30am & 6pm. Built after the original church on this site was destroyed by earthquakes in 1704 and 1705, the Iglesia de la Concepción is a grand structure that reflects the wealth of the local community at that time. Its facade is a particularly notable piece of

Arrival and information

From La Orotava's **bus station** at the top of Avda. Jose Antonio – bus #352 and #353 from Puerto de la Cruz (35 daily, 17min) – it's a ten-minute walk west to the old town, where you'll find the **tourist office** (Mon–Fri 8.30am–6pm; ☏922 32 30 41) on Carrera Escultor Estévez 2.

91

Baroque architecture and has been made a Spanish national monument.

Casa de los Balcones

C/San Francisco. Mon–Sat 10am–1pm & 4–7pm. Upper levels €1.50, otherwise free. Calle de San Francisco is known for its impressive seventeenth- and eighteenth-century mansions, the grandest of which is the Casa de Los Balcones. As its name suggests, the house is best known for its splendid, ornately worked Canarian pine balconies – facing both the street and into its pretty courtyard. The ground floor now contains a lace and linen centre, while the upper level has opulent wood-clad rooms, furnished as they would have been in the eighteenth century. A couple of adjoining rooms reconstruct the living quarters of simpler folk at this time.

La Máquina Gofio Mill

C/San Francisco 3. Mon–Fri 8am–1pm & 2–7pm. Free. El Farrobo, the town's old mill quarter, is where the local speciality *gofio* (see p.195) has been produced for centuries. Nowadays, seven of the original *gofio* mills still survive along the phenomenally steep Calle de San Francisco, and one of them, La Máquina, still operates, albeit now with an electric motor. Photos inside depict bygone days when the quarter still clattered with the sound of the mills.

Museo de Artesanía Iberoamericana

C/Tomás Zerolo 34 ☎922 32 33 76. Mon–Fri 9am–6pm, Sat 9am–2pm. €2.50. Housed in the former Convento de Santo Domingo, the Museo de Artesanía lberoamericana devotes itself to exhibiting handicrafts and folk art from Spain and Latin America. The beautiful old convent building itself is as interesting as the displays, which focus on textiles, ceramics and musical instruments but are poorly explained.

PLACES La Orotava

▲ LA OROTAVA

Hotels

Alhambra

C/Nicandro Gonzales Borges 19
☎ 922 32 04 34, ⓦ www.alhambra
.teneriffa.com. Stylish and highly
recommended villa with
Moorish decor and sea views.
There are six large double
rooms and facilities include a
pool and sauna. €95.

Shops

Casa de los Turistas

C/San Francisco. Mon–Sat 9am–6pm.
Free. One of La Orotava's
Doce Casas, the impressive
Casa de los Turistas is entirely
devoted to peddling Canarian
handicrafts from embroidery
and lace to cigars and wine.
The courtyard sees occasional
pottery and weaving displays
and also has an example of the
floor collages which decorate
the town during Corpus Christi
(see p.89).

Restaurants

Casa Egon

C/Leon 5 ☎ 922 33 00 87.
Tues–Sun 12.30pm–8.30pm. Basic,
inexpensive bistro-style restaurant
specializing in omelettes, tapas
and classic Canarian dishes.

Victoria

C/ Hermano Apolinar ☎ 922 33 26 83.
Mon–Sat 1–3.30pm & 7.30–10.30pm.
The best place to eat in the
old town centre with a lovely
courtyard dining area. Expensive
Canarian dishes are on the menu:
the sole in prawn sauce with
asparagus is especially good.

Garachico and around

Standing at the base of immense cliffs beside a deep harbour, **Garachico** was, along with La Laguna and La Orotava, one of the first towns on the island. The narrow cobbled streets, rough fishermen's cottages and grand town houses belonged to what was Tenerife's most important sixteenth-century port until a series of natural disasters – volcanic eruptions and earthquakes – plagued the town and ultimately ruined its harbour. But for visitors at least the results of these events – lava rock pools in the town's bay and charming old streets frozen in time – are engagingly picturesque.

A good day-trip, particularly during the August Romería, the largest harvest festival-style celebration on the island, Garachico also makes a relaxing, alternative base to the big resorts and gives easy access to the neighbouring town of **Icod de los Vinos** and **El Drago**, the gigantic dragon tree there.

Castillo de San Miguel

Avda. Tomé Cano. Mon–Fri 10am–6pm, Sat & Sun 10am–2pm. €0.60.

One of the town's oldest and most striking buildings is the stocky harbourside fort, Castillo de San Miguel. Built in the sixteenth century to protect Garachico from pirates, the small fort was one of the few buildings to survive the 1706 volcanic eruption and is now home to a vaguely diverting rock and fossil collection. More appealing are the views from the ramparts across the village and out to the Roque de Garachico, a lone rock monolith in the bay.

El Caletón rock pools

One of Garachico's unique attractions is a series of rock pools behind the Castillo de San Miguel. This area of lava is a result of the same eruption in 1706 that closed the harbour and ruined the town, but locals have made the best of it by creating paved walkways between the natural bathing pools. Formed as lava cooled on contact with the sea, these are fed and cleaned by the tidal action – making bathing possible only at low tide during calm seas.

Plaza de la Torre

Narrow Calle Esteban Ponte

Arrival and information

Buses connect Garachico with other towns along the north coast, including Puerto de la Cruz (#363, 16–25 daily, 1hr) and Santa Cruz (#107, 4–6 daily, 1hr 35min). The **tourist office** is at C/Esteban Ponte 5 (Mon–Sat 10am–3pm; ☎922 13 34 61).

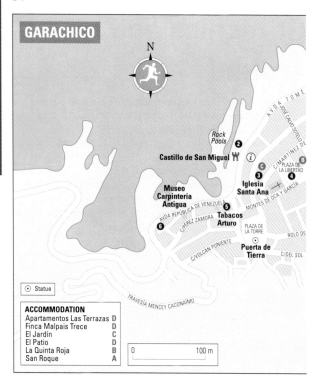

GARACHICO

N

Rock Pools

Castillo de San Miguel

Museo Carpintería Antigua

Iglesia Santa Ana

Tabacos Arturo

Puerta de Tierra

⊙ Statue

ACCOMMODATION
Apartamentos Las Terrazas	D
Finca Malpais Trece	D
El Jardín	C
El Patio	D
La Quinta Roja	B
San Roque	A

0   100 m

divides rows of elegant, largely wooden, town houses as it runs through the centre of Garachico to Plaza de Juan Gonzalez de la Torre. A small park in the square contains the Puerta de Tierra, a one-time gate to the town's harbour, and an old wooden winepress.

Plaza de la Libertad

The town's main square, Plaza de la Libertad, has as its centrepiece a statue of Simon Bolivar, the nineteenth-century South American freedom fighter. His tenuous connection to Garachico is through his grandmother, who emigrated from here after the 1706 disaster. On the western side of the plaza stands the grand Iglesia Santa Ana, the town's

main church, topped by a six-storey belltower and containing a fine wooden ceiling.

Convento de San Francisco

Plaza de la Libertad. Mon–Fri 9am–7pm, Sat & Sun 9am–3pm. €1. This former convent houses the small and ramshackle town museum whose collections include a number of shells, stuffed birds and an exhibit of locks and keys through the ages. More interesting is the information on Garachico's history, particularly its role as a major port, and the chance to see the building's pretty wooden balconies and atriums.

Museo Carpintería Antigua

Avda. República de Venezuela 17.

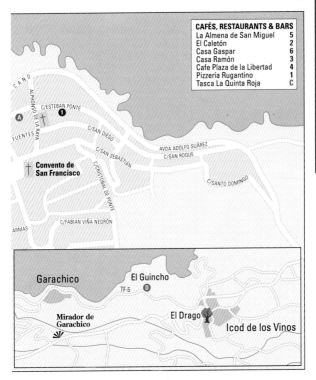

CAFÉS, RESTAURANTS & BARS

La Almena de San Miguel	5
El Caletón	2
Casa Gaspar	6
Casa Ramón	3
Cafe Plaza de la Libertad	4
Pizzería Rugantino	1
Tasca La Quinta Roja	C

Daily 9am–7pm. €1.50. Fans of the elegant woodwork on balconies around Garachico might like to visit the small Museo Carpintería Antigua. Old artisans' tools are beautifully displayed here alongside photos of their work around town, and there's also a small shop selling local products and souvenirs.

El Drago, Icod de los Vinos

Buses #106 & 1#08 from Santa Cruz, 15 daily, 1hr 10min–1hr 35min; #354 & #363 from Puerto de la Cruz, 32–41 daily, 1hr 10min; #363 from Garachico, 16–25 daily, 15min. El Drago, the world's oldest and biggest specimen of the endemic giant yucca-like dragon tree, towers above the main road on the western side of Icod de los Vinos. Its dimensions are impressive enough – seventeen metres high with a six metre trunk circumference – but its true claim to fame arises from its age, thought to be at least 500 years – which means it pre-dates even the oldest buildings that surround it.

The tree stands in a garden (daily 9.30am–6.30pm), to which admission is charged (€4), but most visitors are content to view it from an adjacent elevated shady square where the Baroque interior of the late sixteenth-century Iglesia de San Marcos is also worth a look.

The Dragon Tree

Once common around the Mediterranean, successive ice ages pushed the **dragon tree** (*dracaena draco*) further south around twenty million years ago, restricting its habitat to the climatically stable Canary Islands.

The tree's unusual characteristics – gnarled wood and geometric buds – and its longevity earned it much reverence in the past. Guanche elders and kings held court beneath their canopies and believed the tree foretold the future – a fine blossom pointing to a fine' harvest. The dragon tree's most striking feature, the red rubbery sap, or dragon's blood, not only gave the tree its name but has also been put to a variety of uses: the Guanches incorporated it into healing salves and even used it in their mummification process, while more recently it has been used to dye toothpaste, marble and Italian violins. However, high demand for the sap meant that many dragon trees were tapped to death, and today there are few large specimens left on the island.

Hotels

Finca Malpais Trece

El Guincho ☎922 83 00 64 ⊕922 13 30 68. Large old farmhouse on the same estate as the *Hotel El Patio* (see below) which has incredible views across plantations to the coast from its courtyard and sun terrace. Bathing is possible in a rocky bay, a ten-minute walk through the banana groves. €80.

▼ EL DRAGO

El Patio

El Guincho ☎922 13 32 80, ⓦwww .hotelpatio.com. Inconspicuously signposted from the road to Icod de los Vinos at El Guincho, this sixteenth-century hotel is tucked away in the middle of a massive banana plantation. Its airy rooms are set around a grand and impressively lush courtyard, and facilities include a swimming pool. Rates include breakfast. €100.

La Quinta Roja

Plaza de la Libertad ☎922 13 33 77, ⓦwww.quintaroja.com. Recently opened hotel in a refurbished sixteenth-century building noted for its wonderful woodwork and airy courtyard. Rooms are simple, with minimalist furnishings complementing traditional design. Facilities include a sauna, solarium and jacuzzi and a programme of tours and hiking trips. €120.

San Roque

C/Esteban Ponte 32 ☎922 13 34 35, ⓦwww.hotelsanroque.com. Once the home of the town's leading family, this atmospheric old town house is now an elegant hotel. No two rooms are the

▲ FINCA MALPAIS TRECE, GARACHICO

same, but all are equipped with TV, video and minibar, and there's also a gourmet restaurant, rooftop terrace and pool. Some singles available and all rates include breakfast. €160.

Pensions

El Jardín

C/Esteban Ponte 8 ☎ 922 83 02 45, ⓦ www.argonautas.org Impressively creaky and atmospheric old town house set around a sociable central courtyard with its own little bar. Rooms are large and simple, and most share bathrooms. The owners speak English and also let a couple of apartments. Rooms €30; apartments €42.

Apartments

Apartamentos Las Terrazas

El Guincho ☎ & ☎ 922 13 31 20 or 619 13 31 20. A small, modern block of self-catering apartments tucked away in a peaceful banana plantation (see *Hotel El Patio* opposite). The roomy units are simply and stylishly furnished, and have private balconies with views towards the coast. Weekly rates available. €36–48.

Shops

Tabacos Arturo

Avda. República de Venezuela 6, Garachico. ☎ 922 38 91 18. The painstaking process of lovingly hand-rolling cigars can be observed in this tiny shop. There's also plenty of advice on hand to help you decide between its stock: with a range of qualities and dimensions to choose from.

Cafés

El Caletón

Avda. Tome Cano, Garachico. Wonderfully located between the Castillo de San Miguel and the rock pools, this café is the ideal place for a drink and light snack while you enjoy the view. There's also a more substantial selection of reasonably priced fish (from €7) and meat dishes.

Café Plaza de la Libertad

Plaza de la Libertad, Garachico. Kiosk surrounded by outdoor seating in the town's leafy central square, where families and friends gather to sit and socialize at any time of day.

▲ CAFÉ PLAZA DE LA LIBERTAD

Restaurants

La Almena de San Miguel
Avda. República de Venezuela 4,
Garachico. Unprepossessing
first-floor restaurant that's
nevertheless an excellent choice
for fresh seafood at low prices
– as the regular presence of
locals suggests.

Casa Gaspar
Avda. República de Venezuela 20,
Garachico. Closed Mon. More
expensive and grander than
most of the town's restaurants,
this place is a safe bet for
good seafood. There's always a
selection of the local catch on
display, priced by weight.

Casa Ramón
C/Esteban Ponte 4, Garachico. Basic
restaurant that's recommended
not so much for the limited
menu of excellent seafood
dishes, or the distinctive, spicy
home-made *mojo*, but more

for its old, dingy wood-clad
atmosphere and its elderly
proprietor, who makes you feel
as though you've dropped by
your Canarian grandmother's
for lunch.

Pizzería Rugantino
C/Esteban Ponte 44, Garachico. Fri,
Sat & Sun 7pm–midnight. Small and
invariably packed restaurant
that serves arguably the best
pizzas in Tenerife – bargains at
around €6. You may to have to
wait for a table but it's worth
it.

Bars

Tasca La Quinta Roja
Plaza de la Libertad. Open late.
Traditional wood-and-tile tasca
– at the back of the hotel *La
Quinta Roja* – which, in the
absence of any real nightlife in
Garachico, is the best place to
go for an evening drink.

The Teno

The colossal and ancient **Teno Mountains** define Tenerife's northwest tip. They're an excellent area for **hiking**, with steep gorges and ravines carved out of volcanic rock and cutting down to the rugged coastline and a few accessible beaches. Unlike the laurel forests of the Anaga region, the landscape here is largely treeless – most of its timber was cleared to fire sugar mills in the sixteenth century – but this allows clearer views of local peaks like **Montaña Jala**. The premier attraction, however, is the remote village of **Masca**, deep in the middle of the range, from where the region's best-known hike follows the **Barranco de Masca gorge** to the sea.

Buenavista del Norte

Buses #107 from Santa Cruz, 4–6 daily, 1hr 35min; #363 from Puerto de la Cruz, 16–25 daily, 1hr 15min; and #363 from Garachico, 16–25 daily, 15min. Buenavista del Norte is the largest of several uneventful towns squeezed onto the northern coast beside the sheer sides of the Teno massif. As terminus for local and island-wide bus services, it's a useful transport hub and the small collection of seafood restaurants is a boon for weary hikers. A large golf course being completed on the edge of Buenavista looks likely to change the focus for this town that has until now relied

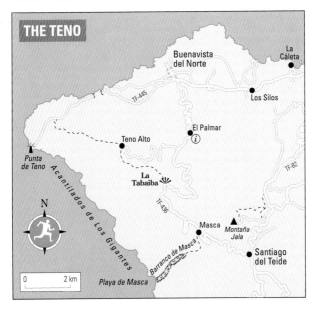

▲ ROAD TO MASCA

on banana cultivation for its income.

Punta de Teno

The Punta de Teno, a jagged volcanic-rock headland jutting into the ocean, is Tenerife's most westerly point. Marked by an old lighthouse, fishing off the headland attracts local fishermen and the clear waters of its sheltered bay invite bathing, but it's the views from the rocky promontory itself that most come for, particularly at sunset when the last rays disappear behind La Gomera and La Palma. Equally impressive are the views eastwards towards the Teno mountains and the huge coastal cliffs.

El Palmar

Bus #355 or #366 from Buenavista, 16 daily, 10min. Among a handful of small rural settlements in the heart of the Teno, the main reason to stop in El Palmar is to visit the park information centre (Mon–Fri 8am–3pm), which hands out free, but fairly simple, hiking maps.

Mirador La Tabaiba & hike

Bus #355 from Buenavista, 4 daily, 20min. The best views over the northern Teno are from Mirador La Tabaiba at its southern edge, with the most spectacular being north towards Buenavista or

west over uninhabited gorges and massive cliffs to the ocean. The viewpoint also marks the start of an excellent ridge walk back to Buenavista, some 11km away. The four-hour hike begins by heading past grazing goats and, in spring, wildflower meadows, to the village of Teno Alto. From here, continue through the village on the minor road that soon becomes a track and gently climbs before finally descending steeply to the road between Buenavista and Punta de Teno. From here you can turn left for an easy 4km return walk to Punta de Teno or right to head 6km along the lightly used road back to Buenavista, with views of the mountains and coast for company.

Montaña Jala hike

Bus #325 from Puerto de la Cruz, 6 daily, 1hr 15min; or Los Gigantes, 6 daily, 30min. The hike up Montaña Jala at the western perimeter of the Teno range is one of the easier walks in this area, climbing through a mix of vegetation – including some prime laurel forest – and rewarded with some great views. The best place to start the hike is the roadside *Restaurant Fleytas* – buses between Icod de Los Vinos and Las Américas stop here and private vehicles can be left in the car park – from where the eight-kilometre loop up Montaña Jala takes around three hours.

The trail begins opposite the restaurant, immediately descending into a wide valley where it passes some ponds and then zigzags up to a ridge on the right, where it splits into three. Take the narrow track straight ahead through thick vegetation; the trail here is overgrown and in places difficult to follow. Look out for a fairly well-trodden path branching off on the uphill side and follow it to a wider track, where you turn right, following it a short way, before climbing again on a small track. This short path soon follows a stream bed before it leads out to a forestry road that circles Montaña Jala. To climb to the summit turn left here; around half an hour later you'll be rewarded with phenomenal views from the summit. The hiking loop ends by descending down the summit road, turning left off it just shy of the main road, then descending on the narrow track that leads back to the ponds and restaurant.

Masca

Bus #355 from Buenavista, 4 daily, 25min; or Valle Santiago, 4 daily, 30min. The village of Masca, in an isolated and picturesque gorge, is considered Tenerife's prettiest village and, outside the hours of 11am–5pm, when crowds and tour buses take over, it's hard to disagree. The village was only connected to the outside world in 1991 by a steep winding road that brings visitors in to see its old stone houses looking out across palm trees and improbably steep ravines towards the Atlantic. The fertile soil here once supported a population of six hundred, but this has dropped to around one hundred today, and many of the buildings have been converted into restaurants or gift shops, with most villagers remaining only to service tourists.

Barranco de Masca hike

One of the best hikes on the island is the strenuous, six-hour return trek down the steep-sided Barranco de Masca. Beginning in Masca village, the route ends at a small beach surrounded by the staggering

▼ MASCA VILLAGE

▲ LOS GIGANTES

Acantilados de Los Gigantes (see p.104) and is a must for any relatively experienced hiker. The path starts just left of the ridge that runs through the centre of town. Keep an eye out for markers along the way as you pass through ravines as high as 600m above the sea. At its narrowest – and most memorable – the gorge is only twenty metres wide, and filled with bizarre, swirling rock formations and curious vegetation.

Several companies (see p.179) offer hiking trips down the valley from the main coastal resorts, costing €35–45 and usually offering a shuttle bus to Masca and a boat to pick you up from the beach at the end. If you want to organize your own transport to the village, but would like to take a boat from the beach to Los Gigantes, contact Excursions Marítimas (☎922 86 19 18) who charge

€9 for this service; the boat leaves the beach at 3.30pm.

Accommodation

El Guanche

Masca ☎922 86 14 05. Basic rooms (with outside toilet) in Masca's old schoolhouse. As the only accommodation in the village it's the best chance to see it without the droves of day-trippers. Rates include half-board. €36.

Café's

El Aderno

C/El Olivio, 1. Los Silos ☎922 84 08 77. Tiny café and confectioners with a well-deserved, island-wide reputation for excellent cakes and tarts. Sit in the basic little café or take away; prices are very reasonable either way. It's located just southwest of Los Silos' town plaza; with another branch in Buenavista del Norte (takeaway only) – again just southwest of its main plaza.

Restaurants

La Fuente

Masca. Daily noon–6pm. Superbly positioned below the main road near the village church, this place has great views over the valley from its terrace and is consequently one of Masca's busiest restaurants. Serves excellent home-made lemonade as well as good Canarian food.

Meson del Norte

Carretera de Masca. Closed Mon. Large rural restaurant, 6km south of Buenavista on the road to Masca, offering inexpensive but top-quality upland Canarian fare – mostly grilled meat and chicken – along with fresh goat's cheese and local wines that are well worth sampling. Other restaurants further up the road to Masca are similar.

El Pescador

C/Los Molinos 27, Buenavista del Norte. Wed–Mon 9am–midnight. In the centre of Buenavista, "The fisherman" has a great range of inexpensive seafood, including succulent king prawns in three different sauces.

The west coast

Though large-scale resort developments are beginning to creep up Tenerife's **west coast**, the main resorts here – **Los Gigantes, Puerto de Santiago** and **Playa de la Arena** – offer a low-key alternative to Playa de Las Américas to the south, and attract those looking for good weather and a quiet resort; nightlife is almost entirely absent here. All three lie at the northern end of this stretch of coast, huddled beside the colossal **Acantilados de Los Gigantes** (Giants' Cliffs), while the smaller, more Canarian, towns further south mostly exist to service the resorts. **Alcalá** is set on a pretty bay and **Playa San Juan** recently invested in a beach and attractive coastal promenade. Inland, this region is thick with (mainly banana) plantations between a series of forgettable towns: only **Adeje**, at the southern end above Las Américas, is worth a visit, particularly to hike up the **Barranco del Infierno**.

Los Gigantes town

Though largely characterized by densely packed low-rise apartment complexes, the town of Los Gigantes has the advantage of a spectacular setting beside the huge cliffs from which it gets its name. A single, one-way main road descends into town and loops around its central collection of shops, which hide a tiny pedestrian plaza in their centre. Below this commercial area is a pleasant marina, crowded with boats and lined with cafés and restaurants, and a black sandy beach, accessed by an alley behind the marina.

Acantilados de Los Gigantes

Beyond the beach on the northern edge of Los Gigantes town rise the sheer rock walls of the massive Acantilados de Los Gigantes (Giants' Cliffs). Formed by lava being squeezed under high pressure through multiple parallel cracks, these astounding formations rise 500m out of the sea. A popular day-trip destination, most visitors explore them on boat tours, which also head out to the Gomeran Channel to see dolphins and stop for a swim. Expect to pay from around €20 per person for these trips, which are hawked by a number

Arrival and information

Buses connect **Los Gigantes, Puerto de Santiago** and **Playa de la Arena** – all just a couple of minutes from each other – with the island-wide network: bus #325 from Puerto de la Cruz (6 daily, 1hr 45min); #473 from Las Galletas (15 daily, 1hr 40min) via Los Cristianos and Las Américas. The local **tourist office** overlooks the beach in Playa de la Arena at CC Seguro de Sol 35 (Mon–Fri 9am–2.30pm; ☎922 86 03 48, ⊛www.santiagodelteide.org).

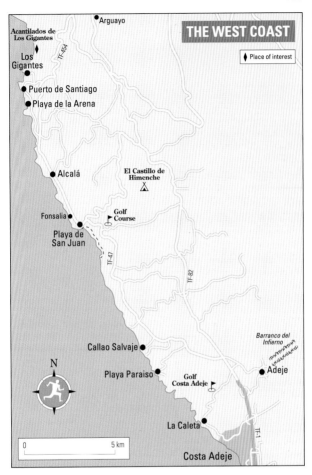

◆ Place of interest

Acantilados de
Los Gigantes

Los
Gigantes

● Arguayo

TF-454

● Puerto de Santiago

● Playa de la Arena

● Alcalá

El Castillo de
Himenche

Fonsalia ●
● Golf
Course

Playa de
San Juan

TF-47

TF-82

Barranco del
Infierno

Callao Salvaje ●

N

Playa Paraiso ●
Golf
Costa Adeje ▶

● Adeje

La Caleta ●

TF-1

0   5 km

Costa Adeje

of operators based beside the
town's marina.

Los Gigantes Lidos

The opportunity to swim
along the coast beside Los
Gigantes is often compromised
by huge waves and dangerous
undercurrents. To compensate,
two private complexes offer pools
and sun terraces on cliffs above
the sea, just south of the marina
in Los Gigantes. The larger
of the two, El Laguillo (daily

10.30am–6.30pm; €3.50, kids
€1.75) has a more imaginatively
laid-out bathing area, with lakes,
waterfalls and islands, than the
nearby Oasis (daily 10am–6pm;
€3, kids €1.50), which is duller
but greener.

Puerto de Santiago and Playa de la Arena

Merging with Los Gigantes
and each other, Puerto de
Santiago and Playa de la Arena
hold an unexciting mixture

PLACES

The west coast

▲ LOS GIGANTES MARINA

of modern, sprawling homes, hotels and apartments with most restaurants, bars and cafés situated along the main seafront road. The local highlight is the small and busy black-sand beach from which Playa de la Arena gets its name.

Alcalá and Playa de San Juan

Bus #473 from Las Galletas via Los Cristianos and Las Américas, 15 daily, 1hr 30min; and Los Gigantes, 15 daily, 10–20min. Set amid banana plantations, the unpretentious town of Alcalá centres on a plaza near the small sheltered harbour and beach which is good for a quiet swim. Further south along the main road, Playa de San Juan is recommended for its large and uncrowded pebble beach and long coastal promenade which snakes its way from the town onto adjoining cliffs for a pleasant two-kilometre hike with excellent views over the ocean.

Adeje

Bus #416 or #473 from Las Américas and Los Cristianos, 36 daily, 30min; bus #473 from Los Gigantes, 15 daily, 40min

and Las Galletas, 60min. Though much of the administrative town of Adeje is bland, its location and modern centre are pretty enough. The only sights are the fortified *hacienda*, Casa Fuerte – sacked by Sir Francis Drake in 1586 and not open to visitors – and the simply decorated sixteenth-century Iglesia de Santa Ursula at the top of the main road, Calle Grande. The church's white washed walls and *Mudéjar* wooden roof protect a copy of the famous Virgin of Candelaria (see p.74).

Barranco del Infierno hike

6km/4hr return hike. Hikers need to book a slot (€3) for the hike at the info centre at the start (daily 8.30am–5.30pm; last access in at 2.30pm ☎922 78 28 85 ✉info@ idecongestion.net) and advance reservations are recommended. Close to Adeje – and the main reason for coming here – is the Barranco del Infierno (Hell's Ravine), the deepest gorge in the Canaries and location of Tenerife's only year-round stream. The path, beginning uphill of the Casa Fuerte in Adeje and beside the panoramic terrace of the restaurant *Otelo*, is easy to follow and involves little steep climbing. The route offers dizzying views down the ravine and passes through a varied landscape where semi-desert gives way to thick stands of willow and eucalyptus trees before finishing at a rather disappointing waterfall which does, however, afford the chance of a cold dip.

Hotels

Barceló Santiago

C/La Hondura 8, Puerto Santiago ☎922 86 09 12, ⊛www.barcelo.com.

Clifftop hotel centred on a massive sun deck and pool. Facilities include a fitness centre and tennis and squash courts, while most rooms have a balcony overlooking the sea with views of La Gomera. Rates include breakfast and more than halve in the off season. €110.

Fonda Central

C/Grande 26, Adeje ☎922 78 15 50. Beautifully restored eighteenth-century Canarian family residence on Adeje's main street. All rooms are on the top floor and look onto a central courtyard. Rates include breakfast. €90.

Playa La Arena

C/Lajial 4, Playa de la Arena ☎922 86 29 20, ☜www.springhoteles.com. Large hotel containing over four hundred air-conditioned rooms, most with balcony and sea views. Facilities include three bars, a restaurant (with a good breakfast buffet), two large pools (featuring waterfalls and a waterslide), tennis courts and a minigolf course. €132.

Pensions

Alcalá

C/Marruecos 2, Alcalá ☎922 86 54 57 ☜www.pensionalcala. com. Bohemian place just north of the harbour, run by an eccentric Gomeran who provides leaflets on his life as a South American revolutionary. The influences of his adventures are evidenced by his abstract paintings on the guesthouse walls, while the rooms, though less interesting, are clean and modern. €31.

Rambala

C/Grande 7, Adeje ☎922 78 00 71. Plain rooms, with bathroom and balcony, on the town's main street. €24.

Pensión Rochil

C/Corpus Christi 29, Adeje ☎922 78 02 52. Scrupulously clean lodgings on a minor road running parallel to the town's main thoroughfare. Good long-stay rates can be negotiated. €22.

▲ BARRANCO DEL INFIERNO

Apartments

Aparthotel Poblado Marinero

C/Poblado Marinero, Los Gigantes
☎922 86 09 66, ⓦwww.elhotelito
.com. Attractive Canarian-
village-style complex beside Los
Gigantes port and with its own
rock pool swimming area. Both
the one- and two- bedroom
apartments have a kitchen,
bathroom and lounge and can
sleep up to six. €48.

Apartamentos Neptuno-Cristina

Avda. Marítima 24, Playa de la Arena
☎922 86 75 67, ⓦwww.aptosneptuno
.com. Large, well-equipped
apartments in a modest complex
containing a small pool and sun
deck next to the black sands of
Playa de la Arena. The friendly
local owners offer one- and
two-bed apartments for weekly
rental (€450), sleeping two or
four people, and there are a
number of shops and restaurants
close to the complex. €64.

Shops

Centro Alfarero

Arguayo ☎922 86 31 27. Tues–Sun
10am–1pm & 4–7pm. For the

chance to watch rough-hewn
traditional pots being made
using thousand-year-old
Guanche techniques, this is the
place to come. There's also a
small shop selling the finished
goods.

Restaurants

La Barrera

C/Los Tarajales, Fonsalía. Closed Sun.
Local tapas bar and restaurant in
a tiny village midway between
Alcalá and San Juan. The TV
might be blaring but the food is
inexpensive and first rate.

Beeches

CC Santiago II, Puerto de Santiago
☎922 86 24 03. Dinner only, closed
Fri. Small restaurant beside the
Hotel Barceló Santiago offering
plenty of fresh gourmet
options, including quite a few
veggie choices. Prices border
on expensive but the food is
prepared with considerable
attention to detail. Reservations
advisable.

Casa Pancho

Avda. Marítima, Playa de la Arena
☎922 86 13 23. Closed Mon & June.
Pleasant, moderately expensive
Canarian restaurant in a great

▼ PLAYA LA ARENA

location directly beside the beach. Among the great fish dishes (most €8–10) is a delicious two-person paella.

Restaurante Marinero

C/Los Gios Playa, Los Gigantes ☎922 86 19 55. Beautifully situated beside the Acantilados de Los Gigantes and accessed via the pedestrian road behind the marina, this friendly restaurant is the highlight of the Los Gigantes dining scene. It specializes in moderately priced fresh fish and seafood – recommended is the fish soup, oven-baked platters and, for dessert, the banana flambé.

Miranda

C/Flor de Pascua 25, Los Gigantes ☎922 86 02 07. Daily 7–10pm. Good and unusually imaginative Canarian restaurant in the centre of Los Gigantes, where local specialities are blended with international cuisine to produce interesting results at above average prices. Vegetarians will find a couple of (odd) choices here too.

Oasis

C/Grande 5, Adeje. Closed Wed. Adeje has a reputation for good upland Canarian food, particularly garlic chicken, and this is the only dish available at *Oasis*, served with salad and fries at crowded tables on the tree-lined main road.

Otelo

C/Los Molinos, Adeje ☎922 78 03 74. Wed–Mon 11am–10.30pm. The unbeatable views over the Barranco del Infierno from its patio make this touristy restaurant the pick of the bunch. The garlic chicken is excellent and prices are very reasonable.

El Pescador de Alcalá

Muelle, Alcalá. Wed–Mon 1–4.30pm & 8–11.30pm. Big place with moderate prices and harbour views that's an excellent option for fresh fish, straight from the restaurant's tanks.

PLACES The west coast

Los Cristianos, Las Américas and Costa Adeje

The seven-kilometre-long string of hotel and apartment complexes along Tenerife's southwest coast may divide into different districts – **Los Cristianos, Playa de Las Américas and the Costa Adeje** – but in reality it's one single conurbation, accommodating two-thirds of the island's visitors and countless expatriates. The districts have characters that range from tacky and down-at-heel to stylish and exclusive, but, with the exception of the core of the old harbour town of Los Cristianos, all of them have been built from scratch since the 1970s – and construction continues on the fringes. Sand was imported to make beaches, sea defences created to protect it, and thousands of gallons of water were piped in to create this holiday city in the desert. While the scale of the achievement is undoubtedly impressive, if you're looking for a holiday to get away from it all or to surround yourself with the island's indigenous culture or charm, you'll be disappointed. Most visitors spend the bulk of their time on crowded beaches, though water sports, including some decent surfing and diving, are also possible and several commercial parks and attractions are within easy reach, most providing free transport. This mega tourist city also has the benefit of good infrastructure, which makes it easy to escape to Tenerife's quieter parts by bus or rental car.

Los Cristianos

Nestling beside Montaña Chayofita, adjacent to its beach and harbour, the old pedestrian core of Los Cristianos is easy to identify and worth a visit. Having grown from fishing village to port and then, since the 1960s, into an agreeable resort, it's still home to many Canarians. Away from the old centre, however, it's a different story, and high-rise apartment blocks dominate here as much as they do elsewhere. A promenade passes the harbour and the Playa de los Cristianos on its route along the town's entire seafront before joining the promenade that runs around Las Américas by the new and relatively uncrowded Playa de las Vistas.

Montaña Guaza hike

3km/3hr. To the east of Los Cristianos, the promenade heads

Arrival and information

Most package holidays include a transfer to your hotel, but there's also a frequent **public bus** from the airport which passes through Los Cristianos and southern Las Américas before heading for the **bus station**, between central Las Américas, San Eugenio and the motorway.

Las Américas has two **tourist offices** and two beachfront kiosks at Playa de las Vistas and Fañabe. Information for the centre and north is covered by the Adeje region office at Avda. Rafael Puig 1 (Mon–Fri 10am–4pm; ☎922 75 06 33), just north of CC Veronicas in central Las Américas, while the south is covered by the Arona region office near the Parque Santiago II building (Mon–Fri 9am–9pm, Sat 9am–1pm; ☎922 79 76 68, ☜www.arona.org). The tourist office in Los Cristianos (Mon–Fri 9am–3.30pm) is downhill from the bus station in the town's cultural centre.

past high-rise hotel blocks and restaurants before finishing just short of the 428-metre Montaña Guaza. The shadeless climb to the peak from this point follows a clear route that crosses arid terrain via a steep rocky path before reaching terraced farmland higher up. The reward for your troubles is a view from the summit that stretches over Los Cristianos, Las Américas and the ocean as far as La Gomera.

Southern Las Américas

Projecting a relatively exclusive image and with some of the least-crowded beaches, southern Las Américas is easily one of the most attractive districts along this stretch of coast. Its pride is the five-star *Mare Nostrum Resort*, whose extravagant 1980s architecture – an oversized pastiche of Mexico's Chichén Itzá pyramids – makes it an eye-catching landmark. Far more natural is the Playa de Guincho,

▲ PUERTO COLÓN

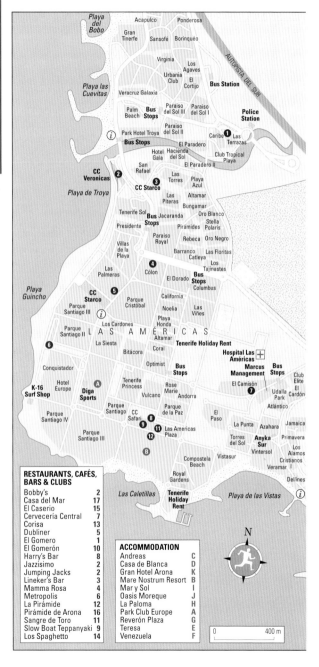

Playa del Bobo

Acapulco Ponderosa

Gran Tinerfe Sansofé Borinquéo

Virginia

Los Agaves

Urbania Club El Cortijo

Veracruz Galaxia

AUTOPISTA DEL SUR

Bus Station

Playa las Cuevitas

Police Station

Palm Beach Bus Stops Paraiso del Sol III Paraiso del Sol I

Park Hotel Troya Paraiso del Sol II

Bus Stops

Caribe ❶ Las Terrazas

El Paradero

Hotel Gala Hacienda del Sol

Club Tropical Playa

El Paradero II

San Rafael

❷ CC Veronicas

❸ CC Starco

Las Torres Playa Azul

Playa de Troya

Las Piteras Altamar

Bungamar

Tenerife Sol Bus Stops Jacaranda Oro Blanco

Presidente Pirámides Stella Polaris

Paraiso Royal Rebeca Oro Negro

Villas de la Playa

Barranco Las Floritas

Catleya Los Tajinastes

Las Palmeras

❹ Cólon

El Dorado

Bus Stops

Columbus

Playa Guincho

CC Starco ❺

Parque Santiago III

Parque Cristóbal

California

Noelia Las Viñes

Los Cardones Playa Honda

Parque Santiago II

LAS AMÉRICAS

Altamar

La Siesta Tenerife Holiday Rent

Bitácora Coral

Hospital Las Américas

Optimist Bus Stops Marcus Management Bus Stops

Club Elite

❻

Conquistador

Tenerife Princess Rose Marie Andorra

El Camisón ❼

El Cardón

K-16 Surf Shop

Hotel Europe Ⓐ Diga Sports

Udalla Park

Vulcano

Parque de la Paz

Atlántico

Parque Santiago IV

Parque Santiago CC Safari ❾ ❽

El Paso

La Punta Azahara Jamaica

Parque Santiago III

❶❶ Las Americas Plaza

❶❷

Ⓑ

Torres del Sol Anyka Sur Primavera

Vintersol Los Alamos

Compostela Beach

Vistasur

Cristianos

Veramar I

Royal Gardens

Dellines

Las Caletillas

Tenerife Holiday Rent

Playa de las Vistas ⓘ

N

0 ———— 400 m

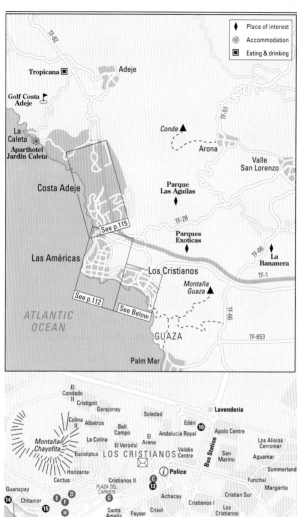

Place of interest
Accommodation
Eating & drinking

TF-82

Tropicana ■

Adeje

Golf Costa Adeje ►

La Caleta ◎

Aparthotel Jardin Caleta

Conde ▲

Arona

TF-51

Valle San Lorenzo

Costa Adeje

Parque Las Aguilas ♦

See p.115

Las Américas

TF-28

Parques Exoticas ♦

TF-66

La Bananera ♦

Los Cristianos

TF-1

See p.112

See Below

Montaña Guaza ▲

ATLANTIC OCEAN

GUAZA

TF-66

TF-653

Palm Mar

El Condado II

Cristigoit

Garajonay

Soledad

Lavendería

Colina II

Albatros

Bell Campo

Edén

⑩

Apolo Centre

Los Alisios Cerromar

Montaña Chayofita

La Colina

El Arena

Andalucia Royal

Eucaliptus

El Verodal

LOS CRISTIANOS

Valdés Centre

San Marino

Aguamar

Horizante

✉

ⓘ Police

Summerland

Cactus

Cristianos II

ⓒ

⑬

Funchal

Guanapay

PLAZA DEL CARMEN

Achacay

Cristian Sur

Margarita

⑭

Chitamar

Ⓔ Ⓓ

Ⓖ

Cristianos I

Los Cristianos

⑮

Ⓕ

Santa Amalia

Fayser

Crisol

Sirena

Chayofita

Ⓗ

Bucanero

Bahia

La Estrella

Princesa Dácil

Atlántida

Reverón

CC San Telmo

⑯

Rosmar

La Chunga

Sur y Sul

Victoria Court

⑰

Playa de los Cristianos

José Bas

El Carmen

La Perla

Ⓘ

Guayero

Ⓙ

Ferry Terminal

Comodoro

Jardines Canarios

Los Angeles

Ⓚ

Costa Mar

Cristamar Paloma Beach

LOS CRISTIANOS & LAS AMÉRICAS

Whale and dolphin watching

Whale- and dolphin-watching trips are a popular excursion from the resorts and companies offering them can be found in harbourside booths in Los Cristianos and in Las Américas at Puerto Colón. As many as twenty-six species of whale and dolphin have been spotted in the channel between Tenerife and La Gomera, though you're most likely to see pilot whales and bottlenose, striped or Atlantic spotted dolphins. Two- to three-hour trips (around €20 per person) head out to the whales and dolphins and stop for a swim and a picnic on the boat. Longer trips – typically five hours for around €40 per person – will also cruise to the imposing cliffs of Los Gigantes (see p.104). The boats used range from old wooden vessels to luxury yachts, but the most important thing to check when booking is whether the trip is actually to do some whale-spotting or if it's just a so-called "booze cruise"; operators will be quite upfront about this. One good whale-spotting option from Los Cristianos harbour is the *Lady Shelley* (☎922 75 75 49 ⊛www.ladyshelley .com), a 35-metre glass-bottomed catamaran which does both long and short trips on different days of the week. The *Tenerife Dolphin* (☎922 75 00 85 ⊛www .tenerifedolphin.com) is similar but leaves from the marina at Puerto Colón. Both offer free pick-up from your hotel. Other operators offer deep-sea fishing trips, starting from around €50 per person for a five-hour trip – check the harbourside booths for info on their irregular sailing times.

beside one of the prettiest stretches of Las Américas' promenade, thanks to the addition of huge iron sculptures and landscaped cactus gardens. The narrow and rocky beach itself, popular with local surfers and bodyboarders, is one of the few natural stretches of coastline on this part of the island.

Northern Las Américas

Northern Las Américas is almost solely responsible for Las Américas' notoriety as a concrete jungle of tackiness and hedonism. Thrown up in the 1970s to cash in on the booming tourist trade, by the mid-1980s it had become tatty and unappealing and has largely remained so, despite attempts at improvement. The bland concrete commercial centres at the heart of the resort – CC Veronicas and CC Starco – house the throbbing nightlife for which the resort is notorious and which forms the main attraction for many young visitors to the island. By day there's not much going on in the bars and fast-food outlets here, but by night the area is packed with clubbers.

Aqualand

San Eugenio ☎922 71 52 66 ⊛www .aqualand.es. Daily 10am–6pm. €22, under-14s €15.50. Free buses from marked stops along the seafront road in Las Américas and near the bus station in Los Cristianos. Along with the usual array of pools, slides and waterfalls, this water park also puts on two daily dolphin shows (Mon–Fri 1pm & 3pm, Sat & Sun 3pm). The complex is best visited on Tuesdays or Fridays – the main flight days when many holidaymakers are busy travelling – and avoided at weekends, when local kids generally take over. The park has several cafés and bars but they're quite pricey so packing a lunch is a good idea.

Costa Adeje

Though in practical terms a continuation of Las Américas, its location in a different administrative district means that the area of resort development north of Las Veronicas is known as the Costa Adeje.

At its southern end lie the overwhelmingly British-dominated adjacent districts of Torviscas and San Eugenio; both successful if dull family destinations where you'll find the small marina of Puerto Colón. The beaches are similarly very popular but generally crowded. Set in a small bay and beside Puerto Colón, Playa la Pinta is marginally the most attractive option, with kayaks, pedalos, jet skis and inflatable bananas all available for hire.

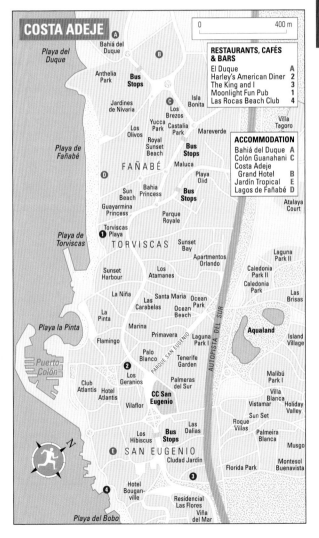

▲ FAÑABÉ

North of San Eugenio is the newer and considerably smarter resort of Fañabé. At the northern end of this district the *Gran Hotel Melia Bahía del Duque* is the island's most luxurious accommodation and the area's most significant landmark. Smartly dressed visitors (no shorts) are welcome to wander around the complex from 6.30pm onwards – worthwhile since several buildings in the complex are reproductions of notable buildings around the island. The Playa de Fañabé beach is relatively quiet and the pick of the bunch along the Costa Adeje.

La Caleta and Golf Costa Adeje

Bus #416 & #441 from Los Cristianos via Las Américas, 11 daily, 35min. Las Américas' string of hotels comes to an end just short of the relatively peaceful fishing village of La Caleta, noted for its fresh fish restaurants and rocky bay offering decent snorkelling. Inland a grid of roads have been laid out to accommodate new developments but for now a stretch of wasteland separates La Caleta and the rest of Las Américas from the large and exclusive golf course, Costa Adeje (see p.114).

Parques Exóticas

TF-66 road, parallel to Autopista del Sur, exit 26. Five free buses daily from Los Cristianos and Las Américas, call ☎922 79 54 24 for locations and times. Daily 10am–6pm. €12, under-13s €6. This well-designed zoo and park is a big hit with kids – and photographers – thanks to its policy of allowing visitors into many of the animal enclosures. One highlight, Amazonia, is a huge tent full of rainforest flora and fauna – including a selection of exotic birds – and while Cactus Park is perhaps only for die-hard cactus fans, the bat cave, butterfly garden, reptile house and monkey area are all worth a visit.

La Bananera

Buzanada. Autopista del Sur exit 26, direction Valle de San Lorenzo ☎922 72 04 03. Daily tours 10am, 11.30am, 1pm, 3.30pm & 4.15pm. €8, under-13s €4. The region's most refreshingly low-key attraction is La Bananera, an adapted family farm giving tours on Tenerife's agriculture with emphasis – as the name would suggest – on explaining banana cultivation. Tours finish with a look at a number of endemic species grown in the farm's gardens, which also produce some of the ingredients used in the good-value set meals offered in the restaurant (daily noon–4pm).

Parque Las Águilas

Chayofa. Autopista del Sur exit 27, direction Arona ☎ 922 72 90 10 🌐 www.aguilasjunglepark.com. Free shuttle buses from Las Américas, Los Cristianos, Puerto de la Cruz and Los Gigantes, call for times and pick-up points. Daily 10am–6pm. €17, under-13s €8. Parque Las Águilas is one of southern Tenerife's premier attractions, with a sizeable collection of animal enclosures chaotically organized amongst the lush vegetation of its replicated jungle. The main attractions are the bird shows, especially the displays of birds of prey who swoop low over the crowds – sit on the lower rows for maximum effect – and there's also an assault course with a bobsleigh run (€2.50 per run) that's popular with kids. Be aware that on windy days the shows are likely to be cancelled, and bring a picnic if you want to avoid the rather overpriced restaurants and cafés.

Arona and Conde hike

Bus #480 or #482 from Los Cristianos, 16 daily, 20min. Arona's tiny centre is good for a stroll and for a quick look at the seventeenth-century Iglesia San Antonio Abad. The town is also the starting point for the hike up the thousand-metre-high flat-topped Conde (4hr return) from where there are rewarding views over southern Tenerife and La Gomera. Most of the shadeless route follows a steep path along an old pack-road though the irregularly spaced painted waymarks occasionally deviate from this. To find the trailhead, leave the plaza in front of the church by the road that runs uphill to the left and cross the main road onto an unmarked road. After a couple of bends this road straightens, leaving town in the direction of the mountain. Turn left at a statue of Jesus and right at C/Vento 30. From here, painted trail markers follow a route that immediately crosses a gorge and then heads up the left-hand side of the hill, the path getting steeper and steeper until it reaches the summit.

Hotels

Andreas

C/Antigua General Franco, Los Cristianos ☎ 922 79 00 12, 🌐 www.hotelesreveron.com. Functional hotel, close to the centre of

PLACES Los Cristianos, Las Américas and Costa Adeje

▲ ROQUE DEL CONDE

town. Many of the ample rooms have balconies, some of which face a busy road, and all have private bathroom. €50.

Colón Guanahani

C/Bruselas, Playa de Fañabé, Costa Adeje ☎922 71 20 46, ⓦwww .colonguanahani.com. Massive and stylish four-star hotel whose 1500 rooms are plush, spacious and have generous balconies. Facilities include a sauna and pool, and guests are offered reduced fees at local golf courses and free Internet access. Substantial reductions for stays of five nights or more. €140.

Gran Hotel Arona

Avda. Marítima, Los Cristianos ☎922 75 06 78, ⓦwww.aronahotel.com. Large classy hotel beside the promenade. All rooms have balconies with sea views as well as satellite TV and a minibar, and there's also an extensive sun terrace and pools. Rates include breakfast. €89.

Gran Hotel Meliá Bahía del Duque

Fañabé ☎922 74 69 00, ⓦwww .bahia-duque.com. Luxurious modern development – in an area largely devoid of amenities – with extensive facilities including eight restaurants, nine bars, an Internet café, a library, an observatory, five swimming pools, a spa and beauty centre, squash and tennis courts and a jogging path. One particularly well-appointed building, the *Casas Ducales*, even has its own butler service. If money is no object, ask for the royal suite at around €1700 per night. €400.

Jardín Tropical

San Eugenio, Costa Adeje ☎922 74 60 00, ⓦwww.jardin-tropical.com. Moorish-style hotel with a sense of taste that's lacking in the surrounding architecture. Its central courtyards are filled with subtropical gardens and facilities include a large fitness centre and five good restaurants, open to non-guests, who can also use the pools for €3 per day in the adjoining *Las Rocas Beach Club*. Low season deals can cut prices by fifty percent. €180.

Mare Nostrum Resort

Avda. Las Américas, Las Américas ☎922 75 75 45, ⓦwww.expogrupo .com. Incorporating five five-star hotels – the *Mediterranean Palace*, *Sir Anthony*, *Julio Cesar*, *Marco Antonio* and *Cleopatra Palace* – this huge complex offers a vast range of facilities including twelve restaurants and cafés, several pools, a volleyball and football area, a nudist zone, tennis and squash courts and a top-notch spa. The location – in the thick of things near Los Cristianos – and

▲ BAHÍA DEL DUQUE

the genuinely friendly staff are unbeatable. €220.

Oasis Moreque

Avda. Penetración, Los Cristianos ☎922 79 03 66, ⓦwww.h10.es. Late Sixties building with fairly swish rooms and good facilities including a pool and tennis courts. Independent reservations are only accepted a couple of days in advance. Rates are generally reasonable – particularly the half-price single rooms – and include a good breakfast. €120.

Park Club Europe

Avda. Rafael Puig, Las Américas ☎922 75 70 60, ⓦwww.europe-hotels.org. Comfortable hotel with good sports facilities, as well as a scuba-diving outfit and the hiking- and mountain-biking tour operator, Diga Sports (see p.179). The reasonably sized rooms boast understated decor and large balconies, and rates halve in low season. €60.

Reverón Plaza

Plaza del Carmen, Los Cristianos ☎922 75 71 20, ⓦwww.hotelesreveron.com. Swanky modern hotel whose amenities include a pool on the roof. There are great views, particularly from the exclusive *Mirador Plaza* restaurant, while the spacious rooms are tastefully decorated and have balconies. Good single rates. €100.

Pensions

Casa de Blanca

C/Ramón Pino 28, Los Cristianos ☎922 75 19 75. Situated in a quiet side-street, this basic, clean pension has rudimentary rooms with shared bathrooms. No singles, but one good-value triple. €25.

La Paloma

C/Paloma 7, Los Cristianos ☎922 79 01 98. Pleasant, if basic, rooms, most sharing bathrooms, in the pedestrianized centre of Los Cristianos. Several singles available. €20.

Teresa

C/Ramón Pino 44, Los Cristianos ☎922 79 12 30. Friendly boarding house on a quiet side-street. The basic rooms all have shared baths. Singles available. €25.

Venezuela

Avda. de Suecia 24B, Los Cristianos ☎922 79 79 31. Located on a busy and noisy road but with clean, spartan rooms (shared bathrooms), this place offers the best deals in town for solo travellers. €23.

Apartments

Aparthotel Jardin Caleta

La Caleta ☎922 71 09 92, reservations ☎922 79 76 61 ⓦwww.hovima-hotels.com. The only accommodation in La Caleta, this unassuming apartment block contains over 200 neat little apartments, sleeping up to three people, that surround a pool and terrace area. €53.

Lagos de Fañabé

C/Londres, Fañabé ☎922 71 25 63, ☎922 71 21 29. Good-value one- and two-bedroom apartments (sleeping up to four). Shared facilities include a pleasant garden and somewhat cramped sun decks and pools with chutes and slides to keep kids busy. €60.

Mar y Sol

Avda. de Amsterdam, Los Cristianos ☎922 79 05 40, ✉marysol@arrakis .es. Unspectacular but well-managed apartment block,

▲ PROMENADE LAS AMÉRICAS

thoughtfully developed so all facilities fully accommodate wheelchair users, for which the resident dive school also caters. Both studios and apartments are offered and the complex's facilities include three pools. €144.

Cafés

Cervecería Central

El Camisón, local 17–18, Las Américas. A branch of the classy and popular Santa Cruz café-restaurant, serving everything from coffees and cakes to filled rolls, omelettes and a good variety of tapas. Moderately priced full meals are available in the evenings.

Restaurants

Casa del Mar

Esplanada del Muelle, Los Cristianos ☏922 75 13 23. Closed Mon. Large, consistently popular, with a good selection of fish and a terrace overlooking the bay and harbour. Prices are above average but the size and quality of the portions make it good value.

El Caserio

Plaza Las Fuentes, Los Cristianos. Open eves only. Simple Canarian place, combining dim lighting

Accommodation agencies

Accommodation agencies can help find vacant apartments in large complexes and generally offer a week's rental (usually the minimum booking period) from around €300. Also check web-based accommodation wholesales for deals (see p.184).

Anyka Sur
Edificio Azahara, Los Cristianos ☏922 79 13 77 or 649 40 85 15. ⊛www .anykasur.com.

Custom Holidays
Aparthotel California 6, Las Américas ☏922 79 60 00, ⊛www.custom-holidays .com.

Marcus Management
Apartamentos Portosin, Avda Penetración, Los Cristianos ☏922 75 10 64, ⊛www .canary-isles.com. ⊛www.tenerife-apts.com.

Tenerife Holiday Rent
Edificio Tenerife Garden, Las Américas ☏922 79 02 11 or 607 14 66 77, ⊛www .tenerife-holiday-rental.com.

Canary's World
CC Bahía de Los Cristianos Loc 15 ☏922 78 85 36, ⊛www.canarysworld.com.

▲ SURFING, PLAYA LAS AMÉRICAS

with wooden furniture and offering traditional, inexpensive food, from stews and rabbit to octopus and a decent choice of fish.

Celso

La Caleta. Tues–Sun 12.30–11pm. One of three fish and seafood restaurants gathered around La Caleta's namesake bay. What generally gives the *Celso* the edge over the others are its competitive prices, large patio area and sea views – all of which encourage locals as well as visitors to eat here. The *Cazuela marinera* (seafood stew) for two people is well priced at €25, and varies according to the day's catch, but is always excellent.

Corisa

C/Antigua General Franco 18, Los Cristianos. Closed Sat. Central restaurant with bright lights and vinyl tablecloths. It serves good, reasonably priced fish, seafood and meat dishes – the €7 *menú del día*, which includes wine, is particularly good value.

El Duque

Gran Hotel Melia Bahía del Duque, Fañabé ☎922 71 30 00. Closed Sun & June. One of the most expensive restaurants on the island, this place serves a changing range of international dishes, including the simple but superb house speciality, seafood lasagne. There's also an extensive wine list. Dress is smart casual.

El Gomero

Edificio Las Terrazas, Las Americás. Mon–Sat 11am–midnight. Speedy service and a menu offering paellas, steaks and cheap but filling set meals are on offer at this straightforward Canarian restaurant.

El Gomerón

Edificio Royal, Los Cristianos. Closed Sun. Inexpensive eatery with stylish chrome tables, popular with locals for its simple Canarian food, including a decent range of fish and seafood and some good steaks.

Harley's American Diner

Torviscas ☎922 71 30 40. Fairly expensive American-style theme-bar and restaurant offering a wide range of cocktails and meals, including nachos, fajitas and some vegetarian options.

The King And I

Local 12B Garden City, San Eugenio
☎ 922 75 03 50. Though a little more expensive than the surrounding restaurants, the quality of Thai dishes here – including tasty green curries and a great papaya salad – makes this place worth the extra.

Mamma Rosa

Apartments Colón II, Las Américas
☎ 922 79 78 23. Smart but expensive Italian restaurant serving delicious pasta and pizza as well as an excellent juicy sirloin steak à la Mamma Rosa – the house speciality.

El Patio Canario

C/Dominguez Alfonso 4, Arona.
Closed Sun & Mon. Run by a Belgian-Canarian family, this place has good dishes from both culinary traditions and moderate prices.

La Pirámide

Pirámide de Arona, Las Américas ☎ 922 79 63 60. Daily 7.30–11pm. Gaudy over-the-top decor but superb – if expensive – food and a pleasantly informal atmosphere make this a good choice. Best time to visit is on the thrice-weekly opera night (Tues, Fri & Sat from 8.30pm) when enthusiastic singers perform arias while you eat. A quartet plays chamber music on other nights.

Las Rocas Beach Club

Hotel Jardín Tropical, San Eugenio.
Clifftop beach club where exclusive dining is offered to visitors as well as hotel guests on a terrace overlooking the sea. The restaurant specializes in rice and seafood dishes – particularly recommended are the paellas, including a vegetarian version.

Rincón del Mero

Esplanada del Muelle, Los Cristianos
☎ 922 79 35 53. Functional restaurant with moderate prices where only fresh fish and seafood grace the menu.

Los Spaghetto

CC San Telmo, Los Cristianos.
Daily 11am–1am. Small Italian restaurant with views over the beach and phenomenal, moderately priced home-made pasta. Leave space for the fabulous Tiramisu, too.

Slow Boat Teppanyaki

CC Safari, Las Américas ☎ 922 79 53 95. Las Américas has long suffered mediocre Chinese restaurants, and the ubiquitous €5 buffet in gaudy surroundings still has wide appeal. Yet local tradition is broken here by the sleek asian simplicity of the dark wood decor and the Pan-Asian menu. The house speciality is *teppanyaki*, a style of Japanese cooking that uses an iron griddle. A choice of set meals (€24–55 per person) gives novices an easy introduction.

Sangre de Toro

CC Safari, Las Américas ☎ 922 79 52 96. The bullfighting theme and decor might be a bit off-putting, but the Iberian fare here is spot on, with everything from sausage platters to paella executed well – but steeply priced. The real deal clincher here is the nightly flamenco performances (usually 8-10pm), which bring the place alive and justify dropping in for a tapas platter.

Bars

Dubliner

Hotel Las Palmeras, Las Américas.

Dependable source of good *craic*, with an enthusiastic live band playing a mix of vaguely contemporary hits to a large, mixed-age crowd. Busiest between 10pm and 4am.

Harry's Bar

Plaza de Américas, Las Américas. Swank African-themed bar that spills onto a lively terrace in the shadow of *Mare Nostrum*'s pyramid. The live music, particularly jazz and blues, most nights attracts mostly thirtysomething holidaymakers. Cocktails are outrageously priced, but the sangria isn't, yet remains potent.

Lineker's Bar

CC Starco, Las Américas. Fun party atmosphere in a bar owned by former England footballer Gary Lineker and run by his brother. It tends to get going earlier (around 10pm) than those over the road at CC Veronicas.

Jumping Jacks

CC Las Veronicas, Las Américas. As good a place as any on the Veronicas strip to quaff an intoxicating beverage, particularly since the large bar's open-air street level seating gives ringside seats for watching the strip's many touts ply their trade and arriving punters gear up for a big night out.

Clubs

Bobby's

CC Las Veronicas, Las Américas. Daily 9pm–6am. Thanks to exposure in a TV docusoap, this dark, first-floor club is the most famous in Veronicas. It shares a landing

▲ GOLF COSTA ADEJE

with the similar *Busby's* and both get busy from about 2am, pumping out run-of-the-mill dance music.

Jazzissimo

CC Las Veronicas, Las Américas. Mon–Sun 10pm–3am. Immeasurably civilized by local standards, this stylish oasis of calm in an ocean of binge-drinking bars, offers the chance to soak up live jazz, soul and Motown whilst sipping on a martini in neon-lit avant-garde surroundings.

Metropolis

Beside Hotel Conquistador, Las Américas. Large club that's packed and fun at weekends and patronized overwhelmingly by Canarians.

Shows

Moonlight Fun Pub

Pueblo Torviscas. Consistently popular bar drawing a mixed-age crowd to its seafront location. Cheesy nightly shows feature Billy Idol and Tina Turner lookalikes.

Pirámide de Arona

Mare Nostrum Resort ☎ 922 79 63

▲ PIRÁMIDE DE ARONA SHOW

60. The flamboyant musical shows here – involving over thirty dancers – marry flamenco to produce polished and entertaining renditions of classic tales such as Carmen, Don Juan and Romeo and Juliet. Tickets, bought through agents and hotels, can be cheaper than those at the venue.

Tropicana

Costa Adeje ☎ 902 33 12 34, ✉ reservas@tropicanaatlantico.co. Tues, Thurs & Sat. Dinner 8pm, show 9pm. €45 including drinks, €52 including meal and drinks. Vivacious Cuban dance show followed by an after midnight disco for up to 1500 that has a huge following among the local Canarian populace.

The south coast

Tenerife's **south coast** is where mass tourism on the island began. Built in the 1960s, the vast *Ten-Bel* hotel complex, beside the small workaday town of Las Galletas, was one of the first large-scale holiday centres, and the bland Costa del Silencio resort has grown up beside it. East of here is the Golf del Sur, a new resort centred on two large golf courses, while further east still is the most picturesque town along this stretch of coast, **El Médano**, whose vast, windswept beaches are the only significant natural ones on the island. The monotony of the landscape is broken by a number of hills – Rasca in the west and Roja and Pelada in the east – that are designated nature reserves, offering opportunities for hiking and mountain biking. Down on the coast, meanwhile, numerous diving concerns operate out of Las Galletas and El Médano.

Las Galletas and the Costa del Silencio

Buses #115 from Santa Cruz, 4–12 daily, 1hr 10min; #467 or #473 from Los Cristianos and Las Américas, very frequent, 45min; and #473 from Los Gigantes, very frequent, 1hr 40min.

Though largely given over to the tourist industry, Las Galletas still has the feel of a small coastal town with a handful of shops, bars and restaurants along its main pedestrian street and the short seafront promenade. Here you'll find a narrow pebble beach, where waves crashing along the rocky shoreline attract local surfers and body-boarders. Eastern Las Galletas merges into the Costa del Silencio, an ironic name given that it consists of a couple of kilometres of almost uninterrupted development along a slim spit of shingle beach, with numerous expat businesses in charmless commercial centres.

▼ COSTA DEL SILENCIO

Malpais de la Rasca hike

12km/3–4hr from Las Galletas to Los Cristianos, returning on bus #467 or #473 (very frequent, 45min).

Following the rugged coastline west of Las Galletas through the wild natural landscape of Malpais de la

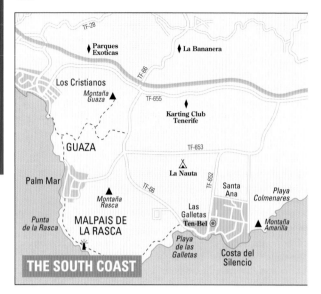

TF-28
Parques
Exoticas
La Bananera
TF-66
Los Cristianos
Montaña
Guaza
TF-655
Karting Club
Tenerife
GUAZA
TF-653
Palm Mar
La Nauta
TF-66
TF-652
Santa
Ana
Playa
Colmenares
Montaña
Rasca
MALPAIS DE
LA RASCA
Las
Galletas
Ten-Bel
Montaña
Amarilla
Punta
de la Rasca
Playa
de las
Galletas
Costa del
Silencio

THE SOUTH COAST

Rasca, this hike gives a glimpse of how things looked along the coast here before tourism took over. The route is virtually shadeless, so bring plenty of suncream and water.

From Las Galletas, head west along the promenade beside the shingle beach. At its end, and by a Red Cross building, turn left onto a rough, unsigned coastal path. The path is crisscrossed by many others but as long as you keep the coastline in sight, it doesn't matter which one you follow. After half an hour's walk you arrive first at a disused plantation and then at a working one, a clear path passing each on the ocean side. Beyond the second plantation

the Faro de Rasca lighthouse comes into view and you enter the protected reserve area. Follow the obvious track to the lighthouse and then beyond – turning inland for around 100m on an asphalt road before joining a dirt road just in front of it. Around ten minutes beyond the lighthouse, ignore a path that heads right in the direction of Montaña Rasca and continue straight on, only to bear right at the next fork shortly after. The following fork is beside a low wall – bear left here on a track to an abandoned house, then continue on a path that begins behind the building. Passing some disused fields and a low wall, head for the coastal

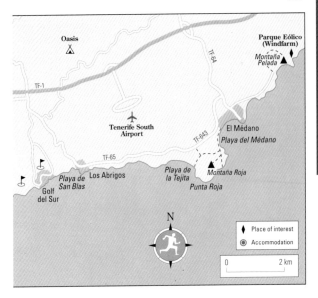

Map showing: Oasis, Parque Eólico (Windfarm), Montaña Pelada, TF-64, TF-1, Tenerife South Airport, TF-643, El Médano, Playa del Médano, TF-65, Playa de la Tejita, Montaña Roja, Los Abrigos, Punta Roja, Playa de San Blas, Golf del Sur, N

Key:
♦ Place of interest
● Accommodation
0 — 2 km

fortification in the fledgling resort of Palm Mar. From the fortification continue to the far side of the bay where a steep path starts to climb between cliffs. The path is marked with a sign announcing the protected area of Guaza and is soon indistinct as it clambers steeply up the rock. Bear slightly left as you head up and you'll see a clear path resuming a zigzag progress up the hill – again bear left at all junctions. Once up on the plateau the coastal path is easily spotted as it dips in and out of several dry gorges. Finally, with views of eastern Los Cristianos visible below, you come to a steep gorge where the path becomes indistinct. Here the choice is to either head inland, cross-country to the clear wide track that heads up Guaza – an extra 20min walk – or to clamber down the gorge and on into Los Cristianos. Once in the town it's a one-kilometre walk along the promenade to the bus

station and services back to Las Galletas.

Montaña Amarilla

East of Costa del Silencio, the unspoilt protected lands around Montaña Amarilla have a wild

▼ MONTAÑA AMARILLA

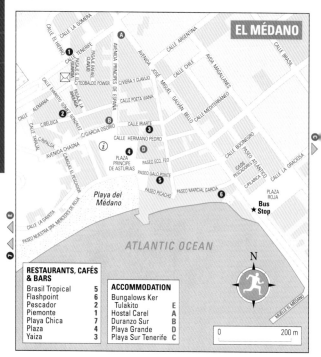

EL MÉDANO

RESTAURANTS, CAFÉS
& BARS

Brasil Tropical 5
Flashpoint 6
Pescador 2
Piemonte 1
Playa Chica 7
Plaza 4
Yaiza 3

ACCOMMODATION

Bungalows Ker
Tulakito E
Hostal Carel A
Duranzo Sur B
Playa Grande D
Playa Sur Tenerife C

and rugged coastline. The short ascent of the hill itself is worth it for the view over both the resort and a rocky piece of scrub where cacti thrive. The striking twisted forms and a sheltered bay around its base are equally alluring, with ladders giving access to turquoise waters, in which it's generally safe to swim.

El Médano

Bus #116 from Santa Cruz, 8 daily, 1hr; from Los Cristianos and Las Américas, 16 daily, 50min. Best known for its sandy beaches and breezy conditions – great for wind- and kite-surfing, not so good for sunbathing – the small town of El Médano has developed into a laid-back resort for sporty types. Though it hasn't escaped the region's ongoing building boom, it has managed to retain a pleasant easy-going atmosphere. The town centres on Plaza Principe de Asturias surrounded by restaurants and cafés and adjacent to the large main beach. From here a boardwalk follows the length of the natural stretch of sand, lined with shops selling clothing and watersports paraphernalia.

Montañas Roja and Pelada

Two distinctive hills of twisted volcanic rock flank El Médano. To the west the 171-metre Montaña Roja is in the centre of a nature reserve protecting a dune ecosystem. One easily followed path from the western end of El Médano's beach leads through this area to the summit, while another rounds the hill on its inland side and leads to a beautiful but windswept beach, Playa de la Tejita.

To the east of town, along a dirt road that follows the coast, is the magnificent crater of Montaña Pelada, shaped by an influx of seawater during a volcanic eruption. A hiking trail begins from the eastern end of the coastal road from El Médano before dropping into a sheltered sandy bay – popular with nudists – before heading up a steep, unmarked route to the crater rim, from where there are good views along the coast. You can follow a trail around the crater rim, returning back down the steep west side, or descend on its northern side to link up with a track that leads east to the Parque Eólico. The eight-kilometre return hike to the Parque Eólico from El Médano takes around three hours.

▲ PARQUE EÓLICO

Parque Eólico

☎ 922 39 10 00, ext.62, ⓦ www. iter.es. Mon–Fri 10am–5pm. Free. Signposted Pol. Industrial Granadilla. An innovative wind farm and renewable energy centre, the Parque Eólico offers visitors a trip along an ecological walkway lined with entertaining exhibits demonstrating principles behind solar and wind power. The topic of domestic power consumption is examined in the "bioclimatic dwellings" – several examples of energy-efficient homes – on the coast below the wind farm.

Hotels

El Médano

Playa del Médano ☎ 922 17 70 00, ⓦ www.medano.es. Sixties hotel, built on stilts over the sea, catering largely for package tourists and not as luxurious as it once was. However, it's in a superb central location and many of the rooms have excellent views. €70.

Playa Sur Tenerife

Playa del Médano ☎ 922 17 61 20, ⓦ www.hotelplayasurtenerife.com. Modern, package-oriented hotel west of the centre at the end of the boardwalk. The seventy

▲ MONTAÑA ROJA

Apartments

Bungalows Ker Tulakito

La Gaviota 17, El Médano ☎ 922 17 70 83. Pretty, well-equipped bungalows, with excellent views over the bay, five minutes west of the town centre. Each has its own garden and terrace and sleeps up to four. The friendly owner speaks English. €60.

rooms are elegantly furnished and the hotel has all the usual four-star facilities, plus some outdoor activities, including hiking. €70.

Duranzo Sur

Avda. Principes de España 1, El Médano ☎ 922 17 69 58, ℻ 922 17 62 99. Unusually spacious and simply equipped apartments, many of which have balconies overlooking the main plaza and the sea. Most sleep up to three, but there are singles too. English spoken. €40.

Pensions

Hostal Carel

Avda. Principes de España 22, El Médano ☎ 922 17 60 66. Simply furnished but clean singles and doubles – some with private bathrooms – in a renovated pension on the edge of the town centre, beside the main approach road. €40.

Pension La Estrella

Avda. del Atlántico, km 1, Las Galletas ☎ 922 73 15 62. A kilometre inland from Las Galletas and on a busy road, this place offers a mix of rooms, some en suite and all at reasonable rates. €23.

Pension Los Vinitos

C/Venezuela 4, Las Galletas ☎ 922 78 58 03. The smarter of the two simply decorated and reliable pensions in Las Galletas; rooms here are a little less cramped and each has a private bath. Some singles too. €30.

Playa Grande

C/Hermano Pedro 2, El Médano ☎ 922 17 63 06, ℻ 922 17 61 68. Swish, modern apartments overlooking the main plaza and sleeping up to four. Along with Scandinavian-style furnishings, they all have telephones, satellite TV, a balcony and access to a roof terrace. €50.

Ten-Bel

Avda. del Atlántico, Las Galletas ☎ 922 73 07 21, ☷ www.tenbel .com. The area's original holiday village has stood the test of time surprisingly well. The modernist 4500-bed complex offers everything from simple studios to apartments sleeping up to seven, most with balconies and some overlooking the sea. Communal facilities include tennis courts and a large salt-water pool by a tiny beach. €40.

Camping

Camping La Nauta

On TF-653, 2km inland of Las Galletas, just off the road to Guaza ☎ 922 78 51 18. One of the island's few campsites, this place has worn facilities including a swimming pool and rudimentary sports area. The tent sites (€4 per person) are dusty and uninviting, but most of the site is given over to basic cabins sleeping up to four (€26).

Oasis

Ciguaña Alta; signposted off a small road off the northern side of the airport motorway junction: Autopista Sur, exit 22 ☎ 922 77 04 14. Small, neat and simple campsite with great views over the coast and friendly owners. Its one drawback is its relative isolation – about 3km from the nearest public transport. Daily charges are €2 each per tent, person and car.

Cafés

Flashpoint

Playa del Médano. Overlooking the beach at the western end of town, this trendy café with a shady terrace serves excellent breakfasts and filled rolls and pizzas in the afternoon. In the evening the bar takes over, serving drinks and snacks against a drum'n'bass soundtrack.

Plaza

Plaza Príncipe de Asturias, El Médano. Popular café taking up one end of the town's main plaza, offering plenty of outdoor seating and views over the sea.

Los Vinitos

C/Venezuela, Las Galletas. One of a number of cafés along the town's pedestrianized street and as good a place as any to head for snacks and light lunches. Along with the budget sandwiches, hamburgers and omelettes, there's also a good range of tapas and fresh-pressed juices.

Restaurants

L'Alpage

La Estrella 7, Las Galletas ☎ 922 73 05 77. Closed Wed. Excellent Swiss restaurant, sporting heavy alpine furnishings and red-check tablecloths. It's a bit of a trek out of town – 1km past *Ten Bel* along Avenida del Atlántico – but worth it for the wonderful fondue and rösti dishes at moderate prices.

Carnaval

Paseo Marítima, Las Galletas. Closed Tues. A dimly lit and atmospheric place in a strip of otherwise functional seafood restaurants. Salads, hamburgers and sandwiches are served for lunch, while the reasonably priced and varied dinner menu includes seafood and more unusual offerings such as ostrich.

Colibri Playa

Paseo Marítima, Las Galletas. Popular with locals, this basic restaurant has one of the largest and least expensive menus of fish and seafood in town. The menu varies according to the day's catch, but portions are always generous.

Pescador

C/Evaristo Gómez Gonzalez 15, El Médano. Closed Tues. Popular with locals, this restaurant serves reliably good, moderately priced fresh fish and seafood dishes at tables decked with cheerful green cloths.

Piemonte

C/Gran Canaria 7, El Médano. Closed Wed & Sat eve. Tucked away in a basement on the edge of the town centre, this stylish, pastel-toned Italian restaurant offers a large menu of top-quality pizza and pasta dishes at above average prices.

Playa Chica

Paseo Marcial García, El Médano. Tues–Sun 7pm–late. Inexpensive tapas and fine views over the bay from the downstairs terrace make this a popular place for a snack; the restaurant upstairs is also good value, serving the usual fish and meat dishes.

Vista Mar

Los Abrigos, 6km west of El Médano. The town of Los Abrigos has a reputation as an outstanding place to eat fresh fish and seafood, and the *Vista Mar* has one of the best selections. Other options include *La Langostera*, a lobster specialist, the more gourmet *Bencomo*, or the cheap and simple *Yaisara*, which also offers a good range of salads.

Yaiza

C/Iriarte 12, El Médano. Daily 6.30–11pm. Elegant restaurant serving creative, expensive gourmet food. The menu includes interesting fish dishes, such as sole in saffron sauce, and various choice cuts of meat – but no vegetarian options.

Bars

Brasil Tropical

Paseo Galo Ponte, El Médano. Snazzy cocktails served in a lively tropical-style bar, just off Principe de Asturias. Open til 2am, this is usually one of the last places in town to close.

Paropo

C/La Arena, Las Galletas. Of several places in the area this is the pick of the bunch – a small, smoky and atmospheric bar where locals congregate to watch sport on TV and eat tapas.

Peanut Disco Bar

CC El Chapparal, Costa del Silencio. Sociable pub offering a little more atmosphere than the glut of places over the road in the CC Trebol.

Clubs

Disco Lord

CC El Chapparal. Closed Tues & Wed. Pumping out the usual array of chart music and also hosting Sixties and Seventies nights, the area's single, low-key, disco is nothing special.

Teide and the interior

Set inside an enormous crater at the centre of the island, the **Parque Nacional Las Cañadas del Teide** dominates a bleak and sun-baked volcanic desert. Used as a set for *Star Wars*, the harsh landscape is often familiar to many of the 3.5 million annual visitors, many of whom come to take the cable car up **Pico del Teide** (3718m), the colossal peak at its heart. One of the highest volcanoes in the world, Teide rises from the lava and pumice plains of Las Cañadas to cast the world's largest shadow over the surrounding ocean and form one of the most enduring symbols of the island. The park is also of considerable interest for its endemic flora, spectacular examples of which occur in May or June when the resilient Teide violet provides a scattering of colour, while the two-metre-high conical Tajinaste rojo blooms with beautiful maroon flowers.

A single east–west road crosses the park with numerous stops providing views and access to walking routes that allow a closer look at the scenery, some of which is only reachable on foot. If you plan to hike, take plenty of sunscreen and water, and don't leave anything on display in a parked car – theft from vehicles is a common problem.

Even if you don't intend to venture far from your car be sure to take an extra layer of clothing to cope with the unpredictable weather, and to have enough fuel in your car. The nearest petrol station to the park is in the traditional village of **Vilaflor** to the south, a tranquil and practical upland base – particularly given the lack of accommodation in the park itself. Spain's highest settlement, the town is also located at the edge of the Canarian pine forest that encircles the park and in sight of some of its largest specimens. There's good hiking in the vicinity, but it's even better on the opposite side of the park – the north side of the island. There, high up in the **La Orotava Valley**, the eye-catching rock face **Los Organos** offers a focal point.

Vilaflor

Bus #482 from Los Cristianos, 3 daily, 1hr 15min. With incredible views, pure upland air and local springs, it's easy to see how this former spa town's charming old brick-and-tile houses once attracted those looking to improve their health. Though less busy nowadays, the town retains

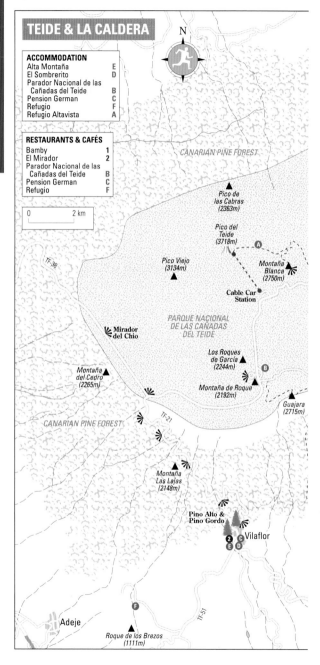

TEIDE & LA CALDERA

N

ACCOMMODATION
Alta Montaña	E
El Sombrerito	D
Parador Nacional de las Cañadas del Teide	B
Pension German	C
Refugio	F
Refugio Altavista	A

RESTAURANTS & CAFÉS
Bamby	1
El Mirador	2
Parador Nacional de las Cañadas del Teide	B
Pension German	C
Refugio	F

0   2 km

CANARIAN PINE FOREST

Pico de las Cabras (2363m)

Pico del Teide (3718m)

A

Montaña Blanca (2750m)

Cable Car Station

TF-38

Pico Viejo (3134m)

PARQUE NACIONAL DE LAS CAÑADAS DEL TEIDE

Mirador del Chio

Los Roques de García (2244m)

B

Montaña del Cedro (2265m)

Montaña de Roque (2192m)

Guajara (2715m)

CANARIAN PINE FOREST

TF-21

Montaña Las Lajas (2148m)

Pino Alto & Pino Gordo

2 C
E D
Vilaflor

F

Adeje

TF-51

Roque de los Brezos (1111m)

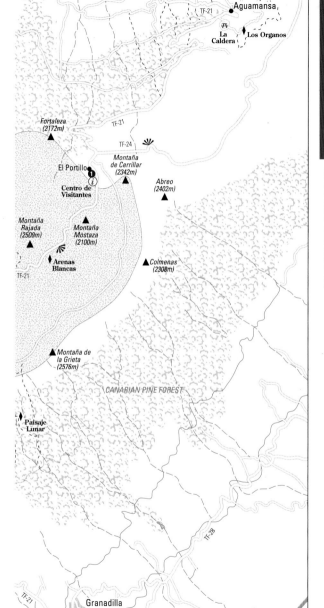

PLACES

Teide and the interior

136

Arrival and information

It's easiest to get to the national park by **car**, though there are daily **buses** from Las Américas and Los Cristianos (#342, 1 daily, 1hr 40min) and from Puerto de la Cruz (#348, 1 daily, 1hr 45min) calling at the Parador, the base of the cable car and the visitors' centre.

Of the four routes to the park the **road from the west** is the fastest. Beginning its ascent near Santiago del Teide, it climbs through a thin belt of pines, passing south of an area of solidified lava from the most recent (1909) eruption of Montaña Chinyero. Beyond the trees the road rises through twisted lava formations, created when the side vent, Las Narices del Teide (Teide's Nostrils), spewed twelve million cubic metres of molten rock in 1789. The vent is technically part of Pico Viejo (3134m), a peak in its own right that rises out from the side of Teide.

From the south a busier road climbs to the national park via Vilaflor and through impressive stands of Canarian pines, with good views over southern Tenerife and La Gomera.

Coming **from the east** visitors take the relatively long and impressive route along the **Cumbre Dorsal**, the mountain backbone of the island. Climbing quickly through La Esperanza, the road ascends through some of the largest sections of pine forest on the island with a number of viewpoints. Once past the trees the route passes the **Izaña Observatory**, home to the Instituto Astrofísica de Canarias (ⓦ www.iac.es).

The busy **road from the north** twists around countless hairpins before rising into the dense vegetation on the damp side of the island, where low cloud often obscures the views. This road passes La Caldera, the start of the hike around the geological wonder of Los Organos (see p.141).

The main **visitors' centre** (daily 9am–4pm; ☎922 37 33 91) is at the eastern end of the park and has displays on geology, flora and fauna, plus maps and leaflets about the generally well-marked hiking trails. The centre also organizes free **guided hikes** of varying difficulty. There's a second centre (same hours) beside the Parador on the south side of the park that concentrates on the park's human heritage. Lastly, two tiny booths, with unpredictable opening hours, field general enquiries and distribute leaflets: one is at the junction of the roads from the west and the south, the other at the junction of the roads from the east and north.

something of its appeal with a friendly, traditional Canarian atmosphere. The main street, Calle Santo Domingo, heads up to a large plaza with the plain but imposing seventeenth-century Iglesia de San Pedro at its heart. From the plaza it's a short, steep walk up to the viewpoint, Mirador San Roque (just west of the road to Teide), which provides a spectacular view over the slopes of southern Tenerife.

Paisaje Lunar hike

6km/2–3hr beginning 9km northeast of Vilaflor or 14km/6hr return hike from Vilaflor. One of the best hikes you can do through the Canarian pine forest goes to the Paisaje Lunar – a moonscape of eroded rock that comprises two small areas of tall, thin and smooth rock columns.

The dirt road to the trailhead is marked by a wooden sign on a bend in the road to the Parque Nacional, not far above Vilaflor. From here it's a two-hour walk, or half-hour drive to the trail proper. The road is hard on cars – if you're in a rental, check that your insurance covers you off sealed roads.

▲ PIÑA ALTO, PINE FOREST

Marked by white-painted rocks, the hike from the dirt road to the columns begins on a narrow woodland trail, but the trees soon thin out to reveal good views of Tenerife's southern coast 17km away and the ridge-like rim of the vast Las Cañadas crater 2km ahead. After 3km you arrive at the first of the Paisaje Lunar's columns, eroded stone whose wide bases support tapering pillars with delicate looking, top-heavy tips. A clear trail runs past them turning downhill and southeast to the second group across an area of volcanic ash. From here an obvious path continues down, following the contours of the hill and some water pipes, before dropping into a children's summer camp. Take the dirt track at its base, which leads to a dirt road back to Vilaflor – bear right to get to the start point about 1km away.

Los Roques de García hike

3.5km/1hr–1hr 30min circular hike.
The best short hike in the centre of the national park loops around the bizarre and twisted Roques de García, a line of huge rocks that serve as a reminder of the erosive forces that helped shape the park. Formed from magma forced through near-vertical underground cracks, Los Roques are volcanic dykes that solidified into walls of stone. Much harder than the surrounding rock, this cooled magma has remained while the softer surrounding material has eroded away. Where softer rock forms a horizontal layer near the base, a top-heavy structure like the Roque Cinchado – a precariously balanced formation – emerges.

The route that takes in these formations is best done anticlockwise, heading out of the car park beside Roque Cinchado in the direction of Teide then following a

▲ PAISAJE LUNAR

The Canarian pine forest

The grand forest of Canarian pines that all but encircles the Parque Nacional begins just north of Vilaflor and it's here that the biggest specimens are found including one, Pino Gordo (Fat Pine) with a trunk circumference of 9.3m and, opposite, Pino Alto (Tall Pine), the highest on the island at almost 50m.

While the proportions of the Canarian pine are impressive, the species' characteristics are even more so, showing impressive adaptation to its environment. Long needles trap moisture from the clouds, introducing vital water into the island's arid ecosystem, while to stop other species from taking advantage of this, the needles degrade slowly and have an acidifying effect on the soil, meaning little else can grow. The tree has also developed a mechanism for dealing with the fires that are common on volcanic islands: a thick bark that protects the tree's heart from the flames making it common to see badly scorched trees sprouting healthy new branches.

well-trodden path to the northernmost rock in the line before dipping to follow a rougher trail back down the other side of the landforms. The final section of the route passes the massive rock monolith, La Catedral, with its striking geometric patterns, before returning steeply back to the car park.

Guajara hike

5km/4hr circular hike. Part of the ancient crater rim that forms the park boundary, Guajara (2715m) stands over 700m above the crater floor, from where it looks more like a series of cliff faces than a mountain. Though a fairly strenuous hike, it's without a doubt one of the best walks on the island. The path climbing across its sheer north face has excellent views over the whole national park and is a good perspective from which to make out the most recent lava tongues on the slopes of Teide, while on clear days the panorama at the summit includes La Gomera, La Palma, El Hierro and Gran Canaria.

The trail begins just a few metres south of the *Parador* beside a sign depicting park footpaths. The narrow track soon crosses a dirt road beyond which the reasonably well-trodden trail heads straight up, marked by occasional paint spots. Around 500m beyond the road the path bears left and begins to steepen as it crosses

▼ LOS ROQUES DE GARCIA

Las Cañadas geology

At only 3 million years old, the area protected by the national park is in the youngest part of Tenerife, having joined up the older volcanic ranges to the north, west and south to form a large island backbone, the **Cumbre Dorsal**. Volcanic activity in the centre of the island reached a peak around 300,000 years ago in a volcano of spectacular proportions whose sixteen-kilometre-wide crater now forms the boundary of today's park. Exactly what geological event destroyed this volcano is unclear – subsequent eruptions and thousands of years of erosion make it difficult to tell – but the crater rim is still clear in the south of the park where the steep-sided mountain of **Guajara** is its highest point.

the base of a cliff face and leads out onto the crater rim. From this point the route steepens further, leading up to the foot of a row of cliffs that mark Guajara's northern face. The path climbs beside, and then passes over, the cliffs (follow the irregular and faded paint markings carefully to find the quickest way to the summit), past a triangulation point to the summit and a large wind shelter. The descent is to the east of here – paths to the south lead in the direction of Vilaflor and Paisaje Lunar, but to return to Las Cañadas continue along the line of the crater rim. This path, which is steep and loose with small pumice rocks, heads down to a saddle just over a kilometre away where it's crossed by another path. From here you have two options: head north around 500m back downhill to reach the crater floor and follow the wide track along the base of Guajara back to the *Parador*; or right at this junction will take you south to Paisaje Lunar from where you can easily hike to Vilaflor, in around three hours (13km; see p.136).

Teide by cable car

☎ 922 01 04 45. Daily 9am–4pm. €20 return, €10 one-way. Not for those with vertigo, the ride up Teide by cable car is nonetheless one of the most spectacular

eight-minute journeys you can make anywhere. Following a near-vertical, thousand-metre climb, the trip affords spectacular views back down the side of the mountain and around Las Cañadas, before depositing passengers 200m below the summit. From here easy walks lead to two viewpoints, giving the best views of the park, island and entire archipelago (on a really good day). Permit holders (see p.140) can, of course, make the short steep climb to the summit of Teide (around 30min one way). High winds, snow and occasional maintenance can close the cable car at short notice so if in doubt, call ahead. In summer, it's also worth getting here as early as possible, as substantial queues soon build up. Be sure to bring plenty of warm clothes too, as temperatures at the summit often hover around freezing.

Teide on foot

12km/7–8hr return hike. An alternative to the cable car and the obvious challenge for fit visitors is the hugely strenuous ascent of Teide on foot. The hike up takes around four hours, with another three needed for the descent – though many hikers catch the cable car to save their joints the strain of the descent. There is only one permissible route

The summit permit

Only **150 visitors a day** are allowed up to the eight-metre wide crater rim on the summit of Teide and the tiny sulphurous vents that surround it. To get one of the free permits, apply in person with your passport and a photocopy of the photo and details page at the **ICONA park administration** in Santa Cruz (C/Emilio Calzadilla 5; Mon–Fri 9am–2pm; ☎922 29 01 29). You need to book the time you'll be visiting the top, but it's generally OK if you turn up outside this time, though you may have to wait if there are people on the summit. Note that if there's snow, the peak closes to visitors. Note: plans are afoot to create an online, or at least email-based, reservation system; check on the latest status by writing to ✆teide @oapn.mma.es.

up the peak, obvious from the summit of Montaña Blanca (see below), which quickly becomes rough, narrow and steep as it zigzags its way up through the solidified lava flows on Teide's flanks. There are no real landmarks in this desolate landscape and few distractions from the gruelling climb, so the *Refugio Altavista* (☎922 53 37 20; €12 per person; closed Nov–March), an hour and a half's hike beyond Montaña Blanca, is a welcome sight. Reservations are advsiable if you plan to stay here and though there are some cooking facilities, water can be in short supply so bring plenty of your own, plus a sleeping bag to combat the low night temperatures. From the *refugio* it's roughly another hour straight climb to the top through a similar craggy area, though the grade of ascent begins to ease. After around twenty minutes a short detour is possible (marked by a pile of stones) to the Cueva del Hielo (Ice Cave), where a slippery metal ladder leads down into a small cavern in which numerous stalactites grow. From the turn-off it's another thirty minutes' walk to the top cable-car station. It you have permission (see above) to ascend to the summit, follow the obvious stone path near the cable-car station to the pale sulphurous pit that constitutes the volcano's crater from where you'll have unrivalled views over the island and, in all likelihood, the entire Canarian archipelago. Note that the high altitude of Teide means lower concentrations of oxygen which make altitude sickness, in the form of a headache or dizziness, common. Slowing the pace is usually enough to solve such problems but if this doesn't work then you need to head back down.

Montaña Blanca hike

6km/2hr return hike. Beginning at a roadside car park, 4km east of the cable-car station, Montaña Blanca (2740m) is a great destination in itself, though for many hikers it's just a stop on the way to or from Teide. The path up is well graded and wide, and takes in vast swathes of beige pumice gravel dotted with huge dark, lava boulders, their shape earning them the name Huevos de Teide (Teide's Eggs). The mountain's smooth rounded summit is a particularly good place to enjoy the sunset (after which there's just enough time to get back down before dark) when the immense, triangular shadow of Teide covers the valley floor.

La Caldera and Los Organos

Bus #345 from Puerto de la Cruz, 12 daily, 55min. Beyond the densely settled slopes of the upper Orotava Valley, the island's largest pine forest takes over, nourished by the mists that regularly shroud these heights. The area is crisscrossed by many paths, most of them wide forest tracks that can be linked to form good hiking routes. A useful starting point for walks in the area is La Caldera, a picnic spot in an old volcanic crater, 2km south of the village of Aguamansa and some 6km southeast of La Orotava. A kiosk beside the crater also does light meals, including fresh trout from a local fish farm. From just past the kiosk and signposted "Pista Monte del Pino", it's a very easy ten-minute walk down a flat dirt road to view Los Organos, a row of massive basalt pillars moulded by crystallization into organ-pipe shapes.

Los Organos hike

16km/5hr circular hike. Strenuous but rewarding, this hike is easily the most exhilarating walk in the pine forest on the northern side of the island, with views on clear days stretching down to Puerto de la Cruz. Even in poor weather the eerie drama of lichen-draped pine trees in the mist is wonderfully memorable. The route forms a loop beginning and ending along the "Pista Monte Del Pino".

About one kilometre from La Caldera, bear right when you arrive at a forest shelter onto an uphill path signed "Pedro Gill". It climbs steeply for around 40min – ignore a narrow track crossing it almost halfway up – to an area of more widely spaced pines and a T-junction, beyond a short section that follows a dry stream bed. Turn left at this junction following a good, simple-to-follow path that turns slightly downhill at first for approximately 6km (2hr). This trail ducks in and out of a number of dry gorges and includes some short narrow sections where ropes have

▲ LAS CAÑADAS

been attached for support. Not long after the last of these is the easily missed turn-off to the left, where the trail heads past a rocky outcrop before zigzagging steeply downwards. The narrow path soon joins a wider and winding track on which you should keep left before turning right at the T-junction further down. This leads into increasingly dense and lush forest on a trail that doubles back on itself until you reach another T-junction with the Pista Monte Del Pino. A left turn here will lead you back along the dirt road to La Caldera in around 45min, passing Los Organos on your left as you reach the final stretch.

Hotels

Alta Montaña
C/Morro del Cano 1, Vilaflor ☎922 70 90 00 ⓦwww.summitclub.de. Just outside the centre of Vilaflor across the Teide road, this stylish hotel has en-suite double and single rooms, a garden with a swimming pool and splendid coastal views. €60.

Parador Nacional de las Cañadas del Teide
Parque Nacional Las Cañadas del Teide ☎922 38 64 15, ⓦwww.parador.es. Stylish, state-run hotel in a fantastic and unique location in the national park. All the rooms have great views and there's a small pool, sauna, lounge and restaurant. €85.

El Sombrerito
C/Santa Catalina 15, Vilaflor ☎922 70 90 52. Smart but simple hotel in the centre of Vilaflor. Rooms here are all en suite and some have a balcony overlooking the quiet main street. Rates include breakfast. €50.

Pensions

Pension German
C/Santo Domingo 1, Vilaflor ☎922 70 90 28. Friendly, well-run pension in the centre of Vilaflor, with clean inexpensive rooms – some with private bathroom – including some singles. €40.

Refugio
Close to Ifonche ☎922 72 58 94. Only a practical option if you have your own transport, this B&B is in a small house by the road to Ifonche, west off the Arona–Vilaflor road. It has stupendous views over the coast, simple rooms and is run by keen hikers and paragliders, who are happy to advise (in English) about local routes and conditions. €50.

Restaurants

Bamby
El Portillo. A large outdoor terrace with splendid views over Teide makes this the best of three restaurants – all bus-tour favourites – near the visitor centre in the hamlet of El Portillo. Average Canarian food at reasonable prices.

El Mirador
Mirador San Roque, Vilaflor ☎922 70 91 35. Vilaflor's best restaurant, just below the viewpoint, isn't too pricey, considering the grand views and the quality of the Canarian and international cuisine available.

Parador Nacionál de las Cañadas del Teide
Parque Nacional Las Cañadas del

▲ TAJINASTE ROJO, GUAJARA

Teide ☎922 38 64 15 or 922 37 48 41. Large and expensive restaurant with a rather sterile atmosphere, but serving good Canarian cuisine and a particularly tasty local stew (*puchero*). The hotel also has an overpriced café and a lovely bar that's ideal for a celebratory drink after a hike.

Pension German

C/Santo Domingo 1, Vilaflor. Inexpensive restaurant in one of the town's pensions, good for typically hearty upland Canarian fare, like the thick vegetable stew, *escaldón*.

Refugio

Ifonche ☎922 72 58 94. Closed Wed, Sat & Sun. If you have your own transport, try the rustic restaurant at this small house-cum-pension. There's a limited range of tasty, though relatively expensive, home-made dishes, including great gazpacho, and fantastic views over the coast from the patio.

San Sebastián and around

La Gomera's busiest transport hub, **San Sebastián,** was the first Spanish settlement on the island and is now its capital and largest town, with a population of just 5000. Central to the town's role is its sheltered harbour, home to yachts and ferries from Tenerife. The harbour also witnessed La Gomera's most famous hour when, on September 6, 1492, Christopher Columbus left here on his first voyage to the Americas – an event with which all of the town's modest sights emphasize their connections. Most buildings have been destroyed and rebuilt several times since then, following repeated pirate attacks, but the old streets are worth a visit, as are the town's sandy beaches.

Most visitors soon move on to quieter parts of the island, but San Sebastián is easily the island's most practical base. All island bus and ferry routes radiate from here and the selection of bars and restaurants makes it a fine place to retire to after a day in the mountains or at the resort of **Playa de Santiago**, a few kilometres southwest. And with mass tourism almost entirely absent, it's also a great place to sample small-town Canarian life.

Casa Aduana

Plaza de la Constitución. Mon–Fri 9am–1.30pm, Sat & Sun 10am–1pm. Free. The seventeenth-century Casa Aduana (Customs House) houses the town's tourist office and a couple of rooms displaying information about Columbus's voyage to the Americas. Scale models of his three ships are worth a look, but the most famous connection with the explorer, in the courtyard of the building, is the Pozo de la Aguada, the well from which Columbus took his water supplies to subsequently "baptize" the New World.

Arrival and information

San Sebastián is connected to Tenerife by three **ferry companies**, one of which operates a passenger service on to Playa de Santiago and Valle Gran Rey (see p.149 & p.153). The town's **tourist office** (Mon–Sat 8.30am–1.30pm & 4.30am–6.30pm, Sun 8.30am–1.30pm; ☏922 14 01 47) is in the old Customs House, on the corner of C/del Medio and Plaza de la Constitución. There's also a much smaller office on Playa de Santiago's Avda. Maritima (Mon–Fri 10am–2pm; ☏922 87 02 81).

Beatriz de Bobadilla

Although La Gomera's most famous association is with Christopher Columbus, its most infamous is with the aristocratic Beatriz de Bobadilla. Beatriz was, by reputation, a vicious medieval nymphomaniac, and by all accounts – including her portrait in San Sebastián's Parador Nacional – a great beauty.

Once a mistress of King Ferdinand of Aragon's, Beatriz was instantly disliked by his wife Queen Isabella of Castile, who feared her manipulative powers. Consequently, she was quickly married off to an equally out-of-favour Spanish aristocrat and banished to La Gomera – then the outermost island of the Spanish empire. The couple began a ferocious and brutal rule on the island, which led to uprisings and his death in 1488.

Four years later, in 1492, Beatriz played host to Christopher Columbus, who delayed his first journey to the New World for over a month, giving rise to much speculation about the pair. But eventually Beatriz married Alonso Fernández de Lugo, the conqueror of Tenerife. She lived there, until rumours prompted her to order the execution of Gomera's governor and, as a result, was promptly summoned to the Spanish court by Isabella. Within days of arrival Beatriz was found poisoned in bed; no real effort was made to investigate the death of the ruthless beauty.

Torre del Conde

Tues–Sat 10am–1pm. Free. San Sebastián's first building of any note was the stocky medieval Torre del Conde fort, built in 1447 as a strategic fall-back during the slow conquest of the island. It proved useful, serving its purpose when Beatriz de Bobadilla, the wife of the murdered governor Hernán Peraza, barricaded herself in during a 1488 uprising until help arrived. Today the fort contains displays on Gomeran history with maps from 1492 showing how, at the time when Columbus was striking out into unknown waters, most of the Gomeran interior was still uncharted – and would remain so until the seventeenth century. A copy of the 1743 demand by English naval officer Charles Windham, ordering that San Sebastián give up arms and surrender, is also here, along with the defiant reply of Diego Bueno, representative of the citizens of San Sebastián, and a print of the subsequent British retreat.

Iglesia Nuestra Señora de la Asunción

C/del Medio. Mass Mon, Wed, Fri & Sun 11am & 1pm. Before setting off on his voyage, Columbus supposedly visited the town's main church for a final session of prayers. Construction of the building started in 1490 and took twenty years to complete, so it's difficult to imagine what it would have looked like in 1492. In any

▼ IGLESIA NUESTRA SEÑORA DE LA ASUNCIÓN

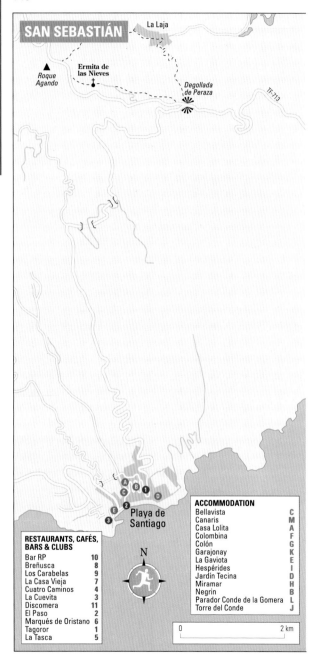

SAN SEBASTIÁN

La Laja

▲ Roque Agando

Ermita de las Nieves

Degollada de Peraza

TF-713

ACCOMMODATION

Bellavista	C
Canaris	M
Casa Lolita	A
Colombina	F
Colón	G
Garajonay	K
La Gaviota	E
Hespérides	I
Jardín Tecina	D
Miramar	H
Negrin	B
Parador Conde la Gomera	L
Torre del Conde	J

Playa de Santiago

N

RESTAURANTS, CAFÉS, BARS & CLUBS

Bar RP	10
Breñusca	8
Los Carabelas	9
La Casa Vieja	7
Cuatro Caminos	4
La Cuevita	3
Discomera	11
El Paso	2
Marqués de Oristano	6
Tagoror	1
La Tasca	5

0   2 km

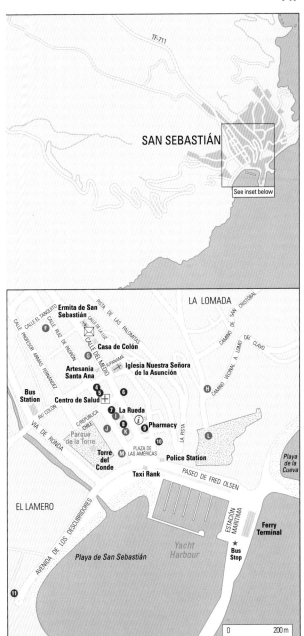

case, an attack by Algerian pirates in 1618 destroyed all but its basic structure, so today's church dates mostly from the seventeenth century – a brick-and-lime, mostly Gothic-style construction, with some Baroque elements, particularly in the carvings of the impressive wooden altars. A large faded mural on one wall of the church depicts the successful repulse of Windham's naval attack on the island (see Torre del Conde, p.145), cause for great celebration in a town weary of rebuilding after repeated pirate attacks. The archway to the left of the main entrance is called the Puerta del Perdón which the Guanches were invited to step through for a full amnesty after their 1488 uprising. Hundreds came only to find they had been tricked and were subsequently either executed or sold as slaves.

Casa de Colón

C/del Medio 56. Mon–Fri 9am–1pm & 4.30–7.30pm, Sat 9am–1pm. Free. A quaint, wooden-balconied seventeenth-century house, the so-called Casa de Colón (Columbus's House) was actually built over a hundred years after the explorer's death. Even so, maps of the voyage, pieces of Peruvian pottery, and small rotating exhibitions of contemporary Gomeran art are worth a visit.

Ermita de San Sebastián

C/del Medio. Built in 1450, the tiny Ermita de San Sebastián was the island's first chapel, but, like most buildings in the town, it was not spared by marauding pirates who destroyed it three times. Recent restoration has returned the building to its original form. One of the few decorations on display

– fourteen iron crosses on the wall – represent the Stations of the Cross.

Playa de San Sebastián and Playa de la Cueva

San Sebastián's central plazas overlook the bay, harbour and a promenade beside the island's longest (400m) sandy beach, Playa de San Sebastián. At the eastern end of the promenade, just beyond the marina and around a headland, is the town's second, more secluded beach, Playa de la Cueva. Also sandy, it's less disturbed by harbour traffic and has great views across to Tenerife and Mount Teide.

Degollada de Peraza, La Laja and Roque Agando

9km/4hr hike. Bus #1 or #2 from San Sebastián, Mon–Sat 4 daily, 25min; or Valle Gran Rey, Mon–Sat 2 daily, 1hr 30min; bus #2 from Playa de Santiago, Mon–Sat 2 daily, 20min. Public buses, though infrequent, allow you to spend the day hiking in magnificent upland scenery. Ask the driver to drop you at Degollada de Peraza and you'll be at the spot that witnessed the 1488 murder of the island's governor, now home to Bar Peraza (where drivers can leave their cars). From here, a 100-metre walk west along the road leads to a viewpoint; a further 100m along on the north side, there's a series of stone steps which climb onto a well-defined track. This track gradually widens, passing a lone house on a ridge before reaching a T-junction. Turn right onto what becomes an asphalt road, following it for five minutes or so to the Ermita de las Nieves, a tiny chapel surrounded by a huge plaza and viewing platform. Picnic tables here make it an ideal spot for a break. Head round the church to follow a narrow track that climbs through stands of laurel trees before dropping down to the main road near Roque Agando. Continue 200m towards this huge rock, looking for a clearly signed turn-off to La Laja (3km) on the north side of the road. This steep, marked path drops through pine forest and groves of palms and orange trees to the scattered village of La Laja. From La Laja, San Sebastián is a pleasant but tiring 8km/3hr downhill hike away, following a lightly used minor road past a series of dams. A better alternative, though dependent on the bus services, is to continue the loop back to Degollada de Peraza, following the marked uphill path at a fork just above the village. If you're early or late for the bus, consider calling a taxi from *Bar Peraza*.

Playa de Santiago

Bus #2 from San Sebastián, Mon–Sat 2 daily, 40min. Ferries arrive to Valle Gran Rey, 3 daily, 20min; and San Sebastián, 3 daily, 25min. Though technically the second largest resort on the island, Playa de Santiago remains a tiny harbour town where only the presence of a few extra restaurants suggests tourism on any scale. Looming over it all, from a spectacular clifftop vantage point, is the

gigantic five-star hotel *Jardín Tecina*. If you're not staying at the hotel, there's not much to do here, though you may be content to enjoy the island's sunniest weather on several large pebble beaches in a series of coves – some popular with nudists and hippies who sleep rough – that beckon just east of the *Tecina*. Most local hikes are dull by Gomeran standards, so the best excursion is to take a boat trip (€36; see p.156) on the *Siron* to Los Organos – a series of organ-pipe shaped cliffs on the northeast side of the island – which leaves on Tuesdays, Thursdays and Sundays at 9am. Tickets can be purchased at *Bar Info* beyond the eastern end of Avenida Marítima.

Hotels

Garajonay

C/Ruíz de Padrón 17, San Sebastián
☎922 87 05 50, ☎922 87 05 50.
Big, four-storey hotel in the centre of town, with 56 clean and simple, pine-furnished, en-suite rooms. The hotel usually has vacancies and also has some singles and triples. €42

Jardín Tecina

Playa de Santiago ☎922 14 58 50,
ⓦwww.jardin-tecina.com. Luxurious

▼ PLAYA DE SANTIAGO

self-contained resort with over four hundred rooms, five pools and restaurants, four bars, a spa and extensive sports facilities – which include tennis, paddle and squash courts and a verdant eighteen-hole golf course. Prices are for half-board. €142.

Parador Conde de la Gomera

Lomo de la Horca, San Sebastián ☎ 922 87 11 00, ⊕ www.parador.es. Graceful four-star Canarian-style mansion, high above town with breathtaking views. The hotel is consistently full and reservations should be made several weeks in advance. €116.

Torre del Conde

C/Ruíz de Padrón 19, San Sebastián ☎ 922 87 00 00, ☎ 922 87 13 14. Central hotel with simple elegant rooms – including some singles – all with TV and air-conditioning. Many also have balconies and there's a rooftop terrace equipped with sunloungers. Prices include breakfast; full- or half-board deals also available. €58.

Pensions

Casa Lolita

Laguna de Santiago, Playa de Santiago ☎ 922 89 55 50. The cheapest

▲ TORRE DEL CONDE

choice on the island – and blessed with fine views – has mattresses on the floor of the "student" rooms and windowless doubles (for married couples only) sharing a bathroom. €13.

Colombina

C/Ruíz de Padrón 83, San Sebastián ☎ 922 87 12 57. Reception open 7.30am–1pm & 4–7.30pm. Functional, clean and quiet property with friendly owners and a lovely roof terrace. Rooms come with bath and there are some triples and good-value singles too. There's often room here when elsewhere is full. €36.

Colón

C/del Medio 59, San Sebastián ☎ 922 87 02 35. A collection of simple, clean and tastefully decorated rooms – though those with a balcony look out onto a noisy road and those without are windowless and dark. Some rooms have their own bathrooms and there are singles and triples available. If there's nobody in reception, ring at the green door for attention. €22.

La Gaviota

Avda. Maritima Playa de Santiago ☎ 922 89 51 35. Playa de Santiago's best pension, though more expensive than the rest. Some rooms are en suite and have a small balcony. Enquire at the restaurant below. €24.

Hespérides

C/Ruíz de Padrón 42, San Sebastián ☎ 922 87 13 05. Clean, basic, good-value pension right in the thick of things. Rooms have sinks but share bathrooms and there are some cheap singles beside a roof terrace, too. Ring at the door on the first floor for attention. €24.

Bus #1 from San Sebastián (Mon–Sat 2–5 daily, 2hr 15min) stops in La Calera, Vueltas and La Playa. Ferries (3 daily) from Los Cristianos (1hr 20min), San Sebastián (35min) and Playa de Santiago (20min) dock at Vueltas. The valley's **tourist office** (Mon–Sat 9am–1.30pm; ☏922 80 54 58) is in La Playa, on the road that runs parallel to the promenade.

Apartments

Bellavista
C/Santa Ana, Playa de Santiago ☏922 89 55 70, ⓦwww.casacanarias.co.uk. Complex of eleven attractive, English-run apartments of varying sizes – up to two bedrooms – all with sea views and some with balcony. €37.

Canaris
C/Ruíz de Padrón 3, San Sebastián ☏922 14 14 53. Roomy, central and modern apartments, some with views over the Torre del Conde. Both the apartments and studios sleep two; the studios are particularly good value. €24.

Miramar
Orilla del Llano 3, San Sebastián ☏922 87 04 48. These smart, pine-furnished apartments are beyond the noise and bustle of the town centre. Units can sleep three and lets are for a minimum of three nights. If there's no answer, try *Bar Curva* next door. €36.

Negrin
Laguna de Santiago, Playa de Santiago ☏922 89 52 82. Modern and very basic apartments, sleeping up to three, with roof terraces offering good bay views. The apartments are in three separate blocks, of which Negrin 2 and 3 are quieter. €24.

Shops

Artesanía Santa Ana
C/del Medio 41, San Sebastián. Housed in a sixteenth-century former chapel, this is the largest of a series of tasteful souvenir shops along the Calle del Medio.

Cafés

Los Carabelas
Plaza de la Constitución, San Sebastián. Mon–Fri 7am–11pm. One of many cafés scattered in and around San Sebastián's two adjoining central plazas. This one is shaded by a couple of vast laurel trees, attracts an even mix of locals and visitors and has some of the best tapas around. Prices are moderate.

▲ FLOWERING CACTI

Restaurants

Breñusca

C/del Medio 11, San Sebastián. Closed Sun. Wood-furnished bar serving good, basic Canarian food – try the tasty stews such as *rancho canario* or the spicy rabbit in a garlicky *salmorejo* sauce. Open from 9am for breakfast.

La Casa Vieja

C/República de Chile 5, San Sebastián. Small simple bar where the TV blares football and you can choose inexpensive tapas from a chalkboard menu listing dishes such as octopus, rabbit and goat.

Cuatro Caminos

C/Ruíz de Padrón 36, San Sebastián. Closed Sun. Tiny restaurant in a bar that's a popular local gathering place. The grilled fish is cheap and fresh.

La Cuevita

Avda. Marítima, Playa de Santiago. Closed Sun. Located in a candlelit natural cave, this restaurant has a massive selection of fish and meat including fine steaks and the good local fresh fish *vieja*. There's also a big and unusually imaginative dessert selection.

Marqués de Oristano

C/del Medio 24, San Sebastián ☎922 87 00 22. Restaurant in a stylish eighteenth-century house offering several good dining options to suit all budgets and appetites. A great selection of tapas is served in a pleasant courtyard; a restaurant in the back serves simple grilled meat dishes, while the first-floor restaurant serves pricey Canarian food with a decidedly gourmet twist.

El Paso

Avda. Marítima, Playa de Santiago. *El Paso* serves huge portions of beautifully cooked food making is justly popular with locals. Some spectacular photos show the 1999 storms, when the sea tore through the town.

Tagoror

Hotel Jardín Tecina, Playa de Santiago. With excellent views over the harbour and bay, *Tagoror* serves good tapas and has a large wine selection but otherwise its moderately expensive food – the usual fish, meat, paella and pizza – is nothing special.

La Tasca

C/Ruíz de Padrón 34, San Sebastián. Eves only. Multilingual menus indicate a mostly tourist clientele in this old, dimly lit Canarian house, where prices are reasonable and there are lots of fish and meat dishes plus a great mixed salad. Try the excellent spicy tomato soup to start.

Bars

Bar RP

Plaza de la Constitución, San Sebastián. Mon–Sat until 2am. One of the town's few nightlife spots, this is a sociable and hip bar with thirty-five varieties of beer available.

Clubs

Discomera

C/El Lamero 15, San Sebastián. Wed–Sat 11pm–3am. At the west end of the seafront promenade, this semi-outdoor club, playing chart music, only really gets busy on Fridays and Saturdays.

Valle Gran Rey

A deep gorge carved out of La Gomera's ancient rock, **Valle Gran Rey** contains a number of villages along its length and some low-key resorts where the valley reaches the ocean. In the late 1960s this area became the destination for German hippies, who have now been replaced by German students and professionals seeking an "alternative" beach holiday. Most of the upper valley is still terraced for agricultural use, but the comparatively large earnings from tourism have proved irresistible to locals who have built small apartment blocks for visitors near the coast. The three main villages, **Vueltas, La Calera** and **La Playa,** offer little more than the chance to relax on the sand-and-pebble beaches or in the pleasantly laid-back restaurants and bars. For something more active, sensational hiking is not far away.

Vueltas

The biggest and busiest of the three main villages in the valley, Vueltas is an untouristy place, where Canarians outnumber visitors and the few New-Agey shops and late-night bars do little to detract from the laid-back atmosphere. The beaches here are not terribly attractive however, the town's quiet harbour is enticing for the chance to swim in the calm and generally clean waters.

Argaga tropicfruitgarden

☎ 922 69 70 04. Tues & Fri: April–Sept 10am–5pm; Oct–March 11am–4pm. €9. The tropical orchard Argaga tropicfruitgarden is a

▼ BEACH, VUELTAS

LA PLAYA

Fisch & Co
La Rueda
(Car rental)
El Fotógrafo

0   100 m

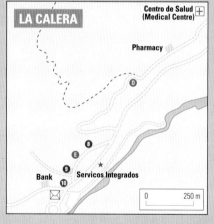

LA CALERA

Centro de Salud
(Medical Centre)

Pharmacy

Servicos Integrados

Bank

0   250 m

*Playa
del Inglés*

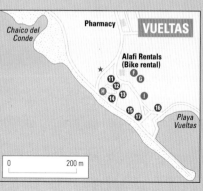

*Chaico del
Conde*

Pharmacy

VUELTAS

Alafi Rentals
(Bike rental)

*Playa
Vueltas*

0   200 m

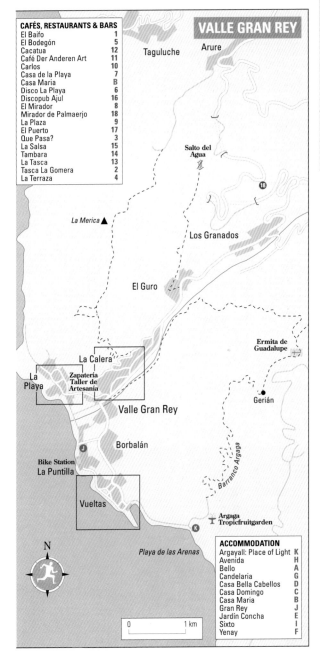

CAFÉS, RESTAURANTS & BARS
El Baifo	1
El Bodegón	5
Cacatua	12
Café Der Anderen Art	11
Carlos	10
Casa de la Playa	7
Casa Maria	B
Disco La Playa	6
Discopub Ajul	16
El Mirador	8
Mirador de Palmaerjo	18
La Plaza	9
El Puerto	17
Que Pasa?	3
La Salsa	15
Tambara	14
La Tasca	13
Tasca La Gomera	2
La Terraza	4

VALLE GRAN REY

Taguluche   Arure

Salto del Agua

La Merica ▲

Los Granados

El Guro

Ermita de Guadalupe

La Calera

Zapatería Taller de Artesanía

La Playa

Valle Gran Rey

Gerián

Borbalán

Bike Station
La Puntilla

Barranco Argaga

Vueltas

Argaga Tropicfruitgarden

N

Playa de las Arenas

0   1 km

ACCOMMODATION
Argayall: Place of Light	K
Avenida	H
Bello	A
Candelaria	G
Casa Bella Cabellos	D
Casa Domingo	C
Casa Maria	B
Gran Rey	J
Jardín Concha	E
Sixto	I
Yenay	F

Boat trips

Boat trips to the impressive cliff face of Los Organos, with its high wall of six-sided basalt columns, depart daily – except in rough weather – from Vueltas harbour. The standard six-and-a-half-hour trip is done by the *Siron* (☎922 80 54 80; Tues–Sun 10.30am; €30) and the *Tina* (☎922 80 56 99; daily 10.30am; €30), and also includes a stop so passengers can have a swim off a small beach only accessible by sea. Food is provided and you may also see dolphins and whales. For specifically whale-watching jaunts, tailor-made yachting, deep-sea fishing trips and visits to Hierro and La Palma, enquire at the Bait and Tackle shop (closed Sun) just inland of the plaza in Vueltas.

fifteen-minute walk south of Vueltas – following first the cliffs opposite the harbour and then a track a short way up the Barranco Argaga (past the "private" signs). Originally developed by enthusiasts as an organic garden for fruits and flowers, visitor interest has led to the orchard being opened for frequent, pleasantly informal tours (in English on request). These concentrate on sampling around a dozen of the exotic fruits grown here, accompanied by salient information on their cultivation.

Barranco Argaga hike

Beyond the Argaga tropicfruitgarden the steep and narrow Barranco Argaga gorge is an amazing sight and offers great hiking. For the energetic, there's a strenuous but excellent loop from Valle Gran Rey, along which the interesting terrain and great views make it one of the island's premier hikes. A marked, but unsignposted, path clambers steeply up Barranco Argaga to the hamlet of Gerián. From here, fork left onto an unmarked but obvious water-channel path to the chapel Ermita de Nuestra Señora de Guadalupe, high on the south slope of the gorge. The path continues from the chapel, dropping gradually into the ravine bed – ignore a marked path on the right to Chipude.

▼ ARGAGA TROPICFRUITGARDEN

▲ PROMENADE, LA PLAYA

Once at the base of the ravine the route climbs again and continues straight over the ridge ahead – ignore turn-offs to the right and left along the ridge – then descends steeply into Valle Gran Rey. Turn left along the path at the bottom of the valley, following a dry stream bed back to La Calera.

Playa de las Arenas

Playa de las Arenas refers to a series of coves, southeast along the coast from Valle Gran Rey's main settlements. Home to a collection of hippies who call it Rainbow Beach and have painted a rainbow on the rock at its entrance, local expatriate Germans prefer to know it as *Schweinebucht* (bay of pigs), unequivocally expressing their feelings about its residents. The beaches are popular with nudists. To get here, follow the coast south of Vueltas and be prepared for some scrambling over loose tracks and rock faces.

La Playa and Playa del Inglés

A collection of modern buildings, clustered around a beach and short promenade, La Playa has an easy-going seaside atmosphere. It's well positioned to take advantage of Valle Gran Rey's best beaches, the most crowded of which is the sand-and-pebble strand that stretches out in front of the resort. From La Playa, a dirt track – the only one leading north out of the village – leads to the most popular nudist beach, Playa del Inglés.

La Calera and La Merica hikes

Two hikes: 2hr & 3–4hr. At the point where the narrow valley opens out towards the sea, a cluster of houses have clawed their way up a cliff to form La Calera, the quietest of the three main villages in the valley. Here, steep steps and winding alleys connect the old buildings enjoying great valley and sea views, while above, the magnificent peak La Merica offers strenuous hiking on rocky trails with tremendous views. A well-trodden track starts from the high road at the up-valley end of La Calera, marked by a large wooden sign. After winding up treeless, volcanic cliffs, the path branches off to a viewpoint near the top – marked by a windsock – with La Playa almost vertically below and an inaccessible collection of steep gorges to the north. This hike can also form part of an excellent half-day hike from Arure at the head of the valley. By taking the bus (or hitching) up to this village, you can head east along an unsigned but obvious dirt road that later becomes a rough track following the stunning ridge south, via the summit of La Merica and the viewpoint described above before finally dropping back down to La Calera.

Salto del Agua hike

3km; 2–3hr return. Despite being one of La Gomera's best short hikes, the island's trademark stunning views are surprisingly absent on here. Instead this clamber up and down a rocky, and largely dry, stream bed leads through dense and atmospheric vegetation to the delightful little waterfall that crashes down the rocky headwall of this minor valley. The trek starts at El Guro, on the inside curve of the large sweeping bend in the road, just below the village proper: the trailhead has been thoughtfully indicated by the words "Wasserfall" on a palm tree beside the road. From here the route initially crosses the dry creek bed and climbs between houses for around 50m before cutting northeast between terraced fields – where blue and yellow trail paint daubs begin to mark the route. These come and go, but generally the route is

easy to find; if in doubt clamber up along the stream bed, until marks reappear.

Hotels

Argayall: Place of Light

Playa de las Arenas ☎922 69 70 08, ⓦwww.argayall.com. New Age centre, 15min walk from Vueltas in an isolated spot by the beach. Both singles and doubles are available and prices include vegetarian full board. A broad activity programme includes meditation, reiki, yoga, African dance and drumming. Reception is open 10am–1pm, but closed Tues. €84.

Gran Rey

La Puntilla ☎922 80 58 59, ⓦwww.hotel-granrey.com. This large waterfront hotel offers the valley's most luxurious accommodation. Facilities include tennis courts, a pool and a large roof terrace, and the en-suite rooms have air-conditioning and TVs. Some singles available. Prices include breakfast. €114.

Pensions

Candelaria

Vueltas ☎922 80 54 02. Simple,

Accommodation Agencies

Valle Gran Rey's **apartment agencies** are the easiest way of finding a rental property. Try to book at least three weeks in advance – longer over Easter or Christmas – though all the following will also try to help at short notice.

Manuel Trujillo y Trujillo
La Puntilla ☎922 80 51 29.

La Paloma
Vueltas ☎922 80 60 43, ⓦwww.gomera.info.

Servicos Integrados La Gomera
Edificio El Contero/La Finca, La Calera ☎922 80 58 66, ⓦwww.gomera-service .com.

very popular pension with a large sun deck and good sea views from the roof, on one of the backstreets of the old port. There are rooms of various sizes, styles and prices – plus some basic apartments (from €25 per night for two) – some with private bathrooms. €20.

Casa Bella Cabellos

Calera ☎ 922 80 51 82. Restored old Canarian home with wooden balconies, surrounded by lush vegetation. Run by an amenable old lady, this place has simple doubles, a studio and a four-bed apartment. The house is a bit off the beaten track on the old village road. €30.

▲ EL FOTÓGRAFO

Casa Maria

La Playa ☎ 922 80 50 47, ©casa-maria@terra.es. Excellently positioned in front of the beach, above a large restaurant (see p.160), the highlight of this pension is the roof terrace overlooking the sea, while the simple rooms (some tiny) share basic bathrooms. €20.

Jardín Concha

La Calera ☎ 922 80 60 63. Elegant, hotel-quality lodgings in the first place in the valley to rent rooms to foreigners. Views from the patios are superb. The pension runs a couple of functional apartments nearby. En-suite doubles €27.

Apartments

Avenida

Vueltas ☎ 922 80 54 61. Four-storey apartment block in a splendid

waterfront location, with sea views from all balconies. Units are equipped with kitchenettes and sleep two. €20.

Bello

La Playa ☎ 922 80 51 15. Spacious, well-equipped, modern apartments with balconies, beside the promenade. All sleep two, and while some overlook the beach, others face the wall of an apartment block and are thus darker but less expensive. Enquire at Bar Yaya below. €30.

Casa Domingo

La Playa ☎ & ☎ 922 80 51 31. Bright, clean, pine-furnished apartments, sleeping two to four people, close to the beach in a four-storey house surrounded by banana groves. €30.

Sixto

Vueltas ☎ 922 80 53 32. Well-worn but good-value apartments in the centre of Vueltas, run by a friendly elderly Canarian who often comes down to the quay to meet arriving boats. Apartments are spacious, sleep up to three and share a small roof terrace. €22.

Yenay

Vueltas ☎ 922 80 54 71. Large basic block with standard apartments, studios and a couple of basic windowless rooms. The roof terrace has great views. €20.

Shops

El Fotógrafo

La Playa ☎ 922 805 654. The best source of original postcards in La Gomera. The shop is also useful for hiking maps and guides (most in German) and has a photo-processing service.

Zapatería Taller de Artesanía

By the road between La Calera and La Playa. Old-fashioned cobblers' where shoes are made to measure (around €50), repaired or widened. Off-the-peg handmade shoes are also available, as are other leather goods.

Cafés

Café Der Anderen Art

Vueltas. Daily except Thurs 10am–1pm & 5pm–midnight. Small trendy café in the centre of town, serving good continental breakfasts, plus cakes and crêpes all day.

Carlos

La Calera. Mon–Sat 9am–7pm. *Carlos*'s tiny outside terrace overflows with people watching the valley's busiest road while they sample the ice cream and freshly pressed fruit juices.

Casa de la Playa

La Playa. Mon–Sat 10am–10pm. Consistently busy, large, shady terrace beside a banana plantation on the edge of La Playa – the place to hang out at sunset. Serves good snacks and *bocadillos* along with ice cream, shakes and juices.

Tambara

Vueltas. Daily except Wed 5pm–1am. Small café-bar with great views over the sea. Spots on the tiny terrace are hard to come by but the interior, decorated with Turkish mosaics, is almost as nice. The tapas are better value than the overpriced sandwiches and cocktails.

Restaurants

El Baifo

La Playa ☎ 922 80 57 75. Closed Fri & July. Excellent, moderately expensive Malaysian restaurant that makes the most of local fresh fish to offer an alternative to the usual Gomeran cuisine. Vegetarians are well catered for.

Casa Maria

La Playa. Closed Tues. Popular restaurant on the beachfront, below the pension of the same name. Large portions of home-made food include a massive Spanish omelette, a tasty paella and a superb grilled chicken breast (each around €6–8). Check the blackboard for the fresh dishes of the day.

El Mirador

La Calera. Closed Thurs. Large moderately priced restaurant with great valley views that's a good place to start or finish the day. Breakfasts include *bocadillos* and fresh juices; the tapas and salads make for a good light lunch; and dinner sees the usual fish and meat options, served with *papas arrugadas* and excellent home-made *mojo*.

Mirador de Palmaerjo

Head of the valley ☎ 922 80 58 68. Open Tues–Sat. Designed by Canarian artist César Manrique, this restaurant-cum-viewpoint provides dizzying views of Valle Gran Rey. The relatively expensive gourmet variations on old Canarian favourites are worth a stop on the way back from hiking in the uplands, but only if you have access to a car or taxi. Book ahead to get the best views.

La Plaza

La Calera. Closed Thurs. Basic, unexciting bar on the main road by the taxi rank, popular thanks to its low prices and large portions of food like rabbit and chicken *en salsa*.

El Puerto

Vueltas. ☎ 922 80 52 24. Harbourside restaurant that is a favourite with locals. Food is suitably basic – the €6.50 menu of the day typically includes salad, a tuna steak and ice cream. The grilled fish platter (€15) for two people is the restaurant's speciality.

La Salsa

Vueltas ☎ 922 80 55 18. Nov–April 6–11.30pm, closed Wed. Bright and trendy restaurant with bold colour schemes and great vegetarian food. The varied menu includes tacos, Thai curry and tofu dishes. Though a bit pricey by local standards, the big portions are worth it.

La Terraza

La Playa ☎ 922 80 54 90. Large enclosed terrace visited exclusively by holidaymakers, this place specializes in big, good-value portions of pork chops with *papas arrugadas*, pizzas and paella.

Bars

Bar La Tasca

Vueltas. A tropical atmosphere permeates this bar, with the best cocktails in the valley and board games on each table. Empty before 10pm.

Bar Que Pasa?

La Playa. Laid-back friendly hangout with ethnic decor, good tapas, fine cocktails and a large library of books.

El Bodegón

La Playa. Closed Sun. Though chiefly a mediocre restaurant, this place is also popular with local men who occasionally gather here to play melancholy Gomeran folk music – and some salsa too. Performances are ad hoc, so keep an eye out or ask if anything's planned.

▼ LA CALERA

Cacatua

Vueltas. Closed Mon. Easily the most popular cocktail bar in the valley, with several spacious rooms, a big patio and a lively vibe. It tends to get going a little later than elsewhere.

Tasca La Gomera

La Playa. Well-run pub with pleasant tiny outdoor terrace and occasional live music.

Clubs

Disco La Playa

La Playa. Wed–Sun 10pm–5am. Free. La Playa's late-night venue can be fun at the weekends or if there's live music. On other nights the scene can be a bit desperate, though, and don't arrive before 1am or you're likely to have the place to yourself.

Discopub Ajul

Vueltas. Tues–Sun 10.30pm–4.30am. €3. Nondescript disco that livens up at the weekend and on Thursdays when the hippies from Playa de Las Arenas get their drums out and add even more colour to the mix of chart, trance, salsa and reggae played here.

Northern La Gomera

Atlantic trade winds regularly bring clouds and misty rain to **northern La Gomera**, making its damp, lush valleys the island's most fertile. Bananas grow here in large quantities, particularly around Hermigua, and much of the tiny population on this side of the island is involved in agriculture. At the head of these valleys lies one of the world's most ancient forests and La Gomera's most outstanding attraction, the **Parque Nacional de Garajonay**. Apart from a mass of moss-cloaked laurel trees, this UNESCO World Heritage site contains around four hundred species of flora and is one of the last vestiges of an ecosystem that was once widespread around the Mediterranean. As the area has few specific attractions and unreliable weather, visitors don't tend to base themselves here – which is a pity as this part of the island is highly rewarding, particularly for hikers, who can enjoy the eerie atmosphere of the park's overgrown trails and the wild and picturesque coast.

Garajonay hike

5km/2hr return hike. Bus to Pajarito: Linea #1 from San Sebastián, Mon–Sat 4–5 daily, 30min; or Valle Gran Rey, Mon–Sat 2 daily, 1hr 30min. The most obvious excursion in the national park is the moderately strenuous hike to its highest point, which offers superb views over the dense tree canopy and beyond to neighbouring islands – weather permitting.

To climb the peak, head up from Pajarito (the road junction where the bus stops), where the route is signposted "Alto de Garajonay 2.5". The path climbs steeply through a laurel forest until eventually the trees thin and you arrive at a T-junction on a ridge and a signpost to "Alto de Garajonay" and "Contadero". Turn left for the Alto and you soon arrive at the summit where in good weather there are views of the islands of El Hierro and La Palma. From the summit simply retrace your steps back to Pajarito

Alto de Contadero to Hermigua hike

9km/4hr hike one way. Bus to Pajarito: Linea #1 from San Sebastián, Mon–Sat 2 daily, 30min;

▼ LAUREL FOREST, GARAJONAY

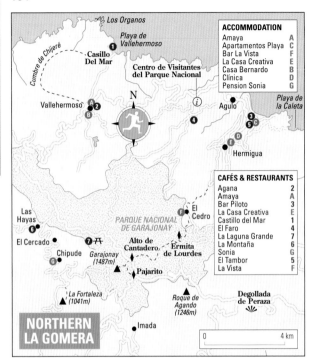

ACCOMMODATION

Amaya	A
Apartamentos Playa	C
Bar La Vista	F
La Casa Creativa	E
Casa Bernardo	B
Clínica	D
Pension Sonia	G

Los Organos

Playa de Vallehermoso ❶

Cumbre de Chijeré

Casillo Del Mar

Centro de Visitantes del Parque Nacional

Vallehermoso ❷
A ❷
B

Agulo

Playa de la Caleta

❸ ❺ C
D
E ❹ D
Hermigua

N

CAFÉS & RESTAURANTS

Agana	2
Amaya	A
Bar Piloto	3
La Casa Creativa	E
Castillo del Mar	1
El Faro	4
La Laguna Grande	7
La Montaña	6
Sonia	G
El Tambor	5
La Vista	F

Las Hayas ❻

El Cercado

Chipude G

PARQUE NACIONAL DE GARAJONAY

❼ 🎋

Garajonay (1487m) ▲

Alto de Contadero

El Cedro F

Ermita de Lourdes

Pajarito ●

La Fortaleza ▲ (1041m)

Roque de Agando (1246m) ▲

Degollada de Peraza ⌁

NORTHERN LA GOMERA

Imada ●

0   4 km

or Valle Gran Rey, Mon–Sat 2 daily, 1hr 30min. This scenically spectacular and wonderfully varied hike is easily the best in La Gomera, and made even more attractive by being almost entirely downhill. The hike is not easily incorporated into a loop, so you have to rely on using the island's bus services to complete a round-trip from

San Sebastián, or get a taxi back to your base.

The first part of the hike follows the route above to Alto de Garajonay as far as the T-junction where you turn right for Contadero. From here it's around 1km descending to a wide dirt track. A right turn here soon brings you to the main road and the lay-by Alto

The legend of Garajonay

The mountain Garajonay is named for Gomera's answer to Romeo and Juliet, **Gara** and **Jonay**. Gara was a Gomeran princess and Jonay a humble peasant boy from Tenerife who visited his princess by paddling over on inflated goatskins – or so the Guanche legend goes. Neither family were keen on the couple's relationship but their love ran far deeper than their differences in status, and so, determined never to be parted, they clambered to the top of Garajonay and ran each other through with lances of laurel wood, choosing death rather than separation and naming the mountain in the process.

de Contadero. Follow the trail signposted "El Cedro 4.8" which drops through overgrown ancient forests along one of the most magical sections of this walk. Around 3km down this trail you come to a fork where you should follow signs to "Arroyo de El Cedro". The track crosses La Gomera's only stream (*arroyo*) several times on the way to a parking area on a dirt road. The *Mudéjar*-style chapel Ermita de Nuestra Señora de Lourdes is a short way beyond this on paths marked "Caserío de El Cedro". Continuing on to El Cedro you arrive at a dirt road on the edge of the hamlet. Turn right here and then left at a T-junction, following signs to *Bar La Vista*. The dirt road snakes its way to the bottom of the valley before arriving at a small ford. Just to the right is an entrance to El Cedro's water tunnel (see below), while the main path carries on across the ford and to the right, following the stream.

The hamlet is soon left behind as the distinct path passes a small waterfall, and then spectacular views of the Hermigua Valley. Descending steeply, the path is clear as it passes a couple of dams and an old *gofio* mill – the grindstone is still there.

Further down the valley, as banana plantations take hold, the path follows a pipeline which you leave only at some short steep steps to a minor sealed road. Turn right here and walk until you reach some stairs that come just before a sharp bend in the road, where benches are set into a concrete road-barrier. Descend here to a plaza where buses will stop if you flag them down or there's a phone to call a local taxi (☎922 88 00 47 or 922 88 00 09).

El Cedro

Set amid lush cultivated terraces and dense laurel thickets, El Cedro is the national park at its best. This modest hamlet makes a good place to stop on longer hikes or, as the only place to stay in the park, a destination in itself. Other than the spectacular surrounding scenery, El Cedro is known for an exciting short hike through a claustrophobic 575m underground water tunnel – allow an hour, bring a torch and expect wet feet. The tunnel took 26 years to chisel by hand and was used to help irrigate Hermigua's thirsty banana plantations. The entrance to the tunnel is just southeast of the dirt road where it crosses the base of the valley. Going through it brings you out within sight of the Hermigua–San Sebastián road, to which you can hike on a steep and twisting path (around 1hr) and flag down a bus.

Hermigua

Linea #3 from San Sebastián, Mon–Sat 2 daily, 25min; or Vallehermoso, Mon–Sat 2 daily, 45min. Scattered the length of a pretty ravine, and fed by water from La Gomera's only stream, the small town of Hermigua is in the island's lushest valley. The presence of a relatively plentiful supply of water here has encouraged prolific banana cultivation for over a century. The town broadly divides into an upper and lower village. The former, Valle Alto, is marked by the sixteenth-century Iglesia de Santo Domingo (rarely open) beside a convent of the same name. The lower village, Valle Bajo, has at its centre a small plaza beside the modern Nuestra Señora de la Emancipación church. Another collection of buildings is further down the valley by the large pebble beach, but huge Atlantic rollers and strong undercurrents mean that the only spot to swim here is the large seawater pool.

Playa de la Caleta

The quiet black-sand-and-pebble La Caleta beach (6km/1hr east of Hermigua) is generally a safe option for a swim. A little restaurant, open on fair-weather days between April and October, serves fish caught by fishermen living in nearby huts. The dirt road to Playa de la Caleta begins near the plaza in Valle Bajo and heads east up a steep road to the top of a headland, from where it descends into a valley before arriving at the beach.

Agulo

Linea #3 from San Sebastián, Mon–Sat 2 daily, 30min; or Vallehermoso, Mon–Sat 2 daily, 40min. Huddled on a tight shelf above the sea and below some mighty cliffs, the charming seventeenth-century village of Agulo holds a maze of cobbled alleys and whitewashed houses making it well worth a quick visit. If you arrive by car, it's better to park on the main road rather than try to negotiate the narrow streets.

Centro de Visitantes del Parque Nacional de Garajonay

☎992 80 09 93. Tues–Sun 9.30am–4.30pm. Free. Bus Linea #3 from San Sebastián, Mon–Sat 2–4 daily, 35min; or Vallehermoso, Mon–Sat 3–5 daily, 35min. Located well outside the national park, the visitor centre is near Agulo, a two-kilometre uphill hike from *Las Rosas* restaurant bus stop on the main road. The centre has a few displays on the park, a supply of books and maps (there's a wider range in San Sebastián and Valle Gran Rey) and a diverting little museum of folk history with a reconstructed traditional Gomeran home. Ask the staff about their free weekly English guided hikes.

Vallehermoso

Linea #3 from San Sebastián, Mon–Sat 2 daily, 1hr 10min. The setting of Vallehermoso, "beautiful valley", is undoubtedly picturesque; the town nestles between steep ridges, and below the towering volcanic monolith Roque Cano. Its focal point is the Plaza de la Constitución, a small plaza surrounded by bars, shops, banks (with ATMs), a post office, a medical centre and a petrol station.

▼ AGULO

Playa de Vallehermoso

An hour's hike (3km) down a quite road to the seaside north of Vallehermoso, is Playa de Vallehermoso. Formerly the town's harbour and beach, it's now home to an elegant pool and a vibrant cultural facility (see below). The harbour here was once among La Gomera's busiest and where the island's first car – a Model-T Ford – was brought ashore in 1910 in an era when the large sandy beach here made an ideal bathing spot. Unfortunately the removal of its white sands for use in cement, means that, today, gigantic rollers pound fist-sized pebbles and discourage bathing. Thankfully, a seawater pool (admission €3), complete with sun lounging area and café, fills the gap.

▲ CUMBRE DE CHIJERÉ

Castillo del Mar

☎ 922 80 54 77, ⊛ www.castillo-del -mar.com. Tues–Sun 11am–sunset. A short walk beyond Playa de Vallehermoso, beside towering cliffs and with wonderful views of Tenerife and Teide, is the atmospheric and bohemian cultural centre Castillo del Mar. Originally built in 1890 as a banana-packing warehouse, the building fell into ruin after the demise of the industry and until 2003 when it was transformed into a cultural centre by a German photographer. The structure has been shored up by local craftsmen using traditional techniques, and its decoration with funky iron sculptures gives the place a whole new feel and purpose; making it an ideal spot for leisurely drinks and tapas (see p.169) and a great venue for the performing arts (see p.171). As well as soaking up the vibe, you can get an insight into the Castillo's history and restoration in the onsite exhibition centre; in the museum shop there's a chance to buy outstanding postcards and prints from the owner's exceptional photographic collection.

Cumbre de Chijeré hike

10km/4hr hike. To gain an appreciation of the beauty of the valley and magnitude of the cliffs on this side of the coast, take the excellent looping hike along the Cumbre de Chijeré. From Vallehermoso head north towards the sea, leaving the road to ascend a steep-sided gorge a few hundred metres shy of the beach. Weaving between three houses, the trail – soon marked by blue arrows and red dots – zigzags its way up the rocky arid slopes, with views of rugged cliffs and Teide on Tenerife in the distance. As the path reaches the top of the Cumbre de Chijeré ridge, a landscape of ochre rock eroded into swirling shapes is revealed. A dirt road, which leads as far as the viewpoint on the tip of the ridge nearby, runs inland past a tiny chapel. Once past the chapel, follow a narrow track off to the right, through woods with more great views over the cliffs to the west. The path rejoins the main track at another chapel, where a short way further on another narrow path turns off to the left (east), snaking its way through dense Laurasilva forest, then descending through terraces back into the centre of Vallehermoso.

Chipude

Linea #1 from San Sebastián, Mon–Sat 2 daily, 1hr; or Valle Gran Rey, Mon–Sat 2 daily, 45min. Until two hundred years ago Chipude was La Gomera's largest town, but there's little trace of this former grandeur today. Only the sixteenth-century Moorish Iglesia de la Virgen de la Candelaria, dominating the central plaza, hints at the bygone importance of the town. Otherwise there are a couple of bars offering basic food and accommodation, making the town the most readily accessible base in the uplands.

La Fortaleza

4km/2hr hike. Bus to Chipude Once a place of considerable spiritual significance to the Guanches, and still the most impressive landmark in the uplands, La Fortaleza mesa makes a superb two-hour round-trip from Chipude. Starting out along the road south to La Dama, the track up the hill to the left of the road is obvious. As the trail ascends the final section to the summit plateau it becomes less clear and it's a case of making your own route over bare rock – a head for heights is essential. The top of the hill is almost uniformly flat, and blustery winds are common, but excellent views over Chipude, the national park and El Hierro island compensate. For Guanches, this was an important place of retreat and worship and remains of stone circles have been found here, along with bone fragments, suggesting sacrifices.

Pensions

Amaya

Vallehermoso ☎922 80 00 73. Bar and pension with basic single and double rooms sharing bathrooms, or more luxurious options with private bath, TV and fridge. €20.

Bar La Vista

El Cedro ☎922 88 09 49. Offers simple rooms and runs a small campsite (€2 per site) – the island's only one, and the only place you can legally pitch in the park. €24.

Casa Bernardo

C/Triana 4, Vallehermoso ☎922 80 08 49. Excellent-value pension whose friendly, relaxed owners speak English and offer clean and simple singles and doubles, along with use of a communal kitchen. Two apartments (€28) on the roof are also good options, but require a three-night minimum stay. €20.

Clínica

Carretera General 72, Hermigua ☏ & ℻ 922 88 10 40. Five rooms are offered in this former clinic turned pension. It's a sociable place and well set up for groups (up to eight people) with a communal kitchen, eating area and pleasant little garden. Single rooms available. €20–25.

Pensión Sonia

Chipude ☏ 922 80 41 58. Bar on the church plaza with modern and scrupulously clean, hotel-quality, en-suite rooms. €22.

Apartments

Apartamentos Playa

Hermigua ☏ 922 88 07 58. Clean basic apartments sleeping two and overlooking the shingle beach. Run by the neighbouring bar *Los Prismas*. €24.

La Casa Creativa

Carretera General 58, Hermigua ☏ 922 88 10 23. Well-equipped, German-run apartments, sharing a pleasant terrace and small pool; offers the option of full-board deals at a wholefood restaurant (see p.170). €41.

Shops

Artesanía

Plaza de la Constitución, Vallehermoso. Mon–Fri & Sun 8.30am–1pm & 5–8pm; Sat 8.30am–1pm. Small shop beside *Bar Central* selling lots of local produce at reasonable prices. The Gomeran goat's cheese (*queso del país*) is particularly recommended. There are also

musical instruments, cigars and spirits.

Centro de Visitantes del Parque Nacional de Garajonay

☏ 992 80 09 93. Tues–Sun 9.30am–4.30pm. The centre's craft workshops produce and sell pottery, musical instruments – tambourines and castanets – and baskets.

Alfarería Tradicional

El Cercado. Daily 9am–2pm & 4–7pm. The small village of El Cercado is home to several pottery shops and workshops specializing in *alfarería* – a traditional technique in which pots are made without a wheel and rubbed with red earth before glazing.

Los Telares

C/General del Norte, Hermigua. Daily 9am–6pm. Weaving studio in a renovated house where rugs are the speciality among all manner of reasonably priced crafts and souvenirs.

Cafés

Amaya

Plaza de la Constitución, Vallehermoso. Overlooking the plaza, this consistently busy café-cum-bar serves coffees, basic food and tapas and has outdoor seating on the town's main square. Great smoothies (€2) and burgers – try the *Super Big*, which includes a fried egg and slice of ham (€2).

Castillo Del Mar

Playa de Vallehermoso. Delicious tapas and excellent German cakes are served in unique and wonderful seafront surroundings – to views of Tenerife and Mount Teide – in this cultural centre (see p.167).

Restaurants

Agana

Avda. Guillermo Ascencio 5,
Vallehermoso. Wed–Mon 10am–
11pm. This combined bar
and restaurant is one of few
eating options in Vallehermoso
and serves a range of simple,
inexpensive traditional meat and
fish dishes.

Bar Piloto

Hermigua. Closed Sun. Inexpensive
bar food served to three small
tables that look out to sea. The
menu changes daily, but often
includes fresh tuna and a good
home-made *mojo*. The Canarian
potatoes with sesame and palm
honey is a unique local spin on
an old favourite.

La Casa Creativa

Carretera General 58, Hermigua
☎ 922 88 10 23. Daily 9am–11pm.
Moderately expensive restaurant
that creatively and successfully
blends German wholefood
fare with traditional Gomeran
cuisine.

El Faro

Hermigua. Noon–4pm & 7–10pm.
Closed Wed & June. At the sea
end of town above *Bar Piloto*,
this place serves substantial
but moderately priced meals
including a great fish paella
(pre-order in the morning) and
meat dishes such as lamb with
papas arrugadas.

La Laguna Grande

La Laguna Grande. Tues–Sun 9am–
6pm. In a large former crater
that's now a popular picnic
spot, this restaurant serves good,
moderately priced stews and
some excellent *mojo* and is often
busy with day-trippers from
Tenerife.

La Montaña

Las Hayas. Sun–Fri 8am–8pm.
Serving superb, reasonably
priced vegetarian cuisine, this
bar puts the uneventful hamlet
of Las Hayas on the map. It
specializes in stews made from
home-grown and picked-to-
order ingredients. The almond
cake drizzled in palm honey is a
delicious and typically Gomeran
way to finish the meal.

Sonia

Chipude ☎ 922 80 41
58. No-frills bar with
inexpensive, basic
Gomeran food – large
dishes of *gofio* stand
on tables ready to
accompany the menu
that's limited to one
daily soup and main
course.

El Tambor

Centro de Visitantes. Tues–
Sun 11am–6pm. Simple,
rustic and inexpensive
restaurant with great
views from a small
patio and excellent

▲ RESTAURANT EL TAMBOR

no-frills Gomeran food, which can be washed down with the local Garajonay wine, or a shot of the palm-honey liqueur Gomeron.

La Vista

El Cedro ☎922 88 09 49. In the centre of El Cedro hamlet, this bar has picturesque views over the Hermigua Valley and hearty, inexpensive Gomeran food. A great place to try the traditional rustic staple *potaje de berros*.

Live Music

Castillo Del Mar

☎922 80 54 77 ⊛www.castillo-del-mar.com. From about 9pm onwards on weekend nights this cultural centre puts on live music concerts. There's usually some traditional Gomeran music on the bill, though South American bands and an eclectic mix of international acts also make appearances. Check the website too for details of movies screened here and for info on the wild all-night full-moon parties, which involve various techno rhythms and extravagant light shows. Concerts and events are usually priced around €10 and connected to Valle Gran Rey by shuttle bus – tickets from the El Fotógrafo shop (see p.160) in La Playa.

Essentials

Arrival

The majority of international flights to Tenerife land at **Tenerife South Airport** (Reina Sofía), near El Médano, with **Tenerife North** (Los Rodeos), near La Laguna and Santa Cruz, handling largely domestic traffic. **La Gomera's airport** receives no international flights, and with exorbitant prices for domestic connections, the most ecomonical option is to fly to Tenerife and take a ferry from Los Cristianos to San Sebastián.

Tenerife

The majority of holidaymakers have a free transfer to their hotel included in their package. For those travelling independently, taxis and frequent public buses run from each airport to major local towns.

Tenerife South (Reina Sofía)

☎922 75 90 00, ⓦwww.aena.es. Bus #341 to Santa Cruz, 23 daily, 50min; #340 to Puerto de la Cruz, 4 daily, 1hr 25min; #487 to Playa de Las Américas and Los Cristianos 15 daily, 45min. Approximate taxi fares: Santa Cruz €48; Puerto de la Cruz €70; Las Américas €16.

Tenerife North (Los Rodeos)

☎922 63 56 35, ⓦwww.aena.es. Buses #107, #108 & #109 to Santa Cruz, 27–30 daily, 30min; #340 to Puerto de la Cruz, 4 daily, 45min. Approximate taxi fares: Santa

Cruz €20; Puerto de la Cruz €40; Las Américas €58.

La Gomera

Three companies make the ferry trip from Los Cristianos to La Gomera and set their timetables in such a way to ensure frequent departures throughout the day. Fred Olsen (☎922 62 82 00, ⓦwww .fredolsen.es; 5 daily, 35min; €21 single) and Trasmediterranea (☎902 45 46 45, ⓦwww.trasmediterranea.es; 2–3 daily, 90min; €17.50 single) head solely to San Sebastián; the Garajonay Exprés catamaran (☎902 34 34 50, ⓦwww.garajonayexpres.com; 3 daily), runs to San Sebastián (45min; €14.50 single), Playa Santiago (1hr; €15.20 single) and Valle Gran Rey (1hr 20min; €17.80 single). You can also make short hops between these three Gomeran towns for €2–4. Though your intended destination and the timetables might decide for you which service you choose, it's worth noting that the Garajonay Exprés is a much smaller vessel than the others – which increases the chances of seasickness in rough seas – and it doesn't allow passengers deck access; with vision through its salt-crusted windows severely limited, you will likely forgo the chance of spotting whales or dolphins in the Gomeran channel.

Fly Less – Stay Longer!

Rough Guides believes in the good that travel does, but we are deeply aware of the impact of fuel emissions on climate change. We recommend taking fewer trips and staying for longer. If you can avoid travelling by air, please use an alternative, especially for journeys of under 1000km/600miles. And always offset your travel at ⓦwww.roughguides.com/climatechange.

Information

The **Spanish National Tourist Office** (SNTO) produces a number of maps and pamphlets on the Canaries. Most of what they have can be picked up at tourist offices on Tenerife and La Gomera, along with a number of local maps, leaflets and accommodation listings unavailable elsewhere. The main and best-stocked offices are at Tenerife South Airport (Oct–June Mon–Fri 9am–9pm, Sat 9am–1pm; July–Sept Mon–Fri 9am–7pm, Sat 9am–noon; ☎ 922 39 20 37) and in Santa Cruz on Tenerife and San Sebastián on La Gomera.

European newspapers reach Tenerife within a day of publication. A big expat presence means that local news and tourist-oriented listings fill the many free English-language newspapers. These include *Island Connections* (Ⓦ www.ic-web.com), *Tenerife News* (Ⓦ www.tennews.com), and *The Western Sun*. Also look out for the expat magazine *Living Tenerife* for its up-to-date features

and the Santa Cruz-focused bilingual listings magazine *Hoy & Today* (Ⓦ www.hoy-today.com), for its thorough performing arts info.

On the **Web**, official sites for the islands – Ⓦ www.webtenerifeuk.co.uk and Ⓦ www.gomera-island.com – are worth browsing for a glossy overview. The Spanish Tourist office site Ⓦ www.tourspain.es also provides a reasonable overview and some useful general links.

Of the many commercial websites, most are preoccupied with selling package holidays, but Ⓦ www.etenerife.com stands out as one of the more informative options. Another decent site is Ⓦ www.sun4free.com, a well-organized online guide to Tenerife, with reasonable detail on all aspects of the island.

Finally, for an entertaining forum with opinions of other holidaymakers go to Ⓦ www.holidays-uncovered.co.uk.

Transport

Getting around Tenerife is straightforward. An excellent island-wide **bus** service operates and is supplemented by plentiful and fairly cheap **taxis**. For added flexibility, and getting off the beaten track, renting a **car** or a **bicycle** is practical and inexpensive. Getting around La Gomera is more difficult: the bus network is skeletal, making renting a car almost essential. If you want someone else to do the driving, a good selection of bus **tours** are widely advertised in hotels and travel agents in the main resorts.

Buses

Local **buses** (locally called *guagua*) offer an inexpensive service all over

Tenerife. Fares are low – Los Cristianos to Reina Sofía Airport, for example, costs €2 – and can be made around a third cheaper by purchasing a Bono-Bus card, a pre-paid ticket available on Tenerife only which is fed into a machine on the bus and, once you've told the driver your destination, has the fare deducted. The cards (from €12) can be bought from newsagents and newsstands.

Timetables are generally attached to main bus stops, which are marked with either the destination of the bus (*destino*) or its origin (*desde*). Most routes stop in the early evening and some don't run on Saturdays. The principal island routes are shown on the book flap, but if you plan to use the network extensively, pick up the excellent map and timetable available from major bus stations, some kiosks and most tourist information centres. Alternatively, call the 24-hour information service – in both English and Spanish – ☎922 53 13 00, or check ⊛www.titsa.com.

La Gomera is served by three public **bus** services, which leave from the ferry terminal in San Sebastián with a stop at the town's bus station on Via de Ronda. Though infrequent, they do offer non-drivers a way to access some of the island's best hikes. Linea #1 heads up to Valle Gran Rey via Chipude (4 daily, 1hr 40min, €4); Linea #2 runs to Playa de Santiago (4 daily, 1hr 10min, €4), and Linea #3 goes to Vallehermoso via Hermigua (4 daily, 1hr 30min, €3.50).

Taxis

Taxis in the islands' major towns and resorts are generally easy to find. The minimum charge is €2, with surcharges added for luggage, travel between 10pm and 6am or on Sundays, and journeys to the airports or docks. Fares also vary according to traffic conditions – make sure the driver uses the meter – but expect to pay €20 from Los Cristianos or Playa de Las Américas to Reina Sofía Airport, and €70 from Puerto de la Cruz.

Taxis can be particularly useful to shuttle you to or from hikes and fares are reasonable if there are several of you to split the cost.

Taxi companies

Las Américas ☎922 71 54 07 or from the ranks on the main seafront road.
Candelaria ☎922 50 01 90.
Los Cristianos ☎922 79 54 14 or from beside the Plaza del Carmen.
Las Galletas ☎922 39 09 24.
Garachico ☎922 83 0056.
Güimar ☎922 51 08 11.
Icod de Los Vinos ☎922 81 08 95.
Puerto de la Cruz ☎922 38 58 18 or at the main rank beside Plaza del Charco.
San Sebastián ☎922 87 05 24 or at the harbour beside Plaza de las Américas.
Santa Cruz ☎922 64 11 22 or at the main rank in Plaza de España.

Cars

Car rental on Tenerife is inexpensive and practical for exploring areas that are poorly served by the bus network – including the national park. Rural roads are often steep, twisting and tiring to drive, but they are at least relatively quiet; in the towns, particularly Santa Cruz, driving can be a hectic experience and finding a parking space often tricky.

To rent a car you need to be over 21 (though some operators won't rent to anyone under 25) and have had your licence for over a year. EU licences (either pink or pink and green) are accepted as are most other foreign licences, though the latter officially need to be accompanied by an International Driving Permit. Most operators also require a €30 deposit or a credit-card number and sometimes an island address as well.

Rates start at around €20 per day for a small hatchback, and all operators offer substantial discounts for rentals of a week or more. You can also save money by using smaller local or regional operators – Auto Reisen (see below) being one particularly good option with extremely competitive prices (one week for €95), online booking discounts, good vehicles and great backup.

Rental usually includes tax, unlimited mileage and full insurance (including collision damage waiver), but these details should be double-checked with any operator – particularly smaller ones who sometimes build odd exclusions into contracts. Most operators will not allow you to island hop with their car and don't include petrol in prices – lead-free petrol (*sin plomo*) costs around €0.80 per litre.

Car rental companies

Auto Reisen Tenerife South Airport ☎922 39 22 16; Tenerife North Airport ☎922 63 59 78 ⊛www.autoreisen.es.
Autos El Carmen Valle Gran Rey ☎922 80 50 29.
Avis Tenerife South Airport ☎922 39 20 56, Tenerife North Airport ☎922 25 87 13, Los Cristianos ☎922 75 35 44, El Duque ☎922 71 44 14, Playa de las Américas ☎922 79 63 53, Puerto de la Cruz ☎922 38 46 98, Santa Cruz ☎922 24 12 94, La

Puntilla Valle Gran Rey ☎922 80 55 27; ⓦavis.es.
Cicar Tenerife North ☎922 63 26 42, Tenerife South ☎922 63 26 42, Santa Cruz ☎922 29 24 25; ⓦwww.cicar.com.
Hertz Tenerife South Airport ☎922 75 93 19, Tenerife North Airport ☎922 25 19 17, Playa de las Américas ☎922 79 23 20, Puerto de la Cruz ☎922 38 47 19, **Torviscas** ☎922 79 75 65, San Sebastián ☎922 87 04 61; ⓦwww.hertz.com.
OrCar Tenerife South Airport ☎922 39 22 16, ⒻFax922 39 22 55, Las Américas ☎922 71 42 80, 922 75 37 71 and 922 71 20 68. ⓦwww.orcarcanarias.com
La Rueda San Sebastián ☎922 87 07 09, La Playa, Valle Gran Rey ☎922 80 51 97; ⓦwww.autolarueda.com.

Tours

The many **bus tours** of Tenerife include circular excursions around the island as well as itineraries that typically go to the mountain village of Masca and the Parque Nacional del Teide or Santa Cruz. Prices are generally €20–30. If you're short on time, there are bus trips around La Gomera too (€50), offered from Tenerife's southern resorts. Note that bus trips that seem extraordinarily cheap are most likely to be outings to the restaurants and gift shops that subsidize them and are best avoided.

Sports and leisure

Tenerife and La Gomera offer a great range of sea- and land-based **activities**, most of which are possible year-round thanks to the archipelago's consistently fine weather. In addition to the natural attractions provided by the waves, winds and mountains, the last decade has seen a boom in the popularity of golf.

Surfing and bodyboarding

The heavy seas all around Tenerife attract thrill-seeking local **surfers** and **bodyboarders** in droves, but it's only along the accessible Playa de Troya in Las Américas that foreigners are tolerated; elsewhere you will certainly get a cold shoulder, and will likely encounter a more aggressive reaction to your presence. Near to the beach in CC Américas, the K-16 Surf shop (☎922 79 84 84, Ⓔk-16surfshop@terra.es) offers gear rental and instruction for all levels of surfers from €19 per day.

Windsurfing and kitesurfing

The coast around El Médano (see p.128) is internationally renowned as premium **windsurfing** and **kitesurfing** territory, with international competitions regularly held here. The conditions are often too difficult for beginners, though the Kitecenter Playa Sur (☎922 17 66 88, ⓦwww.kitecenter.info) offers instruction for €45 for two hours. You can rent equipment here or at a number of places around town, including the Fun Factory El Cabezo, in the *Hotel Atlantic Playa* (☎922 17 62 73, ⓦwww.fanatic.el-medano.com).

Snorkelling and scuba-diving

Some of the more sheltered shores of both islands are suitable for **snorkelling** and there's **scuba-diving** at a number of good sites. The underwater scenery and wildlife aren't world-class, but there are plenty of fish – including sharks – and even turtles, and competition between dive schools has made it relatively inexpensive (around €250) to do the basic PADI or CMAS dive courses. The best sites include the spectacular underwater cliffs just south of Los Cristianos, the so-called Stingray City near Las Galletas and a DC3 plane wreck near Puerto de la Cruz.

Scuba-diving centres

Costa Adeje Barakuda Club ☎922 74 18 81, ⓦwww.buceo-tenerife.com
Garachico Argonaut, C/Esteban Ponte 8 ☎922 83 02 45, ℮argonaut @arrakis.es.
Las Américas Gruber Diving Club, Park Club Europe ☎922 75 27 08, ⓦwww .dive-teneriffa.com; Diversity CC Puerto Colón, local 125, ☎922 71 71 29, ⓦwww.diver-sity.com
Las Galletas Atlantic Divers, Consuelo Alfonso, ☎922 73 55 09, ⓦwww .atlantic-divers.com; Buceo Tenerife, C/Maria del Carmen Garcia 22 ☎922 73 10 15, ⓦwww.buceotenerife.com.
Los Gigantes Los Gigantes Diving Center, Galería de la Marina ☎922 86 04 31, ⓦwww.divingtenerife.co.uk.
Puerto de la Cruz Atlantik Diving Centre, *Hotel Maritim* ☎922 36 28 01, ⓦwww .tenerife-buceo.com
Santa Cruz Seadive, Avda. de Colón, Edif. Botavara, Radazul, ☎922 68 17 05, ⓦwww.subcanaria.com
Valle Gran Rey Fisch & Co, opposite La Playa tourist office ☎922 80 56 88, ⓦwww.fischco.de.

Boat trips, deep-sea fishing and sailing

There's a massive array of **boat trips** on offer from Las Américas, Los Cristianos and Los Gigantes, costing from €12. Most head for the Gomeran channel in search of whales and dolphins, while others stop to allow passengers to swim or snorkel along the coast. Some trips are specifically **fishing trips** (from €48 per person for five hours), with deep-sea fishing – for tuna, swordfish, mako and dorado – especially popular. To join the locals fishing off the seashore

(which doesn't require a permit), there are plenty of bait and tackle shops – the north coast of the Teno range is one of the best places to test your skills.

Chartering a boat is another option and splitting the cost between a group makes the rates more reasonable. Pepino yacht charter, based in Puerto Colón, Las Américas (☎922 29 86 16, ⓦwww.pepinocharter.com), charges around €400 for three hours on a yacht carrying up to eleven people; eleven-person powerboats are also available for charter (3hr, €550).

Hiking

Puerto de la Cruz is traditionally Tenerife's resort of choice for **hikers**. It's well connected by buses and served by a good range of accommodation (and operators offering guided hiking trips), as well as being on the north side of the island where much of the best hiking is to be found. Santa Cruz can also make a good base, as can Los Cristianos if you want to mix hiking with the nightlife, beaches and sunshine of the southern resorts.

Maps and **hiking guides** are available at bookshops in the island's main towns and resorts, but to save time it's worth picking up information before you head out to Tenerife. Two UK publishers produce useful hiking companions: Sunflower Guides publish two books on Tenerife and one on La Gomera, and Discovery Walking Guides publish folded pamphlets with clear, annotated island maps, as well as books that reprint portions of their maps with the addition of further route-finding information.

Hiking companies

Las Américas Diga Sports, Park Club Europe ☎922 79 30 09, ⓦwww.diga-sports.de.
Puerto de la Cruz Call Gregorio ☎922 57 28 67; KWA Guided Walks ☎922 37 15 84, ⓦwww.kwa-guiding-tenerife.com.
Valle Gran Rey Timah, La Puntilla ☎922 80 70 37, ⓦwww.timah.net.

Climbing

Climbers visiting Tenerife will find over a hundred climbing routes on a rough **rock-climbing** medium – with lots of pinch grips, pockets and incut edges. Some of the best climbs are in Las Cañadas – in the Parque Nacional del Teide – particularly around Los Roques and La Catedral.

The climbing guide *Rock Climbs in Majorca, Ibiza and Tenerife* by Chris Craggs should be an essential part of your luggage – it's not available in Tenerife so pick it up before you set off from travel bookshops or online.

Cycling

Tenerife and La Gomera are mountainous islands and many of the narrow roads are very busy, making neither ideal for leisurely cycling. They are, however, well suited to more exciting and challenging day rides – particularly on dirt roads by **mountain bike**. With the exception of areas within the national park, all hiking trails on Tenerife are open to mountain bikes – though many, particularly in the Anaga, are too steep and uneven for even highly skilled mountain bikers. The roads of La Gomera may be quieter but usually involve extremely tough climbs over the 800-metre passes that separate most major towns. Mountain bikers will, however, be pleased to find that once they've climbed to the high ground of the national park at the centre of the island its trails are open to bikers.

Most carriers flying to Tenerife from the UK take bicycles (though there may be a charge of around £20 each way for this), providing they are packed in a box or bag – available from most bike shops. Bagged bikes are also allowed in the hold of buses on both islands, giving you the option of cutting out particularly busy parts of a route.

For a **private shuttle** service contact Diga Sports on Tenerife (see below) or Bike Station on La Gomera (see below), both of whom transport bikes to pretty much anywhere on either island, leaving

riders to make their own way back. They also offer tours and bike rental, as do Fun Factory El Cabezo in El Médano (see below) and Mountain Bike Active in Puerto de la Cruz (see below). Renting a quality front-suspension mountain bike will set you back around €15 per day, €80 per week.

If you are looking for a **guided cycling holiday**, then contact the friendly and efficient Cycling Tenerife (☎922 70 07 23; ⓦ www.cyclingtenerife.com), who offer week-long packages from €420, including accommodation and meals.

Bike rental

Las Américas Cycling Diga Sports, Park Club Europe ☎922 79 30 09, ⓦwww .diga-sports.de.

Los Cristianos Bicisport Edificio el Arenal ☎922 75 18 29.

El Médano Fun Factory El Cabezo ☎922 17 62 73, ⓦwww.fanatic.el-medano.com.

Puerto de la Cruz Mountain Bike Active, C/Mazaroco, Edif. Daniela 26 ☎922 37 60 81, ⓦwww.Mtb-active.com.

Valle Gran Rey Bike Station, La Puntilla ☎922 80 50 82. Alofi Rentals, La Playa ☎922 80 54 82, ⓦ www.bike-station -gomera.de.

Golf

The pleasant climate attracts **golf** enthusiasts year-round to Tenerife and La Gomera's **nine courses**, six of which are dotted around the resorts of southern Tenerife. The professional circuit usually includes at least one annual stop at Tenerife, most notably the Tenerife Ladies' Open held in May. For info on this and a detailed overview of the courses visit the Tourist Board website ⓦwww .tenerifegolf.es.

Green fees typically hover around €80 for eighteen holes, while discounts of up to a third are common between May and September. Most courses rent clubs (around €15) and buggies (around €35).

One company organizing golf holidays is Ultramar Express (☎922 71 74 18 ⓦ www.tui.com). They will take care of all the golfing logistics and arrange flights and accommodation for you.

Golf courses

La Laguna Real Club El Peñón, Guamasa, 2km north of Los Rodeos Airport ☎922 63 66 07, ⊛www.realgolfdetenerife.com, Mon–Fri 8am–12.30pm.

The Teno Buenavista Golf, Buenavista del Norte ☎922 12 90 34, ⊛www .buenavistagolf.es, daily 8am–8pm.

West Coast Abama, Playa San Juan ☎922 12 60 00 ⊛www.abamahotelresort .com, daily 7am–8pm.

Las Américas & Costa Adeje Golf Costa Adeje ☎922 71 00 00, ⊛www .golfcostaadeje.com, daily 7am–7pm. Golf Las Américas, autopista Sur Exit 28 ☎922 552 005, ⊛www.golf-tenerife.com, Mon–Fri 7am–7pm.

South Coast Amarilla Golf & Country Golf, San Miguel de Abona, Autopista del Sur Exit 24 ☎922 73 0319, ⊛www .amarillagolf.es, daily 8am–8.30pm; Golf del Sur, San Miguel de Abona, Autopista del Sur Exit 24 ☎922 73 81 70, ⊛www .golfdelsur.net, daily 8.45am–7.30pm; Palos, Carretera Guaza, Las Galletas, km. 7 Exit 26 from Autopista Sur ☎922 73 00 80, ⊛www.golflospalos.com, daily 8am–midnight.

Playa Santiago (La Gomera) Tecina Golf ☎922 14 59 50 ⊛www.tecinagolf.com, daily 8am–7.30pm.

Karting

The Karting Club de Tenerife (☎922 73 07 03, daily 10am–9pm) has a free shuttle bus from Las Américas to get you – and the kids – to its international standard track. A dozen laps cost €12; kids aged 8–12 pay €5 to use the mini version.

Spectator sports

Traditional Canarian sports such as wrestling and stick fighting are undergoing a renaissance on Tenerife, but it's **football** that attracts most local attention. Times are hard for Club Deportivo Tenerife (⊛www .clubdeportivotenerife.es) as they languish in the second division, so to offer support, head for the Estadio Heliodoro Rodríguez López (ticket office Mon–Fri 10am–1pm & 5–8pm; ☎922 29 16 99 or 922 24 06 13), where seats cost €36, standing €11 and are usually available on match days.

Any sizeable place is likely to have a ring for contests of **Canarian wrestling** (*Lucha Canaria*) and information on fixtures can be gained from the Federación de Lucha Canaria, Callejón del Capitán Brotons 7, Santa Cruz (☎ 922 25 14 52, ⊛www .federaciondeluchacanaria.com), where bouts are held on Friday and Saturday evenings. This relatively non-violent sport involves two barefoot men in a round, sandy ring attempting to manoeuvre each other to the ground by gripping the bottom of the opponent's shorts – kicks and punches are not allowed. There are three rounds and winning two secures a point for the victor's twelve-man team. Bouts continue until one team has the twelve points it needs to win – the whole contest can take around three hours.

A more minor tradition, and one primarily making appearances as a demonstration sport at fiestas, is **stick fighting** (*juego del palo*). This contest, a derivative of Guanche stick-and-stone duels, uses large, two-metre-long staffs to both attack and defend, with the aim of trying to knock an opponent off his perch on a relatively small flat rock.

Festivals and events

January 1
New Year's Day A Spanish public holiday, New Year's Day is traditionally greeted with fireworks and the eating of a grape at every chime of the clock at midnight.

January 6
Reyes Magos (Three Kings). A public holiday, celebrated with processions in major towns the day before. This, rather than December 25, is traditionally the day for present giving.

January 20
Fiesta de San Sebastián (La Gomera) Singing and dancing to celebrate the town's patron saint.

February/March
Carnival The biggest event of the year. Festivities begin in Santa Cruz (see box, opposite), before moving on to other large towns, most notably Puerto de la Cruz.

Late March/early April
Easter week (Semana Santa) Jueves Santo (Maundy Thursday) and Viernes Santo (Good Friday) are both public holidays in Spain and elaborate processions take place on both days in La Laguna, one a silent procession of religious brotherhoods.

April 25
Fiesta de San Marcos, Agulo (La Gomera) A statue of Agulo's patron saint, San Marcos, is surrounded by bonfires through which local young men run in a test of courage.

May
Romeriás Harvest festivals take place throughout the month in the Orotava Valley.

May 3
Día de Santa Cruz Festival celebrating the founding of Tenerife's capital with a procession and lots of traditional entertainment, including Canarian wrestling.

May 30
Canary Islands' Day Public holiday marked by folk dances in the plazas of Santa Cruz.

May/June
Corpus Christi On the Thursday that follows the eighth Sunday after Easter, Corpus Christi is celebrated all over Tenerife. Major events are held in La Laguna and, a week later, in La Orotava – where streets are covered in floral carpets. Note that the actual date for the unveiling of the carpets is exactly one week after Corpus Christi, arrive around noon to see the carpets made, around 7pm to see them trampled by processions.

June 13–29
Los Piques Celebrated in Agulo, La Gomera, this festival includes quarrels in the whistling language, El Silbo.

June 23 & 24
Fiesta de San Juan Herds of goats from the surrounding area are bathed in the harbour at Puerto de la Cruz as part of the midsummer celebrations.

First Sunday of July
Romería de San Benito Abad Celebrations in La Laguna including a major religious procession.

July 16
Fiesta Virgen del Carmen The largest celebrations for the patron saint of fishermen and sailors are in Santa Cruz and Puerto de la Cruz on Tenerife, and in Valle Gran Rey and Playa de Santiago on La Gomera. Celebrations usually include a procession of boats.

July 25
Santiago Day Public holiday in honour of St James the Apostle, patron saint of Spain. The Virgin of Candelaria (see p.74) is paraded in fine robes adorned with gold and surrounded by folk dances and offerings of flowers. Major festivities take place in Santa Cruz too, with citizens also celebrating the anniversary of the defeat of Nelson and his British fleet.

August
Romería de San Roque in Garachico Dates vary for this, one of the largest and most spectacular harvest and folk festivals on Tenerife.

August 15
Fiesta Virgen de la Candelaria The patron saint of the archipelago shares her day with Beñasmen, a Guanche harvest festival – which explains the flowers,

Carnival in Santa Cruz

Santa Cruz's Carnival is one of Europe's most vibrant and colourful festivals, often attracting up to 280,000 people.

Though originally following the religious calendar, the event has now extended deep into Lent itself and each night the Plaza de España and surrounding streets fill with revellers dancing until dawn. Costumes are almost compulsory and many dress in the annual theme.

The highlight of the week is the Grand Procession on Shrove Tuesday – a cavalcade of floats, bands, dancers and entertainers, who march and dance their way along the dockside road. Also popular is the Burial of the Sardine on Ash Wednesday, when the effigy of a sardine is burnt before wailing widows. This burial is really that of the carnival and signifies the approaching end of all the fun – though only after one final blow-out night of partying – and the beginning of Lent with its fasting and praying. The sardine itself is a reminder that many people will now often eat fish; strict Catholics still eschew the eating of meat on certain days during Lent. Traditionally, the sardine's cremation signified the last day of the carnival but the finale actually comes the following weekend – at which point smaller towns around the island often start their own celebrations.

For the latest on the current year's preparations and plans check ⓦwww .carnavaltenerife.com.

greenery, sheep and goats that are paraded behind the statue of the virgin.

September 6
Fiesta de Cristobal Colón Anniversary of the departure of Columbus (Colón) from San Sebastián, La Gomera, on his first voyage to the Americas.

September 7
Fiesta de la Virgen del Socorro Güimar puts on a large procession from the church to the sea in honour of the town's patron saint.

September 7–15
Fiesta del Santísimo Cristo Lengthy religious festival in La Laguna that includes a procession behind a fifteenth-century

Gothic carving of Christ on the Cross, given to the island's conqueror, Alonso de Lugo.

November 1
All Saints Day Public holiday with fiestas in towns around Tenerife.

November 29
Fiesta del Vino Wine festival in Icod and Puerto de la Cruz to celebrate the grape harvest. The highlight is kamikaze sledding (sleds were once used to transport the harvest), with Icod's course the steepest and most dangerous.

December 25
Navidad Christmas Day is a public holiday.

Directory

Accommodation Though accommodation on Tenerife is plentiful, much of it consists of hotel and apartment complexes given over to package tours. Of these, we have listed those that accept independent bookings, though in many cases walk-in rates are substantially higher than pre-booked package prices. There's also a small stock of family-run pensions and

smaller hotels in the main towns and resorts, and a couple of campsites. La Gomera is geared more to independent travel and small, inexpensive apartment blocks have emerged to meet demand. Throughout the Places chapters, prices listed are for the cheapest double room in high season, but excluding Christmas and New Year when rates rocket. In the case of apartments that sleep more than two, the price for the smallest available unit per night is given. Travellers wanting to stay a week or more are likely to find the nightly rate can be reduced a little. Both islands also have a good stock of *casas rurales*: attractive old renovated houses in the countryside that are rented out as self-catering holiday accommodation. Typically, a week in one of these will cost from £200 for a one- to two-bedroom place. The Internet is ideal for finding this kind of accommodation – try Acantur ⊛www .ecoturismocanarias.com/Canarias/uk/islas .htm; Aecan ⊛www.aecan.com; and Top Rural ⊛www.en.toprural.com.

Addresses Common abbreviations are: C/ for Calle (street); Ctra for Carretera (main road); Avda for Avenida (avenue); Edif for Edificio (a large block), and CC for Centro Commercial (a shopping centre or mall, often in an Edificio). An address given as C/Flores 24, 3° means third floor, 24 Flores Street. Derecha and izquierda mean right- and left-hand apartment or office.

Airlines British Airways ☎914 36 59 00, ⊛www.ba.com; Globespan ⊛www. flyglobespan.com ☎922 759 200; Iberia ☎922 75 92 85, ⊛www.iberia. com; Monarch ☎922 75 93 98, ⊛www. flymonarch.com; Thomsonfly ☎914 14 14 81, ⊛www.thomsonfly.com.

Banks and exchange The currency in the Canary Islands is the euro (€). Bank branches, many with ATMs, are plentiful in all the main towns and resorts. Opening hours are Mon–Fri 9am–2pm, Sat 9am–1pm – except between late May and September when banks close on Saturday, and during the Carnival period (February or March) when they close at midday. Outside these times, it's usually possible to change cash at larger hotels, exchange booths and, in resort areas, with real-estate or travel agents. Hotel rates are usually poor, but exchange booths and agents sometimes give better rates than the banks.

Complaints All hotels, restaurants and other businesses have a complaints book (*hoja de reclamación*) in which complaints can be logged. Noted in this form, complaints are treated extremely seriously by authorities and therefore should be used as a last resort.

Consulates Britain, Plaza de Weyler, Santa Cruz de Tenerife ☎922 28 68 63; Ireland, C/Castillo 8, 4ºA, Santa Cruz de Tenerife ☎922 24 56 71. The nearest US consulate is on the neighbouring island of Gran Canaria at Los Martínez de Escober 3, Oficina 7, Las Palmas de Gran Canaria ☎928 27 12 59. The nearest representation for most other English-speaking countries is in Madrid.

Customs The current limits on what can be brought back to the UK from the Canary Islands are 2 litres of non-sparkling wine, 1 litre of spirits, 60ml of perfume, 50ml cologne, 200 cigarettes and up to £145 of other goods and gifts.

Emergency services For police, ambulance and fire brigade call ☎112.

Hospitals Hospital de Nuestra Señora de la Candelaria, off the TF-5 motorway between Santa Cruz and La Laguna ☎922 60 20 00; Clinica Tamaragua, Agustin de Béthencourt 30, Puerto de la Cruz ☎922 38 05 12; Hospital Las Américas, Southern Las Américas ☎922 78 07 59; Hospital El Calvario, San Sebastián ☎922 87 04 50.

Internet Every major town and resort on both Tenerife and La Gomera has at least one café with Internet connections where half an hour on line usually costs around €1.50. The best also have an Ethernet cable or wifi hotspot for you to hook up a laptop.

Mail The postal system in the Canary Islands is quite slow and it usually takes at least ten days for a postcard or letter to reach the UK or mainland Europe (outside Spain). As well as the post offices, most shops selling postcards sell stamps (*sellos*). Post offices can be found in all the main

A bed from the Web

If you are not travelling in a package – just taking a flight – and you want to stay in an apartment complex you should trawl the web for online deals. This will ensure much better rates than you will get by just turning up, and saves the hassle of beating the pavement between the frequently full complexes that are some distance from each other.

Sites worth trying include: ⊛www.go2spain.co.uk; ⊛www.bookings.es; ⊛www .hotelopia.co.uk and ⊛www.ruscotravel; ⊛www.ecanarias.com and ⊛www .abcanarias.com.

towns and villages and are open Mon–Fri
8.30am–2.30pm & Sat 9.30am–1pm.
Pharmacies Farmacias are indicated by
a large green cross and open Mon–Fri
9am–1pm & 4–8pm, Sat 9am–1pm.
Additionally, pharmacies in each area
have a rota to provide 24-hour emergency
cover, details of which are posted on any
pharmacy door.
Telephones Most hotels add surcharges
to calls made from rooms, so it's cheaper
to use a coin- or card-operated payphone.
Various companies offer phone cards –
available from newsagents, petrol stations
and convenience stores – and while some

work out cheaper than feeding in euros,
it's worth checking the small print to see
if there's a connection fee. Mobile phones
work in the Canary Islands but check with
your service provider about coverage and
call costs.
Time Both islands are in the same time
zone as the UK and Ireland, making them
five hours ahead of the US East Coast
and eleven hours behind East Coast
Australia.
Tipping In bars and taxis, rounding up to
the next euro is fine, while with waiters and
hairdressers a 5–10 percent tip is perfectly
adequate.

Chronology

Chronology

20 million years ago ▶ The island of La Gomera is formed, the result of magma oozing through cracks on the ocean floor, before being pushed above sea level by seismic forces.

6 million years ago ▶ The island of Tenerife begins to be recognizable in its present shape, a process cemented by another intense period of volcanic activity three million years ago.

900–400BC ▶ Several waves of human migration see displaced Berber tribes from present-day Morocco settle on the islands to form an aboriginal Guanche society.

c300BC ▶ The earliest known references to the Canary Islands are thought to have been made by Plato (428–348 BC) in his references to Atlantis, a continent sunk beneath the ocean floor in a cataclysmic event which left only the highest mountains above the sea.

40BC ▶ The first written account of a landing in the Canary Islands is made by a fleet serving King Juba II, the Roman client king of Mauritania.

c140 ▶ The Canary Islands appear on maps when Ptolemy (cAD 100–160) draws his world map on which the archipelago forms the edge of the known world.

1312 ▶ The first reliable account of European contact comes when Genoese captain Lanzarotto Malocello is blown off course, landing on – and ultimately lending his name to – the island of Lanzarote.

1404 ▶ French adventurer Baron Jean de Béthencort steps ashore in Lanzarote to a friendly welcome, beginning the process of the conquest of the Canary Islands – he secures La Gomera later that year.

1488 ▶ An island-wide rebellion begins in La Gomera, costing the governor's life; many Guanches are brutally executed or sold into slavery.

1492 ▶ Christopher Columbus stops over in La Gomera supplying his ships with fresh water that he would take all the way to the New World.

1493–1495 ▶ Tenerife is conquered by Spanish conquistador Alonso Fernández de Lugo.

1550–1670 ▶ The production of wine takes the place of sugar cane to become Tenerife's predominant industry.

1797 ▶ Admiral Nelson attempts to take Santa Cruz but suffers his only military defeat and loses his right arm.

1817 ▶ La Laguna university is founded.

1822 ▶ Santa Cruz takes over from La Laguna as the island's capital.

1830–1870 ▶ Tenerife's economy is dominated by the harvesting of a tiny bug, cochineal, whose body fluids are used to make red dye.

1852 ▶ Santa Cruz becomes a free port with associated custom and tax advantages.

1880 ▶ Banana cultivation is introduced to Tenerife and La Gomera.

1880s ▶ Tenerife enjoys increasing popularity as a tourist destination among European Gentry.

1909 ▶ The most recent volcanic eruption occurs on Tenerife.

1927 ▶ Tenerife becomes the seat of government for itself, La Gomera, El Hierro and La Palma; Gran Canaria governs the rest of the Canary Islands.

1936 ▶ Franco launches his coup from Tenerife, sparking the Spanish Civil War.

1959 ▶ The first nonstop charter flights to Tenerife herald a new era of tourism and developments spread around the island like wildfire.

1982 ▶ The Canaries become an autonomous region within Spain.

1986 ▶ The Canary Islands join the EU, though they remain outside the customs union and retain many other economic privileges.

Language

Spanish

Once you get into it, **Spanish** is one of the easiest languages around, and in Tenerife and La Gomera you'll be helped everywhere by people who are eager to try and understand even the most faltering attempt. English is spoken in the main tourist areas, but you'll get a far better reception if you try communicating with Canarian Islanders in their own tongue.

For non-native speakers the easiest difference to notice in the **pronunciation** of Canarian Spanish is the absence of a "lisp" on the the letter "c" before vowels – which is replaced by an "s" sound. Thus Barcelona, pronounced Barthelona in Spain, becomes Barselona. However, in its most casual form, the Canarian pronunciation doesn't even really bother with "s" sounds at all, particularly where these come at the end of a word – so gracias becomes gracia; and buenos días, bueno día.

For more than a brief introduction to the language, pick up a copy of the Rough Guide **Spanish Dictionary Phrasebook**.

Pronunciation

The rules of **pronunciation** are pretty straightforward and are strictly observed.

A somewhere between the A sound of back and that of father.

E as in get.

I as in police.

O as in hot.

U as in rule.

C is spoken like an S before E and I, hard otherwise: cerca is pronounced "sairka" (standard Spanish would pronounce it "thairka").

G is a guttural H sound (like the ch in loch) before E or I, a hard G elsewhere – *gigante* becomes "higante".

H is always silent.

J is the same as a guttural G: *jamón* is "hamon".

LL sounds like an English Y: *tortilla* is pronounced "torteeya".

N is as in English unless it has a tilde (accent) over it, when it becomes NY: *mañana* sounds like "manyana".

QU is pronounced like an English K.

R is rolled, RR doubly so.

V sounds more like B, *vino* becoming "beano".

X has an S sound before consonants, normal X before vowels.

Z is the same as a soft C, so *cerveza* becomes "thairbaitha".

Words and phrases

Basics

Yes, No, OK	Sí, No, Vale
Please, Thank you	Por favor, Gracias
Where?, When?	¿Dónde?, ¿Cuándo?
What?, How much?	¿Qué?, ¿Cuánto?
Here, There	Aquí, Allí
This, That	Esto, Eso
Now, Later	Ahora, Más tarde
Open, Closed	Abierto/a, Cerrado/a
With, Without	Con, Sin
Good, Bad	Buen(o)/a, Mal(o)/a
Big, Small	Gran(de), Pequeño/a
Cheap, Expensive	Barato, Caro
Hot, Cold	Caliente, Frío
More, Less	Más, Menos
Today, Tomorrow	Hoy, Mañana
Yesterday	Ayer
The bill	La cuenta

Greetings and responses

Hello, Goodbye	Hola, Adiós
Good morning	Buenos días
Good afternoon/ night	Buenas tardes/ noches
See you later	Hasta luego
Sorry	Lo siento/Disculpe
Excuse me	Con permiso/ Perdón
How are you?	¿Cómo está (usted)?
I (don't) understand	(No) Entiendo
You're welcome/ not at all	De nada
Do you speak English?	¿Habla (usted) inglés?
I (don't) speak Spanish	(No) Hablo español
My name is. . .	Me llamo. . .
What's your name?	¿Como se llama usted?
I am English / Scottish / Welsh / Australian / Canadian American Irish New Zealander	Soy inglés(a) / escocés(a) / galés(a) / australiano(a) / canadiense(a) / americano(a) / irlandés(a) / Nueva Zelandés (a)

Hotels, transport and directions

I want	Quiero
I'd like	Quisiera
Do you know. . .?	¿Sabe . . .?
I don't know	No sé
There is (is there?)	(¿)Hay(?)
Give me (one like that)	Deme (uno así)
Do you have...?	¿Tiene...?
... the time	... la hora
... a room	... una habitación
... with two beds/ with a double bed	... con dos camas/ con cama matrimonial
... with shower/ bath	... con ducha/baño
It's for one person	Es para una persona
For one night	para una noche
For one week	para una semana
How do I get to...?	¿Por donde se va a...?
Left, right, straight on	Izquierda, derecha, todo recto
Where is...?	¿Dónde está...?
... the bus station	... la estación de guaguas
... the nearest bank	... el banco mas cercano
... the post office	... el correos/la oficina de correos
... the toilet	... el baño
Where does the bus to . . . leave from?	¿De dónde sale la guagua para...?
I'd like a (return) ticket to . . .	Quisiera un billete (de ida y vuelta) para...
What time does it leave?	¿A qué hora sale?

Numbers and days

1	un/uno/una
2	dos
3	tres
4	cuatro
5	cinco
6	seis
7	siete
8	ocho
9	nueve
10	diez

11	once
12	doce
13	trece
14	catorce
15	quince
16	diez y seis
17	diez y siete
18	diez y ocho
19	diez y nueve
20	veinte
21	veintiuno
30	treinta
40	cuarenta
50	cincuenta
60	sesenta
70	setenta
80	ochenta
90	noventa
100	cien(to)
101	ciento uno
200	doscientos
500	quinientos
1000	mil

Monday	lunes
Tuesday	martes
Wednesday	miércoles
Thursday	jueves
Friday	viernes
Saturday	sábado
Sunday	domingo
today	hoy
yesterday	ayer
tomorrow	mañana

Food and drink

aceitunas	olives
agua	water
ahumados	smoked fish
al ajillo	with olive oil and garlic
a la marinera	seafood cooked with garlic, onions and white wine
a la parilla	charcoal-grilled
a la plancha	grilled on a hot plate
a la romana	fried in batter
albóndigas	meatballs
almejas	clams
anchoas	anchovies
arroz	rice
asado	roast
bacalao	cod
berenjena	aubergine/eggplant

bocadillo	bread roll sandwich
boquerones	small, anchovy-like fish, usually served in vinegar
café (con leche)	(white) coffee
calamares	squid
cangrejo	crab
cebolla	onion
cerveza	beer
champiñones	mushrooms
chorizo	spicy sausage
croquetas	croquettes, usually with bits of ham inside
cuchara	spoon
cuchillo	knife
empanada	slices of fish/meat pie
ensalada	salad
ensaladilla	russian salad (diced vegetables in mayonnaise, often with tuna)
fresa	strawberry
gambas	prawns
gofio	finely ground mix of wheat, barley or maize, usually accompanying soups and stews
hígado	liver
huevos	eggs
jamón serrano	cured ham
jamón de york	regular ham
langostinos	langoustines
lechuga	lettuce
manzana	apple
mejillones	mussels
mojo	garlic dressing available in "rojo" (spicy "red" version) and "verde" ("green", made with coriander)
naranja	orange
ostras	oysters
pan	bread
papas arrugadas	unpeeled new potatoes, boiled dry in salted water
papas alioli	potatoes in garlic mayonnaise
papas bravas	fried potatoes in a spicy tomato sauce

pimientos	peppers	salchicha	sausage
pimientos de padrón	small peppers, with the odd hot one	setas	oyster mushrooms
piña	pineapple	sopa	soup
pisto	assortment of cooked vegetables, similar to ratatouille	té	tea
		tenedor	fork
		tomate	tomato
		tortilla española	potato omelette
		tortilla francesa	plain omelette
		vino (blanco/ rosado/tinto)	(white/rosé/red) wine
plátano	banana	zarzuela	Canarian fish stew
pollo	chicken	zumo	juice
pulpo	octopus		
queso	cheese		

Glossary

avenida	avenue	iglesia	church
barranco	gorge	menú del día	daily menu in a restaurant
barrio	suburb or neighbourhood	mercado	market
calle	(usually abbreviated to C/) street or road	mirador	viewpoint
		Mudéjar	Spanish-Moorish architecture
CC (centro commercial)	shopping and entertainment mall	parador	state-run hotel, usually housed in buildings of historic interest
edificio	building		
ermita	hermitage	playa	beach
hacienda	large manor house	plaza	square
guagua	local name for buses	terraza	temporary summer outdoor bar/club
Guanche	aboriginal inhabitants of the Canary Islands		

Visit us online
www.roughguides.com

Information on over 25,000 destinations around the world

- **Read** Rough Guides' trusted travel info

- **Access** exclusive articles from Rough Guides authors

- **Update** yourself on new books, maps, CDs and other products

- **Enter** our competitions and win travel prizes

- **Share** ideas, journals, photos & travel advice with other users

- **Earn** points every time you contribute to the Rough Guide
  community and get rewards

BROADEN YOUR HORIZONS

SMALL PRINT

A Rough Guide to Rough Guides

In 1981, Mark Ellingham, a recent graduate in English from Bristol University, was travelling in Greece on a tiny budget and couldn't find the right guidebook. With a group of friends he wrote his own guide, combining a contemporary, journalistic style with a practical approach to travellers' needs. That first Rough Guide was a student scheme that became a publishing phenomenon. Today, Rough Guides include recommendations from shoestring to luxury and cover hundreds of destinations around the globe, including almost every country in the Americas and Europe, more than half of Africa and most of Asia and Australasia. Millions of readers relish Rough Guides' wit and inquisitiveness as much as their enthusiastic, critical approach and value-for-money ethos. The guides' ever-growing team of authors and photographers is spread all over the world.

In the early 1990s, Rough Guides branched out of travel, with the publication of Rough Guides to World Music, Classical Music and the Internet. All three have become benchmark titles in their fields, spearheading the publication of a range of more than 350 titles under the Rough Guide name, including phrasebooks, waterproof maps, music guides from Opera to Heavy Metal, reference works as diverse as Conspiracy Theories and Shakespeare, and popular culture books from iPods to Poker. Rough Guides also produce a series of more than 120 World Music CDs in partnership with World Music Network.

Visit www.roughguides.com to see our latest publications.

Rough Guide travel images are available for commercial licensing at www.roughguidespictures.com

Publishing information

This second edition published April 2007 by
Rough Guides Ltd, 80 Strand, London WC2R 0RL;
345 Hudson St, 4th Floor, New York, NY 10014,
USA.

Distributed by the Penguin Group
Penguin Books Ltd, 80 Strand, London WC2R 0RL
Penguin Group (USA), 375 Hudson St, NY 10014,
USA
14 Local Shopping Centre, Panchsheel Park, New
Delhi 110017, India
Penguin Group (Australia), 250 Camberwell Rd,
Camberwell, Victoria 3124, Australia
Penguin Group (Canada), 10 Alcorn Ave, Toronto,
ON M4V 1E4, Canada
Penguin Group (NZ), 67 Apollo Drive, Mairangi Bay,
Auckland 1310, New Zealand

Typeset in Bembo and Helvetica to an original
design by Henry Iles.

Cover concept by Peter Dyer

Printed and bound in China

© Christian Williams, April 2007

208pp includes index

A catalogue record for this book is available from
the British Library

ISBN 10: 1-84353-768-0

ISBN 13: 978-1-84353-768-7

The publishers and authors have done their best
to ensure the accuracy and currency of all the
information in Tenerife DIRECTIONS, however, they
can accept no responsibility for any loss, injury, or
inconvenience sustained by any traveller as a result
of information or advice contained in the guide.

1   3   5   7   9   8   6   4   2

Help us update

We've gone to a lot of effort to ensure that the second edition of Tenerife DIRECTIONS is accurate and up to date. However, things change – places get "discovered", opening hours are notoriously fickle, restaurants and rooms raise prices or lower standards. If you feel we've got it wrong or left something out, we'd like to know, and if you can remember the address, the price, the phone number, so much the better.

We'll credit all contributions, and send a copy of the next edition (or any other DIRECTIONS guide or Rough Guide if you prefer) for the best letters. Everyone who writes to us and isn't already a subscriber will receive a copy of our full-colour thrice-yearly newsletter. Please mark letters: "Tenerife DIRECTIONS Update" and send to: Rough Guides, 80 Strand, London WC2R 0RL, or Rough Guides, 4th Floor, 345 Hudson St, New York, NY 10014. Or send an email to mail@roughguides.com

Have your questions answered and tell others about your trip at www.roughguides.atinfopop.com

Rough Guide credits

Text editor: Sarah Eno
Layout: Umesh Aggarwal
Photography: Demetrio Carrasco and
Christian Williams
Cartography: Rajesh Chhibber

Picture editor: Nicole Newman
Proofreader: Karen Parker
Production: Aimee Hampson
Cover design: Chlöe Roberts

The author

Despite falling into the Atlantic off the coast of
Tenerife as a toddler, Christian Williams returned
to the island in 1998, undeterred, to research and
write his first travel guide. He's been working with

Rough Guides ever since and has co-authored
their guides to Skiing and Snowboarding in North
America, the US Rocky Mountains and Canada.

Readers' letters

Thanks to all those readers of the first edition who took the trouble to write in with their amendments and
additions. Apologies for any misspellings or omissions.

Peter Moore, Des & Diane Youngs, Roger G. Thomas and Martin Steibelt.

Photo credits

p.40 Basilica de Nuestra Senora in fore of bay, Candelaria © Richard Passmore / Getty

p.40 Village of Realejos Alto during San Isidro holiday Romeria © Hemis / Alamy

p.44 Basilica de Nuestra Senora, Candelaria © José F. Poblete/CORBIS

p.44 Guanche Statue, Candelaria © Christian Williams

p.46 Wild Orchid, Northern La Gomera © Christian Williams

p.48 Parador Hotel & Guajara, Teide National Park © Christian Williams

p.48 Los Geranios, Puerto de la Cruz © Christian Williams

p.48 Pension Alcalá, Alcalá, West Coast © Christian Williams

p.49 Playa de Vallehermoso, Northern La Gomera © Christian Williams

Places

p.150 Flowering Cacti, La Gomera © Christian Williams

Index

Maps are marked in colour

INDEX

We're covered. Are you?

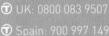

Luke writes with such subtlety. He takes us from the marble throne room of Caesar to the teeming masses of humanity to an unknown man and his wife to an unborn child hidden in the darkness of his mother's womb.

Who would have imagined such ordinary wrapping for God's precious gift? We would have searched everywhere for the Christ child—the ornate chambers of Caesar's royal palace, the sumptuous homes of the heads of state, even the sheltered residences of religious leaders—and brushed right by humble Mary. Just another young mother, another teen in trouble.

Who would have imagined the provincial setting into which the King of Kings was born?

A Miraculous Birth

Luke provides us the modest details:

> And it came about that while they were there, the days were completed for her to give birth. And she gave birth to her first-born son; and she wrapped Him in cloths, and laid Him in a manger, because there was no room for them in the inn. (vv. 6–7)

For centuries, these two simple verses have filled the imaginations of devout artists and writers, who have conjured up the most elaborate scenes. Author Ken Gire paints the scene the way it was meant to be seen—in human terms, without halos and glowing faces.

> By the time they arrive, the small hamlet of Bethlehem is swollen from an influx of travelers. The inn is packed, people feeling lucky if they were able to negotiate even a small space on the floor. Now it is late, everyone is asleep, and there is no room.
>
> But fortunately, the innkeeper is not all shekels and mites. True, his stable is crowded with his guests' animals, but if they could squeeze out a little privacy there, they were welcome to it.
>
> Joseph looks over at Mary, whose attention is concentrated on fighting a contraction. "We'll take it," he tells the innkeeper without hesitation.
>
> The night is still when Joseph creaks open the stable door. As he does, a chorus of barn animals

makes discordant note of the intrusion. The stench is pungent and humid, as there have not been enough hours in the day to tend the guests, let alone the livestock. A small oil lamp, lent them by the innkeeper, flickers to dance shadows on the walls. A disquieting place for a woman in the throes of childbirth. Far from home. Far from family. Far from what she had expected for her firstborn.

But Mary makes no complaint. It is relief just to finally get off the donkey. She leans back against the wall, her feet swollen, back aching, contractions growing stronger and closer together.

Joseph's eyes dart around the stable. Not a minute to lose. Quickly. A feeding trough would have to make do for a crib. Hay would serve as a mattress. Blankets? Blankets? Ah, his robe. That would do. And those rags hung out to dry would help. A gripping contraction doubles Mary over and sends him racing for a bucket of water. . . .

A scream from Mary knifes through the calm of that silent night. Joseph returns, breathless, water sloshing from the wooden bucket. . . . Sweat pours from Mary's contorted face as Joseph, the most un-likely midwife in all Judea, rushes to her side.

The involuntary contractions are not enough, and Mary has to push with all her strength. . . .

Joseph places a garment beneath her, and with a final push and a long sigh her labor is over.

The Messiah has arrived.[3]

A Series of Responses

For a few cherished moments, Joseph and Mary have the tiny Savior all to themselves as the three of them snuggle together against the cold night.

Across the sea, Caesar sleeps warm and secure between silk sheets in a kingly bed. What are his dreams that night? Of his latest conquest? His worshipful public? Little does he know that a greater

3. Ken Gire, *Intimate Moments with the Savior* (Grand Rapids, Mich.: Zondervan Publishing House, 1989), pp. 3–4.

King has just been born, One who will establish an eternal reign of celestial magnitude.

In all the universe, only a few know about the birth, and Luke gives us a peek into their responses.

From the Angels

First are the angels.

> And in the same region there were some shepherds staying out in the fields, and keeping watch over their flock by night. And an angel of the Lord suddenly stood before them, and the glory of the Lord shone around them; and they were terribly frightened. And the angel said to them, "Do not be afraid; for behold, I bring you good news of a great joy which shall be for all the people; for today in the city of David there has been born for you a Savior, who is Christ the Lord. And this will be a sign for you: you will find a baby wrapped in cloths, and lying in a manger." (vv. 8–12)

In the holy temple, Zacharias saw the angel first; then Mary beheld him in her room; and Joseph, in his dream. Now the angel— perhaps Gabriel again—appears to the shepherds in an open field ablaze with an unearthly light. This ragtag group of field-workers becomes an unlikely party of delegates to whom God's angel breaks the greatest news ever given to mankind: *"There has been born for you a Savior, who is Christ the Lord."*

Author Walter Wangerin tells what happens next:

> Suddenly the sky itself split open, and like the fall of a thousand stars, the light poured down. There came with the angel a multitude of the heavenly host, praising God and saying:
> *Glory to God in the highest,*
> *And on earth, peace—*
> *Peace to the people with whom he is pleased!*[4]

Into the calloused hands of these laborers, the news of the ages tumbles like jewels from heaven. Where is the royal Child who

---

4. Walter Wangerin, Jr., *Measuring the Days: Daily Reflections with Walter Wangerin, Jr.*, ed. Gail McGrew Eifrig (San Francisco, Calif.: HarperSanFrancisco; Grand Rapids, Mich.: Zondervan Publishing House, 1993), p. 348.

sends these angelic messengers? Lying in a manger? An animal's feeding trough! How they must have rejoiced—He must truly be the King for the people of the earth.

From the Shepherds

With hearts full of hope, they say to each other,

> "Let us go straight to Bethlehem then, and see this thing that has happened which the Lord has made known to us." And they came in haste and found their way to Mary and Joseph, and the baby as He lay in the manger. And when they had seen this, they made known the statement which had been told them about this Child. And all who heard it wondered at the things which were told them by the shepherds. (vv. 15b–18)

And so the first evangelists to spread the word about God's precious Lamb are, fittingly, shepherds.

From the Mother

In the midst of angels' anthems and shepherds' wonderment, one important person does not escape Luke's notice:

> But Mary treasured up all these things, pondering them in her heart. (v. 19)

Quietly, privately, Mary treasures the moment. She has protected and nourished this little life inside her for nine months. Finally, she gets to meet her intimate stranger face-to-face. She cups His doll fingers in her hand; she lingers over His delicate lips, His pudgy chin, His tuft of newborn hair. Then the Child's eyelids slowly part and she gazes into two pools as soft and deep as the starlit night. The angel's message, Elizabeth's prayer, the shepherd's report all race through her mind—she is cradling deity, the Lord of the universe, her own Creator.

At that moment, Jesus starts to cry. God is hungry. Instinctively, Mary pulls Him close to nurse. A look of wonder supplants her smile, as she suckles the Child and ponders all these amazing things in her heart.

From . . . You!

In the days ahead, others will gaze at Jesus with a similar

expression of awe: Simeon, Anna, the Magi from the East. In the years ahead, Jesus' life will stir a mixed pot of reactions. John will cry out, "Behold, the Lamb of God!" (John 1:36). Peter will proclaim, "Thou art the Christ, the Son of the living God" (Matt. 16:16). The Pharisees will say He's a blasphemer. Pilate will not know what to do with Him (John 18:24–40). Upon seeing Him die, a soldier will respond, "Truly this man was the Son of God!" (Mark 15:39).

As you gaze at the Child through the window of Scripture, who do you say He is?

That's a question every person must answer. And, really, we have only three options. First, we could decide that He wasn't who He claimed to be. He deliberately deceived His followers and taught things He Himself didn't believe. In other words, *He was a liar.* Second, although He wasn't who He claimed to be, He thought He was God. He lived in a fantasy world, and, tragically, His followers were swept up in His delusion. *He was a lunatic.* And third, we could believe that He was who He claimed to be. He said He was the Son of God; and He proved it by His miracles, death, and resurrection. *He is Lord.*[5]

If you subscribe to either of the first two choices, Jesus wasn't a gift at all; He was a curse. But if the third option is true, Jesus is a gift—an indescribably wonderful gift sent directly from God to you.

 Living Insights   STUDY ONE

> *To us, the greatest demonstration of God's love for us has been his sending his only Son into the world to give us life through him.* (1 John 4:9 PHILLIPS)

Have you ever wondered why God hasn't given up on the human race? After a few thousand years of getting snubbed, mocked, and ignored, even God has His breaking point, doesn't He? How much easier it would have been to start over with a new universe rather than patching up the old one.

He probably would have started over, if it hadn't been for one thing. Love.

---

5. These three options were developed by Josh McDowell in *Evidence That Demands a Verdict,* rev. ed. (San Bernardino, Calif.: Here's Life Publishers, 1979), vol. 1, pp. 103–7.

Do you want to touch God's love? Put yourself in the stable. Ask Mary to let you hold her Baby. Look into His eyes. Coo at Him until He gives you a smile. Feel His tiny hand reach for your cheek. . . .

How far from home this Child has journeyed! Max Lucado tells us,

> This baby had overlooked the universe. These rags keeping him warm were the robes of eternity. His golden throne room had been abandoned in favor of a dirty sheep pen. And worshiping angels had been replaced with kind but bewildered shepherds.[6]

Jesus gave up eternity to come to earth. How it must have wrenched the Father's heart to send Him to such a hostile place. That's why the gift is so unspeakably precious—because the cost was so great.

Sometimes, when you're alone and feeling dirty inside, do you ever wonder why God doesn't give up on you? If doubts of your self-worth ever haunt you, cradle the baby Jesus in your arms for a while. He is God's greatest demonstration of love for you.

Won't you receive His gift?

 Living Insights STUDY TWO

After contemplating the Nativity, our hearts yearn to respond to God. Yet how difficult it sometimes is to verbalize the full spectrum of our emotions. If you are at a loss for words, let Ken Gire's prayer voice your feelings toward the One you truly desire to make Lord of your life.

Dear Jesus,

> Though there was no room for you in the inn, grant this day that I might make abundant room for you in my heart. Though your own did not receive you, grant this hour that I may embrace you with open arms. Though Bethlehem overlooked you in the shuffle of the census, grant me the grace, this quiet moment, to be still and know that you are

6. Max Lucado, *God Came Near: Chronicles of the Christ* (Portland, Oreg.: Multnomah Press, 1987), p. 23.

God. You, whose only palace was a stable, whose only throne was a feeding trough, whose only robes were swaddling clothes.

On my knees I confess that I am too conditioned to this world's pomp and pageantry to recognize God cooing in a manger.

Forgive me. Please. And help me understand at least some of what your birth has to teach—that divine power is not mediated through strength, but through weakness; that true greatness is not achieved through the assertion of rights, but through their release; and that even the most secular of things can be sacred when you are in their midst.

And for those times when you yearn for my fellowship and stand at the door and knock, grant me a special sensitivity to the sound of that knock so I may be quick to my feet. Keep me from letting you stand out in the cold or from ever sending you away to some stable. May my heart be warm and inviting, so that when you do knock, a worthy place will always be waiting. . . .[7]

7. Gire, *Intimate Moments with the Savior*, p. 7.

Chapter 7

A SACRIFICE, A SAVIOR, A SWORD

Luke 2:21–38

Many amazing ironies weave silently through the story of Jesus' birth. A tiny infant's frame contains the expanse of deity. Divinity's lungs breathe barnyard dust. Shabby shepherds stand in for angelic courtiers. It's almost too incongruous to comprehend.

Slipping our notice, perhaps, is another irony that appears in Paul's writings:

> But when the fulness of the time came, God sent forth His Son, born of a woman, born *under the Law.* (Gal. 4:4, emphasis added)

Jesus was born a Jew and as a Jew, He was a slave to the commandments He created. Why would He place Himself in bondage to His own Law?

> In order that He might redeem those who were under the Law, that we might receive the adoption as sons. (v. 5)

He redeems us from the Law's judgment, not by getting rid of the Law, but by meeting its demands. He Himself said,

> "Do not think that I came to abolish the Law or the Prophets; I did not come to abolish, but to fulfill." (Matt. 5:17)

So the One by whom all things were created and in whom all things hold together (see Col. 1:16–17) was confined to the requirements of the Law, which His Jewish parents were faithful to perform during His helpless, dependent infancy.

Some Helpful Insights from Ancient Jewish Culture

In the weeks that followed Jesus' birth, Joseph and Mary carefully obeyed God's commands to them as new parents. William Barclay gives us a guided tour of the three ceremonies that were required for the young family:

Circumcision. Every Jewish boy was circumcised on the eighth day after his birth. So sacred was that ceremony that it could be carried out even on a Sabbath when the law forbade almost every other act which was not absolutely essential; and on that day a boy received his name.

The Redemption of the First-born. According to the law (*Exodus* 13:2) every firstborn male, both of human beings and of cattle, was sacred to God. . . . There was therefore a ceremony called the Redemption of the Firstborn (*Numbers* 18:16). It is laid down that for the sum of five shekels . . . parents could, as it were, buy back their son from God. The sum had to be paid to the priests. . . .

The Purification after Childbirth. When a woman had borne a child, if it was a boy, she was unclean for forty days, if it was a girl, for eighty days. She could go about her household and her daily business but she could not enter the Temple or share in any religious ceremony (*Leviticus* 12). At the end of that time she had to bring to the Temple a lamb for a burnt offering and a young pigeon for a sin offering. That was a somewhat expensive sacrifice, and so the law laid it down (*Leviticus* 12:8) that if she could not afford the lamb she might bring another pigeon. The offering of the two pigeons instead of the lamb and the pigeon was technically called *The Offering of the Poor.*[1]

Notice how Jesus' family participates in each of these ceremonies:

And when eight days were completed before His circumcision, His name was then called Jesus, the name given by the angel before He was conceived in the womb.

And when the days for their purification according to the law of Moses were completed, they brought Him up to Jerusalem to present Him to the

1. William Barclay, *The Gospel of Luke*, rev. ed., The Daily Study Bible Series (Philadelphia, Pa.: Westminster Press, 1975), p. 24.

Lord (as it is written in the Law of the Lord, "Every firstborn male that opens the womb shall be called holy to the Lord"), and to offer a sacrifice according to what was said in the Law of the Lord, "A pair of turtledoves, or two young pigeons." (Luke 2:21–24)

Everything was accomplished according to the Law. Eight days after the birth—the circumcision and naming.[2] And on the fortieth day—the redemption or presentation of the firstborn as "holy to the Lord" and the offering of two birds for Mary's purification.[3]

Unlike the other gospel writers, Luke splices these scenes into his gospel to remind us of how highly God values life and how important He considers these special moments of consecration. God has given children to parents as a sacred trust—to name them, shape them, then send them out on their own. What a privilege to share in God's creation and nurturing of human life! In a day in which people so uncaringly toss away young lives through abortion or abuse, it is reassuring to see God ascribing infinite worth to little ones.

As Joseph and Mary took their little One into the temple to offer sacrifices, they encountered two godly people—an older man and woman who had been waiting a long time to meet this Child.

Meet Simeon: An Aging Man of God

To the mass of people swarming through the temple that day, Jesus was just another baby nestled in the arms of a young mother. No one would have noticed Him—no one, that is, except Simeon.

Who He Was

Of the four gospel writers, only Luke gives us a minibiography of this devoted man of God.

> And behold, there was a man in Jerusalem whose name was Simeon; and this man was righteous and devout, looking for the consolation of Israel; and the Holy Spirit was upon him. And it had been revealed to him by the Holy Spirit that he would

2. As instructed by the angel (see Matt. 1:21; Luke 1:31), Joseph and Mary named the baby Jesus—the Greek form of the Hebrew name Joshua, which means "Yahweh saves."

3. Apparently, Joseph could not afford to buy a sacrificial lamb on his carpenter's salary, implying that Jesus came from a family of modest means.

not see death before he had seen the Lord's Christ.
(vv. 25–26)

Like the prophets of the Old Testament, Simeon was uniquely indwelt by the Holy Spirit. During this period when the Scriptures were still under formation, the Spirit sometimes revealed His will to godly people through dreams and visions.[4] Perhaps that is how the Spirit promised Simeon he would live to see the Messiah. It was certainly by supernatural guidance that Simeon came to the temple at just the right time to see the Christ child.

> And he came in the Spirit into the temple; and
> when the parents brought in the child Jesus, to carry
> out for Him the custom of the Law, then he took
> Him into his arms, and blessed God. (vv. 27–28a)

How Simeon recognized this infant as the promised Savior, we don't know. But the moment he saw His face peeking through the folds of the infant's blanket, he knew. And, filled with the Spirit, he took Jesus into his grandfatherly arms and sang a beautiful song of blessing.

What He Said

Simeon's words comprised the fifth song or poem of praise recorded by Luke. Elizabeth's was a song of love (1:42–45); Mary's, a song of faith (vv. 46–55); Zacharias', a song of hope (vv. 68–79); the angels', a song of adoration (2:14); and Simeon's, a song of fulfillment. With his purpose for living accomplished, Simeon is now ready to joyfully enter the Lord's presence a fulfilled man. Eugene Peterson brings out the sense of grateful completion in Simeon's lyrics.

> "God, you can now release your servant;
>   release me in peace as you promised.
> With my own eyes I've seen your salvation;
>   it's now out in the open for everyone to see:
> A God-revealing light to the non-Jewish nations,
>   and of glory for your people Israel."[5] (vv. 29–32)

---

4. Now that we possess the completed Bible, it is best to allow the Spirit to guide us through the words of Scripture rather than look for the kind of extrabiblical revelations the Spirit gave Simeon.

5. Eugene H. Peterson, *The Message* (Colorado Springs, Colo.: NavPress, 1993), p. 120.

Think of the irony of *that* moment! Simeon was praising the Father while cradling the Son in his hands. And as he held up this tiny baby, he was flashing a beacon of salvation not just to Israel but to Gentiles as well. The Savior of the world was here!

Joseph and Mary's eyes must have lit up as Simeon spoke about their special Son. Luke says that they "were amazed at the things which were being said about Him" (v. 33).[6] With each miraculous episode, their minds were opened more and more to their baby's true identity.

With Simeon's next words, though, the sparkle in their eyes would change to tears:

> And Simeon blessed them, and said to Mary His mother, "Behold, this Child is appointed for the fall and rise of many in Israel, and for a sign to be opposed—and a sword will pierce even your own soul—to the end that thoughts from many hearts may be revealed." (vv. 34–35)

This prophecy must have sent a shiver through Mary, who, with motherly instinct, surely yearned to gather up her little One and shelter Him from whatever evils might come. "A sign to be *opposed*"—what could this mean? She had only seen the sun rising on Jesus' future, but now a terrible cloud loomed ahead. Some would receive Him and enter God's favor, yet many would reject Him and fall. And along with that rejection would come opposition and conflict. Through the strife, heartache like a frightful sword would plunge into her soul. From our vantage point, we see her most agonizing moment with stark clarity. One day, she will stand below a blood-stained cross, watching in horror as life spills out of her precious Son.

But for now, these things were just furtive shadows cast against the joy of the occasion. Simeon handed Jesus back to Mary and the smile returned to her face . . . as an elderly woman beaming with delight approached the young family.

---

6. The Greek word for *amaze* can also be translated "to marvel, wonder." G. Abbott-Smith, *A Manual Greek Lexicon of the New Testament*, 3d ed. (Edinburgh, Scotland: T. and T. Clark, 1937), p. 203. It's the same word that would later be used to describe the disciples' reaction when Jesus calmed the raging sea (Luke 8:25) and when He appeared after the Resurrection, saying, "It is I Myself; touch Me and see" (24:39). From beginning to end, Jesus sparked wonder in the hearts of people.

Meet Anna: An Eighty-Four-Year-Old Prophetess

Luke sheds some light on the godly character of this woman.

Her Character

> And there was a prophetess, Anna, the daughter of
> Phanuel, of the tribe of Asher. She was advanced in
> years, having lived with a husband seven years after
> her marriage, and then as a widow to the age of
> eighty-four. And she never left the temple, serving
> night and day with fastings and prayers. (vv. 36–37)

Anna had endured her own heart-piercing experience when she
lost her husband after only seven years of marriage. Like a wounded
bird, she had flown to the hand of her Master and clung to the
Lord in service and devotion. Over the years of working at the
temple, how many parents had she seen come through with their
firstborn sons? Too many to remember. But, like Simeon, she knew
this One was special.

Her Witness

> And at that very moment she came up and began
> giving thanks to God, and continued to speak of
> Him to all those who were looking for the redemp-
> tion of Jerusalem. (v. 38)

Such joy couldn't be contained. He was here—the One of
whom the prophets had spoken! Israel's redemption was at hand.

A Couple of Suggestions for Today

It's a good idea to listen closely when wise, older people speak.
Through their words and actions, Simeon and Anna have something important to say to us.

First, *don't wait for a crisis to occur before you talk about Christ.*
The lostness of humanity has never been more visible than today,
and the human condition never more desperate. Spontaneously
speak up about the wonderful news that Jesus has come.

Second, *don't think that something significant may not happen to shake
up your life.* It may be Christ returning to earth—not as a baby or a
rejected rabbi, but as a warrior, prepared to conquer this world for
His kingdom. Continually look up for His coming. Like Simeon and
Anna, keep watching and waiting for something glorious to appear.

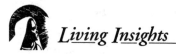 *Living Insights*

According to Simeon's prophecy, one of the Messiah's purposes in coming was so that the "thoughts from many hearts may be revealed" (Luke 2:35). Jesus' life would be like a relentless beam of light, exposing the hidden corners of people's hearts. However, our pride protests against such an invasion of privacy. It protects the heart's shameful secrets and resists the light's uncompromising glare. Jesus talked about this human tendency when speaking to religious Nicodemus, who had come to Him at night under the cover of darkness:

> "And this is the judgment, that the light is come into the world, and men loved the darkness rather than the light; for their deeds were evil. For everyone who does evil hates the light, and does not come to the light, lest his deeds should be exposed." (John 3:19–20)

Although Jesus offers forgiveness and salvation, tragically, people reject His gift of grace because they do not want their deeds exposed.

Does the idea of Jesus revealing the thoughts of your heart cause you to draw back from Him? Have you loved the darkness, perhaps feeling a sense of security there? Express to the Lord some of your fears about letting Him shine His penetrating light into your soul.

_____

_____

_____

What gift of grace might you be rejecting by resisting Christ's purifying presence in your life?

_____

_____

_____

David submitted his pride to the Lord through this humble prayer:

Search me, O God, and know my heart;
Try me and know my anxious thoughts;
And see if there be any hurtful way in me,
And lead me in the everlasting way. (Ps. 139:23–24)

In the quietness of the next few moments, express your own prayer to the Lord, inviting Him to reveal your hidden motives and secret sins and lead you in His everlasting way.

_____

_____

_____

_____

 Living Insights

As a parent, has a "sword" ever pierced your soul?

Perhaps uncaring people have rejected or abused your child. Silently, tearfully, you've had to stand by his or her cross and watch the life drain out of your precious one's spirit.

Perhaps your child's love for the darkness has sent stabbing pains through your heart. Helplessly, you see your son or daughter running from Christ's light into sin's frightful abyss, and your soul aches as if an actual sword had been plunged into your chest.

Would that it were a real sword! At least there would be the hope of healing. But this wound remains open and tender to the touch, no matter how many months go by, no matter how many prayers are cried.

What kind of parent-to-parent comfort do you think Mary, as a fellow sufferer, might give you? Perhaps, if she were here, she might offer you just a listening, sympathetic ear. Perhaps she might also gently lead you to the healing waters of God's mercy. Reread Mary's Magnificat in Luke 1:46–55 from the perspective of a parent in pain. Look for the theme of God's mercy toward those in need and, in the following space, journal some of the strengthening insights the Lord shows you.[7]

7. For parents dealing with their own swords of sorrow, we recommend John White's *Parents in Pain* (Downers Grove, Ill.: InterVarsity Press, 1979).

Journal of Mercy

Chapter 8

THE DAY THE PUPIL STUMPED THE PROFS

Luke 2:39–52

W hat kind of images fill your scrapbook of childhood memories? Our early years should be a time for play and exploration, a time to rub our fingers in the paint and color life with a
bright yellow sun, green shade trees, and family members holding
hands. It should be a time for creativity and fun, for discovering
the ups and downs of our world and ourselves at an easy, summer-
time pace.

Tragically, many people's childhood paintings are smeared with
the dark colors of turmoil and abuse. Some carry with them frac-
tured portraits of themselves trying desperately to hold their families
together or scale the heights of their parents' expectations. For
them, it is as if someone stole away a portion of their soul.

When a thief steals an irreplaceable jewel that has been passed
from mother to daughter for generations, the sense of loss can be
overwhelming. But that loss is only a taste of the heartache we feel
when we are robbed of our most cherished treasure—our childhood.
Sadly, many spend their entire adult lives grasping for lost innocence and joy.

God understands the importance of protecting that treasure.
Perhaps that's why He shows us some snapshots of His own Son's
childhood, as a model of healthy growth. Because the Bible contains
very few portraits of its heroes as children, these pages from the
Father's family album are precious indeed.

Jesus' Childhood . . . A Few Treasured Details

In the last chapter, we took a look at Jesus' baby pictures on
His day of presentation at the temple (Luke 2:21–38). Between
verses 38 and 39, many crucial events happened in Jesus' young life
that only Matthew fills in for us. First, the family returned to Bethlehem and, apparently, settled there for a while. During the next
year or so, magi having seen a star in the east arrived in Jerusalem,
asking King Herod where they could find the One born King of
the Jews (Matt. 2:2). They were directed to Bethlehem, where they

worshiped the Christ child—the city where not long afterward the jealously paranoid Herod had all the baby boys two years and younger slaughtered (vv. 3–18).

Fortunately, an angel had forewarned Joseph of Herod's wicked intent and had sent the young family fleeing to Egypt (vv. 13–15). When the murderous king died, an angel again appeared to Joseph to tell him it was now safe to return. Led by God, Joseph took his family through Judea into Galilee and settled in the safety and obscurity of his and Mary's hometown, Nazareth (vv. 19–23).

The Return to Nazareth of Galilee

Luke picks up the story here, after the family "returned to Galilee, to their own city of Nazareth" (Luke 2:39). What a relief for Joseph and Mary to finally come home. How they must have enjoyed showing the relatives their little Child—a preschooler by now—and settling into a normal routine after so many years on the move.

Jesus' early life reminds us that hardships don't always deprive children of a healthy childhood experience. Abuse and neglect steal away health; but trials can be strengthening to children as long as parents supply abundant security, comfort, and protection.

Growing Up in Nazareth

Luke's photos of Jesus' childhood include one snapshot of Jesus during His grade school years (v. 40), a series of photos from the family's Passover trip to Jerusalem when Jesus was twelve (vv. 41–51), and another snapshot, capturing Jesus as a young adult (v. 52). As we study the first picture of Jesus in verse 40, a few features of His childhood come into focus.

Normal. Luke says almost casually, "the Child continued to grow," as if to imply—"like any other boy." Although the sinless Son of God, He nevertheless had a normal childhood. Mary and Joseph had to potty train Him. They had to teach Him His please-and-thank-yous. When He had chores to do, He probably longed to be out playing with His friends. He was a typical boy who loved chasing lightning bugs and gazing at stars on warm summer nights. The stories that picture Jesus tapping His divine powers to create birds from clay and to command trees to bear fruit are just that, fanciful stories.

Physical. Luke also says that Jesus continued to grow "and become strong" (v. 40a). Physically, He was like any other boy. He caught colds and had runny noses. He felt His knees ache from growing pains. He endured puberty. All the physical bridges we cross en route to adulthood, He crossed too.

Intellectual and spiritual. To this flesh-and-blood image of Jesus Luke adds an intellectual and spiritual dimension: Jesus was "increasing in wisdom; and the grace of God was upon Him" (v. 40b). No doubt "wisdom" includes knowledge, suggesting that Jesus had an appetite for learning. And, like any other child, He was growing in His understanding of Himself, finding out His individual identity, learning how He was gifted and what direction His life would take. These early years of discovery and play were vital to His self-awareness, just as they are to ours.

However, this wisdom of Jesus' went beyond mere knowledge. Uniquely and mysteriously, God was resting His hand of grace on His shoulders and guiding Him toward His divine calling.

It's difficult to know just when Jesus began to understand who He was. "At some time," writes William Barclay,

> Jesus must have discovered His own unique relationship to God. He cannot have known it when He was a child in the manger and a baby at His mother's breast. . . . As the years went on He must have thought [about it]; and then . . . with manhood dawning on Him, there came in a sudden blaze of realization the consciousness that He was not as other men are, that in a unique and special sense He was the Son of God.[1]

Certainly, by the age of twelve, He was starting to see the truth.

Jesus—at the Age of Twelve—in Jerusalem

To us, twelve may seem a young age to be formulating a personal identity and mission. Yet, as we observe Jesus at this age, we clearly see how His Passover trip marked a significant stride in His journey from boyhood to manhood, from innocence to self-awareness. Years later, He would emerge into the full light of His messianic identity, but it is here, during childhood, that the process begins.

Luke hints at this process through different references to Jesus in the passage. In verse 40, Jesus is called "the Child"; in verse 43,

---

1. William Barclay, *The Gospel of Luke*, 2d ed., The Daily Study Bible Series, (Philadelphia, Pa.: Westminster Press, 1956), p. 25.

"the boy"; in verse 48, "Son"; and in verse 52, "Jesus." Each name seems to illustrate a distinct phase in Jesus' development.

The Child. Building on our image from verse 40 of Jesus as a *paidion*, "a young child, a little one,"[2] verse 41 shows Him still dependent on His parents as they plan their annual Passover trip.

> And the Child continued to grow and become strong, increasing in wisdom; and the grace of God was upon Him.
>
> And His parents used to go to Jerusalem every year at the Feast of the Passover. (vv. 40–41)

This year's trip, however, would be different from all the trips they'd made before—Mary and Joseph's little one would never again be a child.

The boy. Jesus, the "boy"—*pais* in Greek—was going to express a measure of independence in keeping with His quietly blossoming identity.

> And when He became twelve, they went up there according to the custom of the Feast; and as they were returning, after spending the full number of days, the boy Jesus stayed behind in Jerusalem. (vv. 42–43a)

As a twelve-year-old, Jesus was only months away from becoming a *bar mitzvah*, "son of the law." "At thirteen years of age," writes commentator E. Earle Ellis,

> a Jewish boy entered into the full responsibilities of adulthood. During the prior year the father was required to acquaint him with the duties and regulations which he was soon to assume.[3]

This year's Passover was a special time of preparation and learning for young Jesus, and when the day came to leave, He wanted to stay. Joseph and Mary, however,

> were unaware of it, but supposed Him to be in the

---

2. G. Abbott-Smith, *A Manual Greek Lexicon of the New Testament*, 3d ed. (Edinburgh, Scotland: T. and T. Clark, 1937), p. 333.

3. E. Earle Ellis, *The Gospel of Luke*, rev. ed., New Century Bible Commentary series (1974; reprint, Grand Rapids, Mich.: William B. Eerdmans Publishing Co.; London, England: Marshall, Morgan and Scott Publishers, 1983), p. 85.

caravan, and went a day's journey; and they began looking for Him among their relatives and acquaintances. And when they did not find Him, they returned to Jerusalem, looking for Him. (vv. 43b–45)

How could they have lost track of their Son? Commentator Leon Morris helps us understand what probably happened.

> In a large "caravan" . . . parents might well not know where a child was. If the later practice was followed, the women and small children went ahead and the men followed with the bigger boys. Joseph and Mary may each have thought that Jesus was with the other. For a full day they journeyed, looking for Him among the travellers before they concluded He must still be in Jerusalem.[4]

It took another full day to return to the city; then, on the third day,

> they found Him in the temple, sitting in the midst of the teachers, both listening to them, and asking them questions. (v. 46)

It wasn't unusual for students to meet teachers of the Law in the temple, plying them with questions and attentively listening to their answers. What was unusual was the way Jesus was answering the teacher's questions! His youthful perceptiveness sparked several reactions. First, from the teachers:

> And all who heard Him were amazed at His understanding and His answers. (v. 47)

The Greek tense suggests that they were amazed over and over again at Jesus' insights. Joseph and Mary responded a bit differently: "when they saw Him, they were astonished" (v. 48a). The Greek word means, "to strike with panic or shock." In modern terms, they were blown away! This was their *son*, going head-to-head with the brightest men of Israel.

The Son. Whatever rush of pride they may have felt quickly melted on the furnace of their emotions, which was fired up with worry. Mary called Jesus, "Son," a name that immediately reminded

---

4. Leon Morris, *The Gospel according to St. Luke*, The Tyndale New Testament Commentaries series (Grand Rapids, Mich.: William B. Eerdmans Publishing Co., 1974), p. 91.

Him that this was His parent speaking:

> "Son, why have You treated us this way? Behold,
> Your father and I have been anxiously looking for
> You." (v. 48b)

"Don't You care that we have been going out of our minds searching for You?" Mary rebukingly asks. She needed to be reminded, though, whose Child He was and that His real Father was with Him the whole time, preparing Him to become the epitome of *bar mitzvah*.

> And He said to them, "Why is it that you were
> looking for Me? Did you not know that I had to be
> in My Father's house?" And they did not understand
> the statement which He had made to them.
> (vv. 49–50)

It was no accident that the Messiah's first recorded words expressed His unique relationship to God. Even Mary and Joseph, who had lovingly parented Jesus through boyhood, had difficulty understanding that mysterious relationship.

Not once, however, did His divine union with God make Him proud. In verse 51, we see Jesus humbly bowing to the will of His earthly parents.

> And He went down with them, and came to Nazareth; and He continued in subjection to them; and
> His mother treasured all these things in her heart.
> (v. 51)

Jesus. Luke's final snapshot of Jesus transports us into His young adult years.

> And Jesus kept increasing in wisdom and stature,
> and in favor with God and men. (v. 52)

This image of Jesus resembles the picture in verse 40, but the main verb is different: instead of "continued to grow," Luke says that "Jesus *kept increasing*." This verb is from the Greek *prokoptō*, which has a more vigorous meaning—"to cut forward . . . to advance, progress."[5] The burgeoning child pictured in verse 40 has

---

5. Abbott-Smith, *Greek Lexicon*, p. 381.

become a young man by verse 52, blazing a trail to His messianic destiny.

Practical Words regarding Children and Childhood

Two principles emerge from our look at these snapshots of Jesus. First, to parents: *the process of growing up is God-arranged and healthy.* God has designed all children to be set free to live for Him on their own. Eventually, we must let go of the rope that ties them to us. Don't try to keep them. Don't manipulate them by making them feel guilty for yearning to sail the open seas.

Now to teenagers: *the awareness of your calling and desire for independence does not nullify your need to submit.* When God's voice of independence starts calling, be careful not to snap the rope out of your parents' hands. By slowly easing away through the teenage years, you build trust. Before long, you'll be an adult, looking back on your childhood through your own scrapbook of fond memories.

 Living Insights STUDY ONE

When Mary looked into the eyes of twelve-year-old Jesus sitting with the men in the temple, she saw a Jesus she hadn't expected to see. Who was this tall, confident person with the face of a boy but the eyes of a man? No longer was He her child, whom she used to rock to sleep and whose tears she once kissed away. Did this new Jesus frighten her? Did she long to grab Him out of time's grasp and forever clutch Him to her breast as her little boy?

"Son, why have You treated us this way?" she said (v. 48).

But we can imagine her heart crying out: "Son, why are You leaving me?"

Most parents realize they must one day let go of their children, but simply knowing that fact doesn't make it any easier. As a parent, have you struggled in this area of letting go? If so, what are some of your fears as you think of your children leaving your side?

_____

_____

_____

Have you tried manipulating them to stay dependent upon

71

you—perhaps through guilt? Do you ever communicate in subtle ways that your happiness depends upon them? Do you sometimes try to live their lives for them? Have you, maybe unconsciously, criticized your children's attempts at self-reliance?

_____

_____

_____

As children grow up, they need us just as much as when they were little, but less and less as hovering parents and more and more as encouraging friends. What are some ways you can encourage your child's self-awareness and independence?

_____

_____

_____

Like Mary, we all need to be reminded of who our children's real Father is. Letting go is ultimately a matter of faith in God, who never lets go of us—or our children.

 Living Insights STUDY TWO

Parenting is the art of striking a balance between extremes—between law and liberty, protecting and exposing, pushing and relaxing. Not letting go of our children may be one extreme, but just as dangerous is hurrying them into adulthood before they're ready.

In his highly acclaimed book *The Hurried Child*, David Elkind describes the pressures our children often face.

> Hurried children are forced to take on the physical, psychological, and social trappings of adulthood before they are prepared to deal with them. We dress our children in miniature adult costumes (often with designer labels), we expose them to gratuitous sex and violence, and we expect them to cope with an increasingly bewildering social environment—

divorce, single parenthood, homosexuality. Through all of these pressures the child senses that it is important for him or her to cope without admitting the confusion and pain that accompany such changes. Like adults, they are made to feel they must be survivors, and surviving means adjusting—even if the survivor is only four or six or eight years old.[6]

How can we help our children savor their childhood before it slips through their fingers? One place to begin is to ask ourselves if we are expecting too much from our children. Are there ways you could be driving your child too hard?

_____

_____

_____

Do you sometimes feel that their social or academic or athletic achievements reflect on you as a parent? Could that feeling be adding pressure to your kids to grow up faster than they're able?

_____

_____

_____

The media compounds the pressures on our children. It feasts on a child's natural desire to grow up, flagrantly exploiting that yearning in order to sell a product or an ideology. What are some ways you can protect the treasure of your child's innocence, which others try so callously to steal?

_____

_____

_____

6. David Elkind, *The Hurried Child: Growing Up Too Fast Too Soon* (Reading, Mass.: Addison-Wesley Publishing Co., 1981), p. xii.

Chapter 9

A Study in Contrasts
Luke 3

Want a surefire method for a successful ministry?

One. Don't go where the people are; make them come to you. Hold meetings outdoors. Let the people sit on the hard, dusty ground; and if it starts raining or gets cold . . . tough.

Two. Deliberately wear stuff that is unattractive. Smelly camel-skin clothing works well. At potlucks, eat insects and honey. Scratch a lot. Don't worry about bad breath. And, certainly, don't have your colors done.

Three. Speak offensively. Assault and insult listeners. A perfect sermon title might be, "Whaddaya Think You're Doin' Here, Ya Buncha Lily-livered Snakes?"

Four. Embarrass top-ranking government officials by exposing their shameful private lives.

Five. When crowds finally start coming, send them away to another minister down the street.

What? You say this method would never work? Well, it worked for John the Baptizer. People streamed out of their villages to be baptized in his waters of repentance and truth. He may have been unconventional . . . OK, strange . . . but he was extremely effective. Even Jesus said, "Among those born of women there has not arisen anyone greater than John the Baptist" (Matt. 11:11a). What made John great? Actually, the answer goes beyond methodology. It's who he was as a person.

Enter: John . . . Who Broke All the "Rules" of Formal Religion

Clothes may make the man, as the saying goes, but the times in which a person lives make great character. The dark backdrop of John's times made his character shine especially bright.

His Times

> Now in the fifteenth year of the reign of Tiberius
> Caesar, when Pontius Pilate was governor of Judea,
> and Herod was tetrarch of Galilee, and his brother

Philip was tetrarch of the region of Ituraea and Tra-
chonitis, and Lysanias was tetrarch of Abilene, in
the high priesthood of Annas and Caiaphas, the
word of God came to John, the son of Zacharias, in
the wilderness. (Luke 3:1–2)

Upon the death of Emperor Augustus in A.D. 14, Tiberius, a
brutish and debauched individual, climbed the steps to the throne
of the Roman Empire. The fifteenth year of his reign would place
the beginning of John's ministry about A.D. 28 or 29.

From the broad panorama of the Empire, Luke telescopes to the
land of Palestine, which had been apportioned to Pontius Pilate,
Herod, and Philip. The political hornet's nest of Judea belonged to
Pilate, the cruelly anti-Semitic Roman governor. Herod—also
called Antipas—and his half brother Philip, were tetrachs, local
rulers supported by Rome. Both governed parts of northern Palestine inherited from their father, Herod the Great. Along with territory, however, their father also passed down to his sons a villainous
legacy that included his scandalous marriages to ten women and
his jealous murder of three other sons.

Also mentioned in Luke's list of rulers is Lysanias, about whom
we know nothing except that he ruled Abilene, a territory north
of Palestine near Damascus.

From heads of state, Luke narrows his focus to religious rulers,
introducing the high priests—Annas and his son-in-law Caiaphas.
Both of them were pompous and power-hungry, with Caiaphas wearing the official vestments but the former high priest Annas pulling
the strings of influence in the country.

Into this morass of moral corruption came John, an individual
honed in the wild, unsullied by fame or power, and consecrated by
God to shatter His four-hundred-year prophetic silence with an
earthshaking message from heaven.

His Message

In resolute obedience to God's Word, John

came into all the district around the Jordan, preaching
a baptism of repentance for the forgiveness of sins.
(v. 3)

To a nation disillusioned by its leaders, John offered a message
of hope: The moment the people cried out to God in repentance,

75

He would wash them clean with His forgiveness. In response they would show the world their change of heart through baptism.[1]

Although convicting, John's message was a fresh wind of good news. He was preaching "the gospel to the people" (v. 18b). Any day now, the Lamb of God would appear—the One "who takes away the sin of the world!" (John 1:29). Get ready for Him! Repent! Soften your hearts! John was "the voice of one crying in the wilderness," as Isaiah had prophesied, the one who would tell the people:

> "'Make ready the way of the Lord,
> Make His paths straight.
> Every ravine shall be filled up,
> And every mountain and hill shall be brought low;
> And the crooked shall become straight,
> And the rough roads smooth;
> And all flesh shall see the salvation of God.'"
> (Luke 3:4–5)

John's responsibilities were threefold: to "clear the way" for the Lord, to "prepare the way" for the Lord, and to "get out of the way" of the Lord![2] He knew the authority that came with his role, but he also understood his limitations.

- He was the voice; Jesus was the Word.

- He was the lamp; Jesus was the Light of the World.

- He was a man; Jesus was the Messiah.

John's sermons whetted the people's spiritual appetites for Jesus' life-giving bread. His job was to make the people hungry for the Savior, hungry enough to change their lives.

However, many people came to the Jordan with no intention of changing. Like vipers smoked from their holes during a forest fire, they had been swept into the wilderness by John's terrifying talk of the Messiah's fiery judgment.[3] Seeing their reptilian hearts

1. Some have thought this verse says that John was baptizing people so they might receive God's forgiveness. But "baptism of repentance for the forgiveness of sins" can mean "*because* of the forgiveness of sins." John was baptizing people as a sign that they were already forgiven.

2. George Goodman, as cited by J. Oswald Sanders in *Robust in Faith* (Chicago, Ill.: Moody Press, 1965), pp. 175–76.

3. According to William Hendriksen, the Greek word translated *viper* can also mean "lizard." See *Exposition of the Gospel according to Luke*, New Testament Commentary series (Grand Rapids, Mich.: Baker Book House, 1978), p. 215.

through the pious veneer, John fiercely confronted them:

> "You brood of vipers, who warned you to flee from the wrath to come?" (v. 7)

Though that's not exactly the best way to win over an audience, keep in mind that John was standing toe-to-toe with the worst kind of religious hypocrites, those who had come to the Jordan merely to make a spiritual show for the audience. Matthew says they were the proud Pharisees and Sadducees (3:7). They believed that their heritage as Abraham's offspring secured them favor with God, but John had news for them.

> "Therefore bring forth fruits in keeping with repentance, and do not begin to say to yourselves, 'We have Abraham for our father,' for I say to you that God is able from these stones to raise up children to Abraham. And also the axe is already laid at the root of the trees; every tree therefore that does not bear good fruit is cut down and thrown into the fire." (Luke 3:8–9)

Pedigrees don't produce fruit. A tree may be lush with religious accomplishments or well-rooted in biblical knowledge, but if it bears nothing of heavenly value, it is destined for the axe. Only genuine repentance brings salvation.

With this simple image, John was indicting the most respected religious leaders of the day, the pious of the pious. If they weren't safe from God's wrath, who was? What "fruit" of repentance was God looking for?

His Answers

"What shall we do?" the people asked as they came to be baptized (v. 10). John's answers were painfully practical—there's no losing his point in theological underbrush. To the general public, he said,

> "Let the man who has two tunics share with him who has none; and let him who has food do likewise." (v. 11b)

To the tax-gatherers, who were notorious for overcharging the people in their districts, he said,

"Collect no more than what you have been ordered to." (v. 13)

And to the soldiers, the thugs of the ancient world, who would muscle money out of people or blackmail the rich through false accusations, John said,

> "Do not take money from anyone by force, or accuse anyone falsely, and be content with your wages." (v. 14b)

Repentance, for John, meant much more

> than taking a dip in the Jordan and having a spiritual experience. It means changing one's life. In all the categories of life—as a spouse, parent, roommate, employee, or boss—we are to practice our Christian beliefs, not just give verbal assent to them. If repentance is true, then it will impact our giving, our attitudes, and our treatment of others. It may begin with a sorrowful heart, but it must end with determined action.[4]

With this kind of down-to-earth teaching, John spoke with authority and integrity. They'd never seen a man like him before, nor had they watched so many despised sinners miraculously transformed. Could *he* be the Promised One (see v. 15)? John's answer was a clear and humble no.

> "As for me, I baptize you with water; but One is coming who is mightier than I, and I am not fit to untie the thong of His sandals; He will baptize you with the Holy Spirit and fire. And His winnowing fork is in His hand to thoroughly clear His threshing floor, and to gather the wheat into His barn; but He will burn up the chaff with unquenchable fire." (vv. 16–17)

The contrasts between John and Jesus abound in these verses. Although John is effective, Jesus will be so mighty that John would not be worthy of a slave's most menial task, untying His shoes.

---

4. From the study guide *John the Baptizer*, coauthored by Bryce Klabunde, from the Bible-teaching ministry of Charles R. Swindoll (Anaheim, Calif.: Insight for Living, 1991), p. 13.

Although John purifies the people with water baptism, Jesus will purify them through Spirit baptism and fire. He will sift people like a farmer sifts wheat. As the farmer tosses the wheat into the air with a winnowing fork, the lighter chaff blows away and is later burned, while the heavier kernel falls to the ground and is gathered for safe storage. Only the Messiah has that kind of power to judge between the righteous and the wicked.

His Courage

One corrupt man whose life would one day blow away like chaff was the weak-willed king, Herod Antipas. Luke illustrates John's courage in exposing the sin in this man's life.

> But when Herod the tetrarch was reproved by him on account of Herodias, his brother's wife, and on account of all the wicked things which Herod had done, he added this also to them all, that he locked John up in prison. (vv. 19–20)

The story behind these verses is a tangled one. Herod Antipas had several half brothers, and one of them had married the beguiling Herodias—the daughter of another half brother. Antipas became infatuated with Herodias, who, being an ambitious woman, agreed to divorce her husband and marry him . . . if he got rid of his present queen. After divorcing and disgracing his wife, Antipas eventually got his beloved Herodias. Only John had the courage to bring this dark affair into the light of day. And for that he was thrown in prison and eventually beheaded at the grisly request of Herodias' daughter, whose seductive dance before Antipas sealed John's fate (see Mark 6:17–29).

But all that was still in the future. In the next verses, Luke switches back to the present, as the Son of God quietly entered the scene.

Enter: Jesus . . . Who Came Quietly and Unobtrusively

One face in a sea of people, Jesus approached John as just another baptismal candidate. His baptism, however, was unique. It wasn't an act of repentance, but an opportunity for the Father to authenticate His Son.

> Now it came about when all the people were baptized, that Jesus also was baptized, and while He was praying, heaven was opened, and the Holy Spirit

descended upon Him in bodily form like a dove, and a voice came out of heaven, "Thou art My beloved Son, in Thee I am well-pleased." (Luke 3:21–22)

In the muddy Jordan waters, the Trinity appeared before all humanity. You could see the Spirit. You could hear the Father. You could touch the Son. Jesus' mission to bring heaven to earth had begun. At the time, He was about thirty years old, "supposedly the son of Joseph" (v. 23). But as His genealogy in verses 23–38 shows, Jesus truly was both "the son of Adam" and "the son of God" (see v. 38).

Exit: You . . . Who Must Enter the World

Flowing like streams from the Jordan are four principles from this passage. First, *those who make an impact must not fear being different.* You stand for things about which others have compromised. Don't be afraid to disagree with the majority.

Second, *those who wish to change should not ignore being specific.* Change takes longer when we deal in generalities. If we truly want to grow, we must ask for God's power in our specific areas of need.

Third, *those who risk confronting dare not forget the consequences.* John courageously confronted a king, and it cost him his freedom and ultimately his life. Throughout history, countless men and women like him have dared to speak God's truth, and they have suffered real and painful consequences. It may very well be the same for us.

Fourth, *those who seek the Savior cannot deny the evidence.* The heavens opened. The Holy Spirit descended in the form of a dove. The Father spoke, "Thou art My beloved Son." We need to take God at His word: Jesus is the Savior of the world.

 Living Insights STUDY ONE

People flocked to the Jordan to hear John speak. They marveled at him. They hung on his words. Yet he never lost sight of who he really was—"The voice of one crying in the wilderness" (Luke 3:4).

John's clarity of vision and humble spirit are remarkable in light of the fame that launched him to celebrity status overnight. As more and more people's lives were touched, it must have been tempting for him to believe in his own power, to think he was indispensable, to become someone he wasn't in order to please the crowds.

Fame has a way of fogging our minds. Actor Kevin Costner, who skyrocketed into international stardom in the eighties, recognizes the dangers of fame. He candidly told an interviewer,

> "I would trade it all for anonymity again. . . . [Fame doesn't] help you get up in the morning. Fame doesn't help clear your mind. Fame doesn't tell you when you're right or wrong. I can't think of anything good that comes out of it."[5]

Perhaps you've received some honor lately, either at work, in the community, or at church. Have these warm accolades felt affirming to you? If so, that's good—that's their purpose. It's when we start depending on them for our self-esteem and identity that problems arise. How much does your self-image rely on your press releases?

_____

_____

_____

For the next few moments, step out of the blinding limelight and try to reclarify your vision of yourself. Can you identify a role for which God has gifted you? Are you fulfilling that role, or have you pursued another role with more status and perks?

_____

_____

What influence do others' expectations have on you? Do they lead you away from God's will for your life?

_____

_____

As quickly as John's star rose, it fell again as the people started leaving him for Christ. When he saw this happening, he said with all honesty: "This joy of mine has been made full. He must increase, but I must decrease" (John 3:29b–30). By keeping his focus on the

5. Kevin Costner, as quoted in the *Press-Telegram*, June 13, 1991.

81

Lord, John anchored himself against fame's pitch and plunge. Following his example can keep you emotionally stable as well. Name some practical ways you can keep your focus on the Lord.

_____

_____

_____

 Living Insights

The religious hypocrite is an expert at hiding sin under the garb of his or her spirituality. But this is an extremely dangerous practice, for as the writer of Proverbs asks, "Can a man take fire in his bosom, And his clothes not be burned?" (Prov. 6:27).

To douse the fiery coal, we must first confess—that is, we must open up our elegant cloaks and reveal our sin to God. But we must also follow James' counsel:

> Therefore, confess your sins to one another, and pray for one another, so that you may be healed. (James 5:16a)

How difficult it is to open up before others and reveal our sin. Yet, really, those who know us best can see its effects in our lives anyway.

Are you attempting to hide some not-so-secret sins? Have you confessed them to God? Perhaps you have, a million times. Is there someone else to whom you could also open up and reveal these smoldering thoughts and actions?

Find that person and start down the road of repentance now. It begins with confession, but it ends with change.

Chapter 10

THE DEVIL NEVER MADE
HIM DO IT
Luke 4:1–13

"The Devil made me do it!" How many of us have shrugged and used that excuse when caught doing something we weren't supposed to? It's a convenient defense, but there's one problem: the Devil *can't* make us do anything. He may be clever, but he's not all-powerful. It may feel that way, however, when we're dangling on temptation's hook, because Satan has a tried-and-true strategy for luring us into his net.

First, he lays out the bait. Satan knows people like a skilled angler knows fish. He notes our habits. He observes our hangouts. Then he prepares a tailor-made lure and drops it right in front of our noses.

Second comes the appeal. He can't make us bite, but he does know what happens inside us when we catch a glimpse of that tantalizing bait. Our fleshly nature draws us to it. We linger over it. We toy with it. We roll it over in our minds until it consumes our imaginations.

Third, the struggle begins. Immediately, our conscience jabs us in the ribs, warning us of the danger. We know it's wrong to take a bite. We may even see the barbed consequences poking through the bait. But Satan's invitation looks so delicious. What to do!

Fourth, the temptation ends with the response. Either we resist or yield; swim away or swallow it whole. Anyone who has resisted knows the feeling of freedom that decision brings. On the other hand, anyone who has yielded knows the feeling of emptiness that follows and the pain of the hook in your cheek.

If anyone knows about Satan's insidious tactics and temptation's staggering power, it is Jesus. The Devil designed some particularly potent bait for Him—bait that could have snagged Jesus' ministry before it even got started.

Two Critical Questions We Must Answer

Before we see how Jesus handled the pressure, we need to settle a couple of questions.

Is the Devil Real?

We often picture the Devil as a little red mischief maker with horns and a pitchfork, but that Devil doesn't exist except in cartoons. The Devil portrayed in the Bible, however, is very real. According to Paul, "Satan disguises himself as an angel of light" (2 Cor. 11:14). He is "the ruler of this world" (John 12:31), "a murderer from the beginning . . . and the father of lies" (John 8:44), "the tempter" (1 Thess 3:5), and "like a roaring lion, seeking someone to devour" (1 Pet. 5:8).

Though we may not be able to see him, he is as real and deadly as electricity surging invisibly through a wire. If we believe in the unseen Spirit who led Jesus into the wilderness (Luke 4:1), we mortals believe in the unseen Devil who tempted Him.[1]

Were Jesus' Temptations Real?

Whether Jesus could really be tempted is an important issue to raise, because on its answer hangs all the consoling truth of Hebrews 4:15:

> For we do not have a high priest who cannot sympathize with our weaknesses, but one who has been tempted in all things as we are, yet without sin.

To sympathize with us, Christ had to have fully experienced the Devil's temptations. Yet, as the Son of God, Jesus had no sin nature; He couldn't sin. So how could He have been tempted to sin?

In the same way that an unconquerable army could still be attacked[2]—and all the more viciously because of its undefeatability—so Jesus' invincible will would nevertheless leave Him susceptible to the Devil's greatest assaults. And one of Satan's heaviest mortar shells was launched at Jesus in the lonely wilds of the Judean wasteland.

Three Actual Temptations Jesus Had to Handle

With His Father's baptismal affirmation still fresh in His heart,

---

1. While both the Holy Spirit and Satan are unseen, the two are far from equal. Satan is a created being, the chief of the fallen angels. Since he can't be everywhere at once like God can, he deploys his legions of demons to do his work of accusing and tempting for him.

2. From Shedd, as quoted by Charles C. Ryrie, in *Basic Theology* (Wheaton, Ill.: Scripture Press Publications, Victor Books, 1986), p. 264.

this beloved Son is now filled with the Holy Spirit and, strangely, led by Him into desolate solitude.

The Setting

The wilderness arena is temptation's opportune setting. The sun's stern eye bears down on the relatively young and probably sheltered thirty-year-old Jesus. The wind's hot breath chafes His skin. The swirling dust whips His face. Only in the jagged crag of a cliff can He find relief. He is by Himself in this forsaken place, where for forty days He has been fasting, praying, and planning His ministry.

When these days end, Luke says, "He became hungry" (Luke 4:2). Hungry! We miss a meal, and we are hungry. After forty days without food, Jesus must be ravenous. Hunger pangs claw His belly. His body screams at His mind to find food somewhere—anywhere. It takes all of His willpower to cage His cravings.

Circling above, Satan sees Jesus depleted and struggling. And with a rustle of vulturous wings, he lands by Jesus' side.

The Assault

The Devil's purpose is simple: to destroy Jesus by drawing Him away from His Father and His mission. With this in mind, the tempter approaches his quarry.

The first test: the temptation of a private nature. Cleverly, the Devil uses Jesus' deity as leverage to ply Him into acting independently of His Father.

> And the Devil said to Him, "If You are the Son of God, tell this stone to become bread."[3] (v. 3)

Oh, the Devil knows who Jesus is. His implication is, "How can You—the Prince of heaven, the almighty Creator—be hungry? Create some bread for Yourself. No one will know. You deserve a little pleasure."

As Jesus pictures the smooth stone as a loaf of hot, buttered bread, His stomach must have rumbled like a roaring lion. With only one thought, He could satisfy it. It's just a piece of bread, hardly a banquet. Who would find out anyway?

Can't we all identify with Jesus! How tempting that secret pint

---

3. The word *if* means "since"—"Since You are the Son of God."

of ice cream is to the deprived dieter alone on a Friday night. Or that hidden, heart-pounding affair to the love-starved person. Or that clandestine pornographic video to the one famished for intimacy. Or that shopping spree to the one with long-unmet needs.

What all these things are to us, the Devil's bread is to Jesus. But, clamping a firm hand over the muzzle of that growling beast within, He turns the offer down with a quote from Scripture:

> And Jesus answered him, "It is written, 'Man shall not live on bread alone.'" (v. 4)

The second assault: the temptation of power. Having failed to lure Christ with self-gratification, the Devil attempts to catch Him with the offer of power.

> And he led Him up and showed Him all the kingdoms of the world in a moment of time. And the Devil said to Him, "I will give You all this domain and its glory; for it has been handed over to me, and I give it to whomever I wish. Therefore if You worship before me, it shall all be Yours." (vv. 5–7)

"Why go to all the trouble and pain of winning the world when it can be handed to You on a silver platter?" Satan proposes. For Jesus, this would mean

> no suffering, no struggling, no sacrifice. Just one little compromise and this world and the crown of power that goes with it are all His.
>
> Then what's the problem? It bypasses the Cross. God wants His Son to rule over all the kingdoms of the world, not with a crown of power given by the enemy, but with a crown of thorns worn on a Cross.[4]

Anyone whose boss has offered cash, perks, and prestige if only a few principles would be set aside understands the seductiveness of this bait. The proposition is simple: just kowtow to the company or the art or the cause, and you can access the fast lane to success. But the problem is, whatever we worship, we must serve. Power has its price.

---

4. From the study guide *Christ at the Crossroads*, coauthored by Lee Hough, from the Bible-teaching ministry of Charles R. Swindoll (Anaheim, Calif.: Insight for Living, 1991), p. 5.

Jesus' price for power would be service to Satan. Once more, the Scriptures guide His response:

> And Jesus answered and said to him, "It is written, 'You shall worship the Lord your God and serve Him only.'" (v. 8)

The third test: the temptation of a public nature.[5] In an instant, Satan fires back with a third ploy and whisks Jesus to the heart of the city in which He will one day be crucified.

> And he led Him to Jerusalem and had Him stand on the pinnacle of the temple, and said to Him, "If You are the Son of God, throw Yourself down from here; for it is written,
> > 'He will give His angels charge concerning
> > > You to guard You,'
> and,
> > On their hands they will bear You up,
> > Lest You strike Your foot against a stone.'"
> (vv. 9–11)

Tired, hungry, beaten by the elements, Jesus needs a little ease right now. He must have longed for a break from the harsh demands of His calling. The jump would be spectacular, a real crowd-pleaser, an absolutely sensational—and easy—way to prove to all that He is the Son of God. So why not merely risk death with an assured nick-of-time rescue rather than actually die? What's wrong with a little pinnacle jumping now and then if it would demonstrate God's power?

The problem is presumption: flirting with danger to prove power; using sensational recklessness in order to show off divine deliverance. To do this draws attention to ourselves instead of to God and creates a circus atmosphere where greater and greater miracles are needed to hold the crowd. We easily become more interested in impressing others than in saving them.

How does Jesus respond? With Scripture again, and a desire to please His Father more than Satan or the crowds.

> And Jesus answered and said to him, "It is said, 'You shall not put the Lord your God to the test.'" (v. 12)

---

5. This section is adapted from Hough, *Christ at the Crossroads*, pp. 4–5.

If Jesus had flung Himself off the pinnacle, His life would most likely have been preserved, but not His mission. The test was to see whether He would draw all people to Himself by relying on the way of sensationalism or the way of the Cross. Jesus chose the Cross.

The Ending

No matter how smoothly the Devil paved the road, Jesus would not be enticed to abandon God's narrow, difficult way. Set in the concrete truth of Scripture, Jesus' resolve expressed itself with firm conviction: no, *no, NO!*

Fended off, Satan retreats—but only temporarily.

> And when the Devil had finished every temptation, he departed from Him until an opportune time. (v. 13)

To be sure, the Devil would be lurking in the shadows, crouching in the alleys. Watching. Waiting for Jesus' next vulnerable moment.

Some Practical Conclusions We Can Form

The Devil and his evil accomplices stalk us as well. Are we aware of their subterfuge? Are we ready for the battle? Here are three words of advice that Jesus' confrontation offers us.

When you are weak—expect a major assault. When we're weak—either physically and emotionally depleted like Jesus, immature in our faith, or drained after a grueling victory—we are ripe for Satan's morsels of temptation. So don't be taken by surprise; look for an attack.

When you resist—be ready for a different approach. Satan's temptations are eminently creative. If one doesn't work, he can always pull five more out of his hat. Keep a wary eye.

When he leaves—count on another attack. Defeat never discourages Satan from trying again and again. Reformer Martin Luther acknowledged the Devil's relentless character:

> The Devil takes no holiday; he never rests. If beaten, he rises again. If he cannot enter in front, he steals in at the rear. If he cannot enter in the rear, he breaks through the roof or enters by tunneling under the threshold. He labors until he is in. He uses great cunning and many a plan. When one miscarries, he

has another at hand and continues his attempts until he wins.[6]

Attack as he may, though, he need never win. For, as Luther also wrote in his ageless hymn "A Mighty Fortress Is Our God," Christ's victory is sure:

> The prince of darkness grim,
> We tremble not for him—
> His rage we can endure,
> For lo, his doom is sure:
> One little word shall fell him.[7]

 ## *Living Insights*

If you struggle with temptation in your private life, the solution may *not* be to pray more, read the Bible more, or "just say no." The answer may be simpler than that. Why don't you try cutting down on your privacy?

"But I have a *right* to my privacy," some may object. That's true, but remember what Jesus said:

> "And if your eye causes you to stumble, pluck it out, and throw it from you. It is better for you to enter life with one eye, than having two eyes, to be cast into the fiery hell." (Matt. 18:9)

The point is, if privacy is destroying your spiritual life, maybe it's not worth having so much of it lying around for temptation to fill.

Here are a few practical suggestions. Take the television out of your bedroom. Leave your door open at work. Travel with a partner. Or if you must travel alone, bring a family picture to keep you company. If you're home by yourself at night, ask someone to call you, or spend the night at a friend's house. When running errands, bring one of your children with you. If you're single, try to find a roommate.

---

6. Martin Luther, as quoted in *What Luther Says: An Anthology* ([St.] Louis, Mo.: Concordia Publishing House, 1959), vol. 1, p. 395.

7. Martin Luther, "A Mighty Fortress Is Our God," from *The Hymnal for Worship and Celebration* (Waco, Tex.: Word Music, 1986), no. 20.

What else can you do to make yourself less vulnerable?

_____

_____

_____

Living Insights

Rather than think of Jesus' temptations in terms of stones and bread, kingdoms and pinnacle jumping, we need to heed the deeper issues of satisfying our needs, hungering for power or wealth, and wanting overnight success. Let's get personal with each of these areas.

In what ways are you tempted to meet your own needs—physical or emotional—apart from God's will?

_____

_____

_____

How do you think Jesus' response to Satan in Luke 4:4 applies to your situation? See also Matthew 4:4.

_____

_____

_____

In what ways are you tempted to trade your heart for riches, fame, or power?

_____

_____

_____

How does Jesus' response to Satan in Luke 4:8 apply to your situation?

_____

_____

_____

In what ways are you tempted to take reckless risks to make your dreams come true?

_____

_____

_____

How would verse 12 apply to your situation?

_____

_____

_____

When you feel the allure of Satan's temptations in these three areas, remember the way Jesus' words cut through to the real issues at stake. When you can hold fast to the greater reality, the surface seducements will lose much of their power.

Chapter 11

FROM THE FRYING PAN INTO THE FIRE

Luke 4:14–30

Beginnings. The difficulties in them often take us by surprise, don't they? You dream of starting a new business, but the problems that were so easy to solve on paper don't work out so neatly on the ledger of reality. You marry your life's love, and suddenly your "I do" turns into "Now what do I do?"

The same is often true in the ministry. You joyfully anticipate serving the Lord and His people, but the joy is not exactly reflected on the bored faces of the congregation as you stumble through your first sermon.

When your head is spinning in those tough and tender times called "beginnings," remember what happened to Jesus at the start of His ministry. He went from the frying pan of the wilderness temptation to the fire of rejection in—of all places—His own hometown.

Back Home: Jesus' Experience in His Own Hometown

Had Nazareth not been Jesus' hometown, the people there might have received Him the way the rest of Galilee's citizens did.

Praise in Galilee

Upon leaving the wilderness of Judea,

> Jesus returned to Galilee in the power of the Spirit; and news about Him spread through all the surrounding district. And He began teaching in their synagogues and was praised by all. (Luke 4:14–15)

According to commentator William Barclay, Galilee was a fertile field in which new movements could easily spring up.

> The name itself means a circle and comes from the Hebrew word *Galil*. It was so called because it was encircled by non-Jewish nations. Because of that, new influences had always played upon Galilee and

92

it was the most forward-looking and least conservative part of Palestine. . . .

. . . Josephus says of them, "They were ever fond of innovations and by nature disposed to changes, and delighted in seditions. They were ever ready to follow a leader who would begin an insurrection."[1]

Although Jesus wasn't preaching rebellion, the people scrambled to hear His revolutionary words of new life. Yet human praise is fickle. One moment people can be applauding God's messengers; the next, they can be looking for stones to hurl at them. Jesus surely knew the balmy breeze of good favor would be short-lived, but who would have anticipated the sudden storm awaiting Him at Nazareth?

Rejected in Nazareth

Luke reminds us that this was the city "where He had been brought up" (v. 16). Ever since His return from Egypt when He was a preschooler, Nazareth had been His home (see Matt. 2:13–23). Down the street was His favorite climbing tree when He was a boy. Across the way was the synagogue His family faithfully attended. Without thinking, He could weave His way through the city's maze of alleys and passageways. He could greet folks by name as He passed them on the streets, and they knew His name. This was His town, and these were His people—the fabric that formed the tapestry of His life.

Yet when He returned, something seemed different about Jesus. He looked leaner and more determined. Then one day,

as was His custom, He entered the synagogue on the Sabbath, and stood up to read. (Luke 4:16b)

It would not have been unusual for Jesus to participate in the service this way. According to Barclay, the synagogue service included three parts:

(a) The worship part in which prayer was offered.

(b) The reading of the scriptures. . . .

(c) The teaching part. In the synagogue there was no professional ministry nor any one person to

1. William Barclay, *The Gospel of Luke*, rev. ed., The Daily Study Bible Series (Philadelphia, Pa.: Westminster Press, 1975), p. 45.

give the address; the president would invite any distinguished person present to speak and discussion and talk would follow.[2]

During the second part, Jesus stepped to the front. A hush of reverence for the Scriptures quieted the congregation as an attendant handed Jesus the scroll of Isaiah.

> And He opened the book, and found the place where it was written,
> "The Spirit of the Lord is upon Me,
> Because He anointed Me to preach the
>   gospel to the poor.
> He has sent Me to proclaim release to the
>   captives,
> And recovery of sight to the blind,
> To set free those who are downtrodden,
> To proclaim the favorable year of the Lord."
> And He closed the book, and gave it back to the attendant, and sat down; and the eyes of all in the synagogue were fixed upon Him. (vv. 17b–20)

Jesus didn't sit down because He was finished but because, in those days, teachers used to sit down to instruct the people. He had read from Isaiah 61, one of the prophet's famous messianic prophecies, and He was getting ready to expound it.

Up until now, according to Luke,

> all were speaking well of Him, and wondering at the gracious words which were falling from His lips; and they were saying, "Is this not Joseph's son?" (v. 22)

They were feeling proud of the hometown boy whom all of Galilee was buzzing about. But they weren't prepared for the bombshell Jesus was about to drop on them.

> And He began to say to them, "Today this Scripture has been fulfilled in your hearing." (v. 21)

With this stunning announcement, Jesus claimed to be the Person Isaiah had written about—the Messiah. But He would not fulfill all of Isaiah's prophecy right away, for, notice, He had only

2. Barclay, *The Gospel of Luke*, p. 46.

read the first line of Isaiah 61:2. If we read one line further, we find that God would send the Messiah

> To proclaim the favorable year of the Lord,
> And the day of vengeance of our God.

Eventually, He would deliver God's judgment; but now was the springtime of God's grace, which God was generously shedding abroad to all nations.

And Jesus wanted His family and friends to be among the first to know about His calling and mission.[3] Yet, as Mark records, "They took offense at Him" (Mark 6:3b). As their approving smiles turned to scornful scowls, He could see skepticism written all over their faces.

> And He said to them, "No doubt you will quote this proverb to Me, 'Physician, heal yourself! Whatever we heard was done at Capernaum, do here in your home town as well.'" (Luke 4:23)

Apparently, Jesus had performed many supernatural feats in Capernaum (see Mark 1:21–2:12). But, true to the rule He would follow throughout His ministry, Jesus refused to whip up a miracle just to impress stony-hearted skeptics.

While He had the floor, though, He had more to tell them. He quoted another proverb, then quickly followed up with two illustrations that cut His audience to the quick:

> And He said, "Truly I say to you, no prophet is welcome in his home town. But I say to you in truth, there were many widows in Israel in the days of Elijah, when the sky was shut up for three years and six months, when a great famine came over all the land; and yet Elijah was sent to none of them, but only to Zarephath, in the land of Sidon, to a woman who was a widow. And there were many lepers in Israel in the time of Elisha the prophet; and none of them was cleansed, but only Naaman the Syrian." (Luke 4:24–27)

Jesus didn't have to spell out what He was saying for them to

---

3. According to Mark's account, Jesus' brothers—James, Joses, Judas, and Simon—and His sisters were present (see Mark 6:1–3).

get the message. He was comparing Himself to the scorned prophets Elijah and Elisha, who reserved God's miracles for a couple of faithful Gentiles (see 1 Kings 17:8–24; 2 Kings 5:1–14). And this congregation was like the stiff-necked Israelites, whom God overlooked because of their unbelief.

With the sharp edge of Scripture, Jesus was slicing open and exposing the prejudices in their Jewish way of thinking. According to Barclay,

> The Jews were so sure that they were God's people that they utterly despised all others. They believed that "God had created the gentiles to be fuel for the fires of hell." And here was this young Jesus, whom they all knew, preaching as if the *gentiles* were specially favored by God.[4]

We can picture the crowd's brewing hostility as Jesus' neighbors and friends began shaking their heads and then their fists at Him: "He's no prophet—He's just a carpenter." "The gall of Jesus to preach to us that way!" "Gentile-lover! Throw Him out!"

> And all in the synagogue were filled with rage as they heard these things. (Luke 4:28)

And in a rush to judgment,

> they rose up and cast Him out of the city, and led Him to the brow of the hill on which their city had been built, in order to throw Him down the cliff. (v. 29)

No warning. No trial. No appeal. In a sudden wave of hate, the crowd crashed upon Jesus and swept Him away to His punishment: death. Amazingly, these were the same people who, moments ago, "were speaking well of Him"[5] (v. 22). Their extreme shift in attitude portends Jesus' last week of ministry, when the happy shouts of "Hosanna" would swiftly turn into the deadly cries of "Crucify Him!" Right from the beginning, the Messiah tasted the cruel rejection of the friends He came to save.

---

4. Barclay, *The Gospel of Luke*, p. 48.

5. In Lystra, Paul and Barnabas would also witness a crowd's violent shift in attitude. When Paul healed a lame man, the townsfolk at first wanted to deify them. But not long after, they almost stoned Paul to death (see Acts 14:8–19).

However, this was not His day to die. The One who would later walk across the surging waters of the Sea of Galilee now parted this violent Galilean crowd, and, "passing through their midst, He went His way" (v. 30).

Here Today: When the Tide Turns against You

Has the tide of public opinion ever turned against you? Perhaps, in a meeting at work, you looked around the table at your coworkers, and their hardened faces told you your reputation and job were on the line.

Perhaps, in your friend's eyes, you once saw an unsettling look of contempt or dislike that you'd never seen before. Maybe you saw it in the eyes of your brother or sister. Or your spouse, or your child. Rejection is a horrible experience. And if anyone knows what it feels like to be drenched in a sea of scorn, it's Jesus. From His example, here are three life preservers you can hang on to.

Number one: don't be surprised. When rejection hits us broadside, shock is a normal reaction: "I can't believe he did that," or, "I can't believe she said that." Being aware that rejection is not unusual will help us handle the shock without freezing up. One pastor, David Roper, has a realistic view of the issue:

> Criticism always comes when we least need it. . . .
> Furthermore, criticism seems to come when we least deserve it. . . .
> And then, criticism comes from people who are least qualified to give it. . . .
> And finally, criticism frequently comes in a form that is least helpful to us.[6]

Just knowing what the tide is like when it turns against you will go a long way toward keeping you calm during the storm.

Number two: don't give up. Jesus passed right through the crowd that intended to throw Him off the cliff. He didn't let one group of people keep Him from pressing on. The majority may be against you, but that doesn't mean you're wrong. Imagine if Jesus had quit that day on the cliff. Don't let opposition keep you from accomplishing what God wants you to do.

6. David Roper, *A Burden Shared* (Grand Rapids, Mich.: Discovery House Publishers, 1991), p. 59.

Number three: don't get sidetracked. After Jesus passed through the crowd, "He went on His way." Literally, He "kept on going." Their rejection couldn't roadblock Him. The path He had begun He intended to follow to the very end, in spite of the difficulties that would be waiting for Him along the way.

 ## Living Insights

While banners are flying, following Jesus feels comfortable. But things get complicated when stones of ridicule start whizzing past our ears and a Nazareth mob begins pressing us toward the cliff.

Jesus says,

> "Are you able to drink the cup that I drink?"
> (Mark 10:38, emphasis added)

To feel like strangers in our own families, to be left out of neighborhood get-togethers, to feel the sting of fiery anti-Christian editorials, to be made to look the fool—sometimes that's what it's like to be a Christian.

Jesus says,

> "If they persecuted Me, they will also persecute you."
> (John 15:20, emphasis added)

There seems to be a double standard today. We can talk all we want about Hitler, Darwin, or Buddha, but one mention of Jesus Christ and we're violating some law. It's infuriating!

Jesus says,

> "These things I have spoken to you, that you may be kept from stumbling." (John 16:1, emphasis added)

Are you feeling the world's tide turning against you because you're a follower of Christ? In what ways?

_____

_____

_____

Jesus spoke very directly about this in John 15:18–16:4. Take a few moments to read His words. How do they challenge you to apply the three concluding points of our lesson?

Don't be surprised: _____

_____

_____

Don't give up: _____

_____

_____

Don't get sidetracked: _____

_____

_____

Living Insights

The world's scorn is heavy enough to carry, but who can bear the rejection from one's own family? For those who must live under such a load, consider Jesus' family. From the scattered information in the gospels, we can piece together a portrait you may never have seen before.

Because Mary appears alone in the gospels after Jesus' childhood trip to Jerusalem, many scholars believe that Joseph died while Jesus was a youth. William Barclay surmises that, as a result,

> Jesus took upon himself the support of his mother and of his brothers and sisters; and only when they were old enough to fend for themselves did he go forth.[7]

As a young man with heavy responsibilities, Jesus probably found work where He could get it, following in Joseph's footsteps as one of the town carpenters. According to Barclay, the Greek word for *carpenter, tektōn,* has a broad meaning.

> It means a *craftsman.* . . . In the old days, and still to-day in many places, there could be found in little

7. William Barclay, *The Gospel of Mark,* rev. ed., The Daily Study Bible Series (Philadelphia, Pa.: Westminster Press, 1975), pp. 139–40.

towns and villages a craftsman who would build you anything from a chicken coop to a house; the kind of man who could build a wall, mend a roof, repair a gate; the craftsman, the handy-man, who with few or no instruments and with the simplest tools could turn his hand to any job. That is what Jesus was like.[8]

If Jesus lived today, we can imagine Him with a tanned face and rough hands, wearing coveralls and work boots, driving a pickup truck loaded with ladders and buckets.

No wonder the people looked at Him slantwise when He came into town acting like a rabbi. His kinfolk thought He had lost His senses. In their minds, Jesus was a fool to abandon a secure business to become a traveling preacher and a lunatic to denounce the religious elite and claim to be the Messiah.

Jesus had become an embarrassment to the family.

Mark says that early in His ministry, they tried to quietly "take custody of Him," perhaps to save Him from Himself (Mark 3:21). Whatever compassion they may have felt toward Jesus, though, turned to rage that day in Nazareth. His brothers may even have been part of the mob that tried to shove Him over the cliff.

Surely, when Jesus passed through the crowd, He walked away from His family and friends with a heavy heart.

Perhaps rejection from your family has burdened your spirit too. In the following space, unload your sorrow to the One who understands how you feel. And take a moment to read His familiar counsel in Matthew 11:28–30. It just might take on a wonderful new meaning for you.

_____

_____

_____

_____

_____

_____

_____

8. Barclay, *The Gospel of Mark*, p. 138.

Chapter 12

MINISTRY AT THE GRASSROOTS LEVEL

Luke 4:31–44

Writing pastor to pastor, David Roper reveals how a little sign on the preacher's side of an old church pulpit shook him to the core of his calling.

> "What in the world are you doing to these people?" the plaque on the old pulpit read. I couldn't get my eyes or my mind off of it. It's one of the best questions I've ever been asked!
>
> What was I doing to the people in my care? Did I have any objective for them? Was there some ultimate purpose, or was I simply being carried along, doing what busy workers do—presiding over solemn traditions, herding sacred cows, doing the usual? What in the world was I doing to these people? I wasn't sure I knew.[1]

Swirling along in a liturgical current, it's easy to lose our sense of direction. What is our purpose for ministry? Fortunately, the apostle Paul hands us a credo we can all hang on to:

> And we proclaim Him, admonishing every man and teaching every man with all wisdom, that we may present every man complete in Christ. And for this purpose also I labor, striving according to His power, which mightily works within me. (Col. 1:28–29)

Our message is Christ. Our methods are admonishing and teaching with insightful wisdom. And our purpose is to help God's people become "complete in Christ." David Roper crystallizes what this means:

> Evangelizing, discipling, counseling, advising, organizing, encouraging, and socializing exist for one

1. David Roper, *A Burden Shared* (Grand Rapids, Mich.: Discovery House Publishers, 1991), p. 49.

101

purpose and one purpose alone: *To encourage women and men to become grown-up disciples of Christ.* There's simply no other reason for doing what we do. (emphasis added)[2]

What can we do to set our bearings toward this goal of maturity? Based on a few observations of churches today, four objectives rise as beacons to guide our way.

Some General Observations on Ministry Today

Noticing what's missing in a church can help us perceive what needs the most attention. The following essentials are often conspicuous by their absence in many ministries.

First, *an emphasis on solid, biblical teaching.* Winsome speakers may attract swarms of people with their spiritual confections, but people will starve spiritually unless they are fed the meaty truth of God's Word (compare Amos 8:11–13).

Second, *a dependence on the power of God.* When mountains need moving, people tend to focus on human talent to do the job and exalt their dynamic leaders. Ministries that are truly effective, though, exalt Christ and His life-changing power.

Third, *the active presence of compassion.* To grow, we must balance our intake of teaching with energetic compassion—reaching out to the troubled, the divorced, the addicted, the struggling, the sick.

Fourth, *a priority on quietness before God.* Dotting the horizon of each tumultuous week should be islands of refuge where we can commune with the Lord in prayer, soul-searching confession, and meditation on His Word. We can't cultivate godliness without time with God.

Like a light in a harbor, Jesus' perfect model guides us toward each of these objectives, as we shall see in our passage.

Specific, Careful Analysis of Christ's Agenda

If that little pulpit plaque had caught Jesus' eye, He would have known exactly what He was "doing to these people."

Teaching the Truth

First, He was teaching them—and notice how they responded.

2. Roper, *A Burden Shared*, p. 50.

> And He came down to Capernaum, a city of Galilee. And He was teaching them on the Sabbath; and they were amazed at His teaching, for His message was with authority. (Luke 4:31–32)

The tense of Luke's verb suggests that Jesus "kept on teaching them." He was *consistent*. He didn't parade into town with a greatest-show-on-earth message, then pack it up and take it to the next village. He stayed around so the people could learn and grow.

Also, He was *clear*. Luke says those who heard Him "were amazed at His teaching." When God's Word speaks directly to us, we can't help but be astounded. It's not verbal gymnastics and clever illustrations that set us on the edge of our seats. What amazes us is clearly seeing how the grand truths of the universe fit into our lives today.

Finally, Jesus taught with *authority*. And Mark adds, "not as the scribes" (Mark 1:22). The scribes' job was to slice the Law into detailed rules and regulations based on tradition. According to William Barclay, a scribe would always begin his lecture like this:

> "There is a teaching that . . ." and would then quote all his authorities. If he made a statement he would buttress it with this, that and the next quotation from the great legal masters of the past. The last thing he ever gave was an independent judgment. How different was Jesus! When he spoke, he spoke as if he needed no authority beyond himself. He spoke with utter independence. He cited no authorities and quoted no experts. He spoke with the finality of the voice of God. To the people it was like a breeze from heaven to hear someone speak like that.[3]

Although we're not Jesus, we can teach authoritatively if we seek to build up our reservoir of biblical knowledge, develop an intimate relationship with the Author of the Bible, share the insights He gives with originality of thought and presentation, and deliver the message with confidence and wholehearted passion.

3. William Barclay, *The Gospel of Mark*, rev. ed., The Daily Study Bible Series (Philadelphia, Pa.: Westminster Press, 1975), p. 32.

Rebuking the Demons

Among those who were stunned by Jesus' authority and power were some of Satan's emissaries.

> And there was a man in the synagogue possessed by the spirit of an unclean demon, and he cried out with a loud voice, "Ha! What do we have to do with You, Jesus of Nazareth? Have You come to destroy us? I know who You are—the Holy One of God!" And Jesus rebuked him, saying, "Be quiet and come out of him!" And when the demon had thrown him down in their midst, he came out of him without doing him any harm. And amazement came upon them all, and they began discussing with one another saying, "What is this message? For with authority and power He commands the unclean spirits, and they come out." And the report about Him was getting out into every locality in the surrounding district. . . .
>
> . . . And demons also were coming out of many, crying out and saying, "You are the Son of God!" And rebuking them, He would not allow them to speak, because they knew Him to be the Christ. (Luke 4:33–37, 41)

No one left the synagogue that day complaining that the service was dull! Jesus' shocking encounters with the forces of darkness illustrate several truths about demons.

- They are able to possess people (v. 33).

- They represent the "unclean" (vv. 33, 36b)—the sinful, the evil. Their delight is to pollute and destroy people with all filthiness.

- They use human bodies to carry out their wicked schemes (v. 33).

- They know who Jesus is (vv. 34, 41).

- They respond in obedience to the authority of the Lord Jesus Christ (vv. 35, 41). It's in His name that we defend ourselves against them.

- They depart when told to do so, but often there is a struggle

(v. 35). So we mustn't play around in the demonic realm or give them an opportunity to gain a foothold.

Stories like this one about demons possessing people always raise the hair on the back of our necks. But we needn't run scared of the enemy. The same blood of Christ that cleanses our hearts from sin has also vanquished the Evil One. We can call upon His name for protection from the forces of darkness whenever we need it.

On the other hand, we don't want to go overboard and look for demons in everything—if we have a flat tire on the way to church, we probably don't need to rebuke the demon of road hazards! The Holy Spirit will sensitize our spirits to the real presence of a demon. And if you do encounter one, don't confront it alone. Find another believer to help support your faith, which is a necessity when dealing with demons (see Matt. 17:14–21).

Healing the Sick

Many times in ministering to people, we won't need to teach or clash with evil powers; we'll simply need to reflect the Lord's compassion.

> And He arose and left the synagogue, and entered Simon's home. Now Simon's mother-in-law was suffering from a high fever; and they made request of Him on her behalf. And standing over her, He rebuked the fever, and it left her; and she immediately arose and waited on them. (Luke 4:38–39)

Sometimes God will heal a person instantly. Other times, healing —whether physical or emotional—comes slowly and arduously. We, as Christ's caregivers, must show patience and compassion. There may be many battles still to fight, but no army abandons its wounded. A ministry that truly reflects Christ's heart makes room for the suffering. And as it does, people will come from all over to experience Jesus' healing love—just as they did when He was on earth:

> And while the sun was setting, all who had any sick with various diseases brought them to Him; and laying His hands on every one of them, He was healing them. (v. 40)

The sun must have lingered as long as it could that day, watching in wonder as its own Creator touched the diseased, the lame, and the castaways of the earth. And He was still touching them when its light finally retreated into the night.

Clearing the Vision

"And when day came, He departed and went to a lonely place" (v. 42a). As much as Jesus' heart broke for the needs of the people, He needed time away to clarify His vision, pray, and draw strength from the Father. And so do we.

Yet problems demand attention, the hurting cry for comfort, the weak need counsel. The voice of panic says, *There's so much to do, you don't have time to pray.* The voice of guilt says, *You said you cared for these people. How can you take time for yourself?*

Jesus, though, refused to let panic or guilt set His agenda. Neither did He let the people deter Him from His Father's path:

> And the multitudes were searching for Him, and came to Him, and tried to keep Him from going away from them. But He said to them, "I must preach the kingdom of God to the other cities also, for I was sent for this purpose."
>
> And He kept on preaching in the synagogues of Judea. (vv. 42b–44)

Jesus' example illustrates three principles worth taping to our calendars:

- Time alone, away from the demands of ministry, is neither selfish nor unimportant.

- Others may not always understand our need to get away. People won't set our boundaries for us; we must set them for ourselves.

- We must guard against a limited scope of ministry. The Lord may lead us to other places, and we must go.

Vital Reminders from the Master's Model

You may not be a preacher standing behind a pulpit every Sunday, but even so you are a minister. You minister to people every day as you respond to their problems or guide them into a deeper understanding of God. Teach them God's truth, not human opinion. Depend on God's power when dealing with the enemy. Touch people with Christ's compassion. And stay balanced by taking time off. That's ministry at the grassroots level.

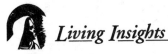

Author Lee Hough lovingly recalls his mother's compassionate touch when he was a boy:

> I remember the times when I was sick. Mom would untie my Buster Browns and gently coax me to the couch. Then the ritual began that I'll never forget: pillows fluffed up and carefully positioned, a comfortable quilt snugly wrapped, a cool washcloth, and the thing I remember best—the tender touch of Mom's hand. Just the warm press of her slender hand on my forehead reassured me that everything would be all right. It spoke the healing truths that I was loved, that I belonged, that somebody cared if I was sick—someone bigger, who understood how to call forth the curative powers of mysterious medicines and ancient home remedies. All that in a touch, a tender, healing hand.[4]

Yes. Yes—that must be how Jesus touched the suffering people who came to Him. He felt compassion toward the sick and dying, like a mother toward her child; not pity, like a king toward his subjects.

"Compassion and pity are very different," writes Paul Roud, author of *Making Miracles*.

> Whereas compassion reflects the yearning of the heart to merge and take on some of the suffering, pity is a controlled set of thoughts designed to assure separateness. Compassion is the spontaneous response of love; pity, the involuntary reflex of fear.[5]

Do you know someone who is suffering? A relative? A neighbor? A coworker? Pitying them, remaining separate, is not Jesus' way. But showing compassion is. Compassion has its risks. It means taking on some of their pain . . . it means touching them.

---

4. From the study guide *You and Your Child*, coauthored by Lee Hough, from the Bible-teaching ministry of Charles R. Swindoll (Anaheim, Calif.: Insight for Living, 1993), p. 77.

5. Paul C. Roud, *Making Miracles*, as quoted in *Reader's Digest*, September 1994, p. 162.

Who is that person, and how can you model Christ's compassion toward him or her this week?

_____

_____

_____

_____

Living Insights STUDY TWO

Have you ever seen one of those blank books? They have beautiful covers but the pages are empty. Whoever came up with that gem is a genius! You can sell thousands of those and never pay a cent in royalties.

The idea, of course, is for you to write your own story. Sort of a do-it-yourself novel. Well, this is going to be a do-it-yourself Living Insight! Below is some space to write your thoughts. You may need a little help to get started, so . . .

Imagine yourself in a lonely place, just you and Jesus. Far away from the crowds, you have His full attention. The sun is just peeking above a Galilean hill, casting the morning in an amber glow. This is your quiet time with Him.

Look into His eyes. What do you admire about Him? Is there something bothering you that you need to talk about? Are there some doubts needling you? Some pains? Some worries? Listen to His Spirit within you. Let Him show you *His* compassion.

_____

_____

_____

_____

_____

_____

_____

_____

Chapter 13

WHAT IT'S LIKE TO FISH WITH JESUS

Luke 5:1–11

It had been a long night on the Sea of Galilee—one that could make a fisherman curse his trade. Under a pallid moon, Simon and his crew had fed their nets into the inky water, stringing them into a circle hundreds of feet around. The light from their torches was supposed to attract the fish into their trap, but when they drew in the bottom lines, pulling with their thick hands and strong sailor's backs, the pulling was strangely easy. Straining their eyes, they searched the black water for any splash of life. But the sea was tauntingly still that night, and the nets came up empty.

Hour after hour, the men repeated the ritual, first here, then there, then across the bay. Still nothing. The night was turning misty gray as the shivering men pulled in the nets for the last time and rowed for home.

We sometimes feel like those discouraged fishermen when our ingenuity proves fruitless and our best efforts come up empty. But it's in those times of weakness that God often surprises us with the bright rays of His power. As a powerless Paul once wrote:

> And He has said to me, "My grace is sufficient for you, for power is perfected in weakness." Most gladly, therefore, I will rather boast about my weaknesses, that the power of Christ may dwell in me. Therefore I am well content with weaknesses, with insults, with distresses, with persecutions, with difficulties, for Christ's sake; for when I am weak, then I am strong. (2 Cor. 12:9–10)

In their moment of weakness, the weary fishermen had a surprise awaiting them. Jesus was coming to the shores that day to shine His light into their gloomy Galilee dawn.

This chapter is adapted from "Boats, Nets, Fish, and Faith," from the study guide *Living Above the Level of Mediocrity*, rev. ed., coauthored by Ken Gire, from the Bible-teaching ministry of Charles R. Swindoll (Anaheim, Calif.: Insight for Living, 1994).

The Setting

For weeks, Jesus had been preaching in the area, healing the sick and casting out demons. People had been crowding Him from all sides, eager for Him to spill out more food from heaven. It was all the Teacher could do to find a few spare moments for Himself. But they would seek Him anyway. The news of His whereabouts would spread, and the crowds would come running.

On this particular day, they cornered Him on the sandy banks of the Sea of Galilee. Yearning to feed all the people, not just the ones in front, He looked around for a way to address the whole crowd.

> Now it came about that while the multitude were pressing around Him and listening to the word of God, He was standing by the lake of Gennesaret;[1] and He saw two boats lying at the edge of the lake; but the fishermen had gotten out of them, and were washing their nets. And He got into one of the boats, which was Simon's, and asked him to put out a little way from the land. And He sat down and began teaching the multitudes from the boat. (Luke 5:1–3)

The Catch

When Jesus asked Simon to turn his boat into a floating platform a little way from shore, Simon and his fishing partners consented. In doing so, they became a captive audience—literally. At the conclusion of His sermon, Jesus planned an object lesson so vivid that the fishermen would never forget its significance.

> And when He had finished speaking, He said to Simon, "Put out into the deep water and let down your nets for a catch." (v. 4)

Simon Peter must have thought Jesus was venturing into waters over His head. After all, fishing was Peter's business, his life; and Jesus was . . . well . . . a preacher.

---

1. "The famous sheet of water in Galilee is called by three names—the Sea of Galilee, the Sea of Tiberias and the Lake of Gennesaret. It is thirteen miles long by eight miles wide. It lies in a dip in the earth's surface and is 680 feet below sea level." William Barclay, *The Gospel of Luke*, rev. ed., The Daily Study Bible Series (Philadelphia, Pa.: Westminster Press, 1975), p. 56.

> And Simon answered and said, "Master, we worked
> hard all night and caught nothing, but at Your bid-
> ding I will let down the nets." (v. 5)

Peter knew the best fishing spots and the most favorable conditions for making a catch, but out of respect for the one he knew
as "Master," he did as he was asked.[2] Little did he realize the extent
of the Master's domain!

> And when they had done this, they enclosed a great
> quantity of fish; and their nets began to break; and
> they signaled to their partners in the other boat, for
> them to come and help them. And they came, and
> filled both of the boats, so that they began to sink.
> (vv. 6–7)

Peter suddenly realized that he stood in the presence of deity.
This Jesus was not simply a preacher with the power to heal; He
was Lord of the sea and the fish, of every realm, of the entire
universe! The words that followed this recognition are reminiscent of
the expressions of Abraham, Job, and Isaiah when they, too, stood
before the awesome presence of God (see Gen. 18:27; Job 42:5–6;
Isa. 6:5).

> But when Simon Peter saw that, he fell down at Jesus'
> feet, saying, "Depart from me, for I am a sinful man,
> O Lord!" For amazement had seized him and all his
> companions because of the catch of fish which they
> had taken; and so also James and John, sons of Zebe-
> dee, who were partners with Simon. (Luke 5:8–10a)

When the Lord takes control of a situation, it amazes everybody
how He can use our weakness for His glory. The thousands of
flopping fish illustrated Christ's great power. But they also depicted
a much larger catch that Jesus had in mind for these men.

The Objective

As the boats filled with fish, the fishermen's hearts filled with

---

2. The Greek word for *master* means "overseer, director, master, implying authority and used
here of one who has the right to give orders." Fritz Rienecker, *A Linguistic Key to the Greek
New Testament*, ed. Cleon L. Rogers, Jr. (Grand Rapids, Mich.: Zondervan Publishing House,
Regency Reference Library, 1980), p. 150.

awe. Speechless, they were now primed for what was to prove a life-changing announcement.

> And Jesus said to Simon, "Do not fear, from now on you will be catching men."[3] (v. 10b)

Jesus wasn't giving these rough, seasoned fishermen a lesson in fishing; His objective was to change their profession—by changing their lives. And change their lives He did.

> And when they had brought their boats to land, they left everything and followed Him. (v. 11)

Everything? The biggest catch these fishermen had ever made? Their boats? Their nets? Their livelihood? Everything. Without an over-the-shoulder glance. Without even a second thought (compare 9:62).

The Application

The lessons we can apply revolve around three pairs of verbs: *chooses* and *uses*, *moves* and *proves*, *conceals* and *reveals*.

1. *Jesus chooses not to minister to others all alone.* Jesus deliberately involves others in His work. He could have rowed the boat and cast the net Himself, but instead He included the disciples. He didn't want a boatload of spectators; He wanted workers accustomed to rolling up their sleeves, feeling the tug on the nets, and sweating side by side. When He recruited them, He didn't say, "Follow Me, and watch Me catch men." He announced, "*You* will be catching men."

2. *Jesus uses the familiar to do the incredible.* Boats, nets, fish— all quite routine for the fishermen. It's in the grind of the everyday world that God reveals His glory. What is your world? What is familiar to you? What is your profession or craft? You will be amazed at how the Lord can use you in your sphere of influence to do an incredible work for Him.

3. *Jesus moves from the safety of the seen to make us trust Him through the risks of the unseen.* Christ took the fishermen past the shallows and into the deep water to cast their nets. If God is calling you to launch a similar boat of faith and you're teetering on the

---

3. The Greek word *zōgreō* means to "catch alive." It appears only one other time in the New Testament, in 2 Timothy 2:26, describing a person "held captive" by the Devil "to do his will." That snaring of humanity will continue until God's people cast their nets and bring those people into the boat of salvation.

brink of that decision, don't be afraid to venture out. The Master of the wind and waves is in the boat with you.

4. *Jesus proves the potential by breaking our nets and filling our boats.* The catch of fish in Luke 5 perfectly illustrates God's ability to "do exceeding abundantly beyond all that we ask or think" (Eph. 3:20). These fishermen had never had such a catch—a catch so great that their nets began to break and their boats began to sink. If you will lay your skepticism aside just long enough to lower your nets, God will amaze you with His ability to fill them.

5. *Jesus conceals His surprises until we follow His leading.* It seemed business as usual for the fishermen to launch their boats and head toward the place where they would cast their nets. The water didn't glow. There wasn't a halo around the boat. . . . The oars were just as heavy as ever. The surprise didn't come until they lowered their nets. That was when Peter realized Jesus was more than just a powerful preacher—He was Lord.

When was the last time God surprised you? When was the last time you took Him at His word and He almost broke your mental nets with a display of His lordship over this world . . . over circumstances . . . over people?

6. *Jesus reveals His objective to those who are willing to relinquish their security.* Only after the disciples gave up the safety of the shore did Jesus finally reveal His purpose: "From now on you will be catching men" (Luke 5:10b). If the Lord is ever going to perfect His power through our weakness, we can't be landlubbers. We have to launch out into sometimes deep waters . . . and that means more than dangling our ankles in the shallows. Fear will bid us, like a seductive siren, to rest secure on the shore. But if we want to fish with Jesus, we're going to have to set sail into the waters of faith.

 Living Insights STUDY ONE

As amazing as the great catch of fish is, the real splash in this story occurs within the deep waters of Simon's heart. Luke records two sentences uttered by Simon that reveal the miracle. Recall what he first said when Jesus commanded him to take the boat out again:

> "Master, we worked hard all night and caught nothing, but at Your bidding I will let down the nets." (Luke 5:5)

Simon Peter obeys out of duty—as a seaman obeys his skipper. But what attitude is he harboring inside?

_____

_____

_____

Do you ever express that same attitude toward the Lord? If so, can you pinpoint why? Do the immediate problems seem overwhelming? Have you already tried and failed? Are you afraid of being disappointed?

_____

_____

_____

It's understandable if sometimes we can muster only enough faith to obey Christ as Master. But He wants us to know Him as Lord—as Someone we can trust with our whole hearts. Do you remember Simon's response when the boats started sinking from so many fish?

> He fell down at Jesus' feet, saying, "Depart from me, for I am a sinful man, O Lord!" (v. 8)

Describe Simon's change of heart.

_____

_____

_____

Could the Lord be working a similar miracle within you? In his book _Intimate Moments with the Savior_, author Ken Gire expresses his heart's desire in a prayer. Is it your heart's desire too? If so, read it to the Lord as if the words were your own.

> Call me, Lord, out from a shallow faith near the shore, which requires no risks and offers no rewards. Call me to a deeper commitment to you.
> And when you call, grant that I would be quick in my boat, swift to my oars, and fast with my nets.

And I pray, grant me the eyes to see who it is who labors by my side—an awesome and almighty God.

Take me to a place where I have worked hard by my own strength and yet ended up with empty nets. Take me there to show me the depths of your dominion and the net-breaking fullness of your power.

Keep me ever aware that you are Lord. And ever aware that I am a sinful person. And in that knowledge keep me ever on my knees before you.

At your bidding, O Master, I will let down my nets. And at your bidding I will leave them forever behind. For what you have to offer is infinitely more than all the seas of this world ever could.[4]

 Living Insights

About four years after fishing with Jesus, Simon Peter would be waist deep in another catch, not of fish but of people. Luke tells us that when he threw out the net of the gospel on the day of Pentecost, he gathered in three thousands souls (see Acts 2:38–41).

Had Peter refused to row into deep waters, he would never have seen the miracle Jesus had in store for him beneath the surface of the sea. And had he refused to leave the fish and follow Jesus, he may never have seen the miracle Jesus had waiting for him on Pentecost.

Consider once again these statements from the chapter:

- Jesus conceals His surprises until we follow His leading.

- Jesus reveals His objective to those who are willing to relinquish their security.

Is there something specific Jesus could be asking you to do? What deep waters could He be calling you into?

_____

_____

Are you going to go?

4. Ken Gire, *Intimate Moments with the Savior* (Grand Rapids, Mich.: Zondervan Publishing House, 1989), p. 33.

Chapter 14

GREAT DEEDS, STRONG FAITH . . . BIG GOD

Luke 5:12–26

Theologian A. W. Tozer launched the first chapter of his epochal book *The Knowledge of the Holy* with this insight:

> What comes into our minds when we think about God is the most important thing about us.[1]

If our God is bigger than the star-strewn universe, then the problems strewn throughout our lives won't seem so overwhelming. On the other hand, if we project God onto a small screen in our minds, life's obstacles can take on giant proportions. We will tremble before them. We will act first and pray later. The twin fists of panic and worry will pummel our hearts with fear.

In his book *Your God Is Too Small*, British pastor J. B. Phillips challenges us not to settle for such a meager concept of God.

> Let us fling wide the doors and windows of our minds and make some attempt to appreciate the "size" of God. He must not be limited to religious matters or even to the "religious" interpretation of life. He must not be confined to one particular section of time nor must we imagine Him as the local god of this planet or even only of the universe that astronomical survey has so far discovered. It is not, of course, physical size that we are trying to establish in our minds. . . . It is rather to see the immensely broad sweep of the Creator's activity, the astonishing complexity of His mental processes which science laboriously uncovers, the vast sea of what we can only call "God" in a small corner of which man lives and moves and has his being.[2]

---

1. A. W. Tozer, *The Knowledge of the Holy* (New York, N.Y.: Harper and Row, Publishers, 1961), p. 9.

2. J. B. Phillips, *Your God Is Too Small* (New York, N.Y.: The Macmillan Co., 1961), pp. 61–62.

How can we begin to absorb "the vast sea" that God is? Understanding our limitations, God poured Himself into the cup of Jesus Christ, and He offers Him to us to come and drink.

Two Brief Glimpses of God's Incredible Presence

According to Hebrews, Jesus "is the radiance of [God's] glory and the exact representation of His nature" (1:3). When Philip asked Jesus, "Lord, show us the Father," He responded, "He who has seen Me has seen the Father" (John 14:8–9).

As Jesus crosses paths with two needy souls in our passage, we'll sense the bigness of deity's presence . . . and find in Him a Person we can trust.

A Leper Cleansed

Jesus first lets deity descend on the lonely life of a leper.

> And it came about that while He was in one of the cities, behold, there was a man full of leprosy; and when he saw Jesus, he fell on his face and implored Him, saying, "Lord, if You are willing, You can make me clean." (Luke 5:12)

Leprosy, according to William Barclay, proliferated in two forms in Palestine.

> There was one which was rather like a very bad skin disease, and it was the less serious of the two. There was one in which the disease, starting from a small spot, ate away the flesh until the wretched sufferer was left with only the stump of a hand or a leg. It was literally a living death.[3]

Surely the worse of the two kinds afflicted this man, for Dr. Luke says he was *full* of leprosy. Compounding the agony of the disfiguring disease were the social stigmas attached to it, burning like salt in his open wounds. Barclay says,

> The most terrible thing about it was the isolation it brought. The leper was to cry "Unclean! Unclean!"

3. William Barclay, *The Gospel of Luke*, rev. ed., The Daily Study Bible Series (Philadelphia, Pa.: Westminster Press, 1975), p. 58.

wherever he went; he was to dwell alone; "in a habitation outside the camp" (*Leviticus* 13:45, 46). He was banished from the society of men and exiled from home. The result was, and still is, that the psychological consequences of leprosy were as serious as the physical.[4]

Death's tentacles had grabbed ahold of his heart as well as his body. When he walked down the street, people kept their distance. Mothers covered their children's eyes. Doctors shook their heads. No one dared step too close to an open grave.

When the leper saw Jesus, he knew this Man held life in His hands. In a desperate lunge of faith, he did the unthinkable—he drew near. Falling in the dust before Jesus, he spoke in a trembling voice: "Lord, if you are willing. . . ." The Greek construction suggests that maybe the Lord would be willing, but maybe not—and if He wasn't, who would fault Him? This was a leper at His feet.

"You can make me clean," the man says, as a simple matter of fact. There's no presumption on his part. No bargaining. No expectations. Just a glint of faith, and that was enough to crack open the floodgates of Jesus' compassion.

> And He stretched out His hand, and touched him, saying, "I am willing; be cleansed." And immediately the leprosy left him. (v. 13)

Did you see what Jesus did? He reached out and *touched* the leper. He could have cleansed him from a distance, as a doctor might prescribe a remedy over the phone. But Jesus came to touch the untouchables, to hold the Father's cup of love to the parched lips of humanity.

The leper drank deeply as the Master reached out His hand. How long had it been since he had felt the tender touch of another human being? How long since he had belonged and been welcome among others?

Then, in the moment it takes to wash dirt from your arm, the sores fell away. This was no gradual getting better; Jesus didn't patronize the leper with a lot of empty promises. The healing was immediate—an unmistakable release of heaven's power. As the leper stroked his smooth, uncrusted skin, he must have jumped for

4. Barclay, *The Gospel of Luke*, p. 58.

freedom's joy. But Jesus put a finger to his lips.

> And He ordered him to tell no one, "But go and show yourself to the priest, and make an offering for your cleansing, just as Moses commanded, for a testimony to them." But the news about Him was spreading even farther, and great multitudes were gathering to hear Him and to be healed of their sicknesses. (vv. 14–15)

How refreshing Jesus' action is! Instead of promoting Himself as a wonder-worker, He promoted respect for God's laws. Yet, with human nature being what it is, how could the people keep quiet about a miracle like this? The news kept spreading farther and farther, and "great multitudes were gathering to hear Him and to be healed of their sicknesses" (v. 15).

In the midst of the fervor, Luke says that Jesus "would often slip away to the wilderness and pray" (v. 16). Today's promoters would cringe to see Him retreat from the public eye—He should stay on the trail, pumping hands, kissing babies, and selling His image. But Jesus wasn't out to win popularity. He was serving His Father, who was big enough to handle the ministry while Jesus found the refreshment He needed.

A Paralytic Healed

Luke next sets a new scene: a stuffy room, bulging with people. Jesus had become a lightning rod, attracting bolts of interest from all over Palestine. But an energy of a different sort crackled in the air on this day. God, who fashions the fires of electricity, was funneling His immense power into His Son.

> And it came about one day that He was teaching; and there were some Pharisees and teachers of the law sitting there, who had come from every village of Galilee and Judea and from Jerusalem; and the power of the Lord was present for Him to perform healing. And behold, some men were carrying on a bed a man who was paralyzed; and they were trying to bring him in, and to set him down in front of Him. And not finding any way to bring him in because of the crowd, they went up on the roof and let him down through the tiles with his stretcher,

119

right in the center, in front of Jesus. And seeing their faith, He said, "Friend, your sins are forgiven you. . . . I say to you, rise, and take up your stretcher and go home." And at once he rose up before them, and took up what he had been lying on, and went home, glorifying God. And they were all seized with astonishment and began glorifying God; and they were filled with fear, saying, "We have seen remarkable things today." (vv. 17–21, 24b–26)

Many powerful elements charged the crowded room: the momentum from Jesus' growing ministry, the enthusiasm from the pressing crowd, the reckless faith of the paralytic and his friends. But nothing surmounted the power of God's presence. His strength healed the man, His grace forgave his sins, and in the end, His name was glorified.

Yet a small-minded group, with a sweep of their self-righteous robes, had pushed God aside.

And the scribes and the Pharisees began to reason, saying, "Who is this man who speaks blasphemies? Who can forgive sins, but God alone?" (v. 21)

With these caustic accusations, Luke introduces us to the infamous antagonists in his gospel drama. This is our first look at these self-proclaimed guardians of right and wrong. For them, William Barclay tells us, rule-keeping equaled righteousness.

A certain section of the Jews . . . desired not great principles but a rule to cover every conceivable situation. From the Ten Commandments they proceeded to develop and elaborate these rules. . . .

The commandment says, "Remember the Sabbath day to keep it holy"; and then goes on to lay it down that on the Sabbath no work must be done (*Exodus* 20:8–11). But the Jews asked, "What is work?" and went on to define it under thirty-nine different heads which they called "Fathers of Work." Even that was not enough. Each of these heads was greatly sub-divided. Thousands of rules and regulations began to emerge. These were called the Oral

Law, and they began to be set even above the Ten Commandments.[5]

The Pharisees spent their lives binding themselves and others with their fetters of legalism, so much so that a spiritual paralysis had set in. Guilt and fear had numbed the Jewish heart toward God—rendering it as dead as the limbs of the man who had laid pitifully on the mat before Jesus. Seeing him there and hearing the Pharisees' whispers behind His back, Jesus had said:

"Why are you reasoning in your hearts? Which is easier, to say, 'Your sins have been forgiven you,' or to say, 'Rise and walk'? But in order that you may know that the Son of Man has authority on earth to forgive sins,"—

and, as we saw earlier, Jesus broke the pharisaical bonds and brought healing and freedom to the paralyzed man (Luke 5:22–24).

Like the Pharisees, when our spiritual lists get longer and our negative mentality gets deeper, our God gets smaller. We resist His acting outside our realm of understanding. We close our minds to Him and shut our hearts. Thank the Lord, though, for those times when He breaks out of our "God boxes" and gives us a glimpse of His glory.

Three Ways to Sustain a "Big God" Mind-set

Because we typically have trouble seeing beyond our limited sphere, developing a "big God" mind-set requires some effort. Try exercising your spirit using these three stretching reminders.

First, *when God is willing, remember there is no area which He cannot touch.* We may carefully mark off what He can and cannot do, but just the time we get Him figured out, He surprises us. So don't draw lines around your needs; God has a way of touching us with His power through avenues we never imagined.

Second, *because God is powerful, remember that there is no limit to His ability.* Perhaps you've given up trying to help a relative or friend who has wandered from God's protective fold. There may be no hope from your perspective, but remember God's cleansing, life-changing power.

5. Barclay, *The Gospel of Luke*, p. 60.

Third, *since God is to be glorified, remember that there is no reason for our seeking the credit.* Or for needing to defend Him either. Whether we're sick or hurting or victims of unfairness and cruelty, because God is big, our tears are not the final chapter. Something far more glorious is coming, which is why we can say along with Paul:

> Christ shall even now, as always, be exalted in my
> body, whether by life or by death. (Phil. 1:20b)

How big is your God? Have you limited Him according to your own limitations? Have you stopped praying because you've stopped trusting? Mark today as the dawn of a deeper faith in the One who balances the earth on His fingertip, yet stoops to touch a leper.

 Living Insights STUDY ONE

Leprosy has long been a poignant illustration of sin's wasting effects in a person's life. Author Ken Gire aptly describes the nature of the disease:

> It begins with little specks on the eyelids and on the palms of the hand. Then it spreads over the body. It bleaches the hair white. It casts a cadaverous pallor over the skin, crusting it with scales and erupting over it with oozing sores.
> But that's just what happens on the surface. Penetrating the skin, the disease, like a moth, eats its way through the weave of nerves reticulated throughout the body's tissues. Soon the body becomes numb to the point of sensory deprivation, numbed to both pleasure and pain. A toe can break, and it will register no pain. And sensing no pain, the leper will continue walking, only to worsen the break and hasten the infection. One by one the appendages of the leper suffer their fate against the hard edges of life.[6]

Like leprosy, sins of the flesh often start as small, unnoticeable specks. Slowly they spread, consuming more and more of our minds.

6. Ken Gire, *Incredible Moments with the Savior* (Grand Rapids, Mich.: Zondervan Publishing House, 1990), p. 31.

Eventually, we notice a bitter attitude encrusting the surface of our lives, a self-focused demeanor, a flared temper. But the worst damage is caused by sin's numbing effect on our conscience. No longer do we wince inside with pain when we do wrong. Our sin may be destroying ourselves and the relationships we hold most dear, yet we feel nothing.

Can you see sin's leprous effects anywhere in your life? If so, in what ways?

_____

_____

_____

How do you imagine Jesus would touch those areas? Do you fear He might shame or ridicule you? What does His treatment of the leper in Luke 5 say to you?

_____

_____

_____

Could it be that He wants to touch you through someone close to you? Your spouse? Your parents? Your friend? Your pastor? Would you be willing to reveal your sin to one of these people so you can feel Christ's understanding and help?

_____

_____

_____

A big God is able to cleanse our sin, no matter how shameful. He can sensitize our consciences; He can restore our spirit. Won't you draw near to Him today?

 Living Insights

A big God is also able to revive a person paralyzed by legalism. According to A. W. Tozer,

The essence of legalism is self-atonement. The seeker tries to make himself acceptable to God by some act of restitution, or by self-punishment or the feeling of regret.[7]

To the legalist bound by a system of rules and regulations, Jesus, in His limitless mercy, says, "Come to Me in faith as the paralytic did. I accept you as you are. I forgive you."

Christ's forgiveness frees us from guilt. It loosens the chains of fear. It liberates us to accept and forgive others. In his sermon at Antioch, Paul announced,

> "Therefore let it be known to you, brethren, that through Him forgiveness of sins is proclaimed to you, and through Him everyone who believes is freed from all things, from which you could not be freed through the Law of Moses." (Acts 13:38–39)

Has legalism paralyzed your spirit? Have you lost your ability to love and laugh and enjoy the life God has given you? Do you fear God's retribution if you waver in keeping your list?

_____

_____

_____

Do you evaluate others by your list? Do you have difficulty accepting those who don't measure up?

_____

_____

_____

Drink deeply from Christ's cup of forgiveness. Pour it over your face. Let it drip from your hair and soak your skin and fill your shoes. Drench yourself in His mercy! It will bring you life.[8]

7. A. W. Tozer, _Signposts: A Collection of Sayings from A. W. Tozer_, comp. Harry Verploegh (Wheaton, Ill.: Scripture Press Publications, Victor Books, 1988), p. 116.

8. If you are interested in learning more about God's wonderful grace and freedom from legalism, we encourage you to read Chuck Swindoll's _The Grace Awakening_ (Dallas, Tex.: Word Publishing, 1990).

Chapter 15

IS IT OK TO PARTY WITH SINNERS?

Luke 5:27–39

Mark Twain, with a twinkle in his eye, once said,

> Having spent considerable time with good people,
> I can understand why Jesus liked to be with tax
> collectors and sinners.[1]

We know what Twain was talking about, don't we? Christians who plume their righteousness like peacock feathers can be annoying—even to fellow believers.

Yet we still tend to build our own little Christian world. We choose Christian doctors, follow Christian celebrities, prefer Christian hairdressers—who give our hair a Christian curl. We attach Christian stickers to the cars we buy from Christian dealers. We read Christian books, listen to Christian radio, watch Christian TV . . . and on and on.

What's going on with us?

A Few Candid Comments about Most Christians' Social Life

Most of us were closer to more non-Christians at the time we were saved than we are now. Our worlds and interests were the same, until we became Christians. Then many of us removed ourselves from that world as quickly as possible. That led to our re-creating our own world—which quite often is a small, protected bubble we can control.

It's understandable why, after being washed clean by Christ, we'd want to avoid all worldly associations. After all, didn't Paul say to "clean out the old leaven" and not "associate with immoral people" (1 Cor. 5:7, 9)? If we read on, though, he explains just who he means by "immoral people":

> I did not at all mean with the immoral people of

---

1. Mark Twain, as quoted by Haddon W. Robinson in *The Christian Salt & Light Company* (Grand Rapids, Mich.: Discovery House Publishers, 1988), p. 59.

this world, or with the covetous and swindlers, or with idolaters; for then you would have to go out of the world. But actually, I wrote to you not to associate with any so-called brother if he should be an immoral person, or covetous, or an idolater, or a reviler, or a drunkard, or a swindler—not even to eat with such a one. (vv. 10–11)

Clearly, the context is church discipline. Paul is not advising us to sever all ties to our non-Christian friends. He's telling us to cut our fellowship with carnal Christians in the hope that they might return to the Lord. Christ's gospel might actually be better served if we stopped hanging around with immoral believers and started hanging around with *unbelievers* instead.

Which is exactly what Jesus did.

A Surprising Discovery: Jesus with the Sinners

Never tentative, as Luke continues to show, Jesus went directly where any respectable Jew would have feared to tread.

Calling a Man Named Levi

And after that He went out, and noticed a tax-gatherer named Levi, sitting in the tax office, and He said to him, "Follow Me." And he left everything behind, and rose and began to follow Him. (Luke 5:27–28)

In only a moment Levi, also known as Matthew, weighed his life as a tax-gatherer against the promise of a life with Jesus. As a tax-gatherer he was considered a traitor, for he earned his bread by taking money from fellow Jews, giving the Romans their due, and hoarding what he overcharged.[2] To follow Jesus, he would be trading a business gold mine for an uncertain life on the road. But Jesus was offering him the bread of life, an eternal and honest treasure.

Without hesitation, the scales in his heart tipped toward Jesus. He grabbed his coat, locked his office door, and never returned. Christ had once again touched an outcast and drawn him near.

---

2. William Barclay tells us that "robbers, murderers and tax-collectors were classed together. A tax-collector was barred from the synagogue." *The Gospel of Luke*, rev. ed., The Daily Study Bible Series (Philadelphia, Pa.: Westminster Press, 1975), p. 64.

Answering a Group of Legalists

Bursting with generosity and gratitude, Levi threw a reception for Jesus and His disciples in his richly appointed home. It must have been a party to end all parties, with music and dancing and the finest food and drink.

> And Levi gave a big reception for Him in his house; and there was a great crowd of tax-gatherers and other people who were reclining at the table with them. (v. 29)

Peeking through the doorway, however, was a group of high-brow Pharisees and scribes who were standing with their arms crossed, disgusted by what they saw.

> And the Pharisees and their scribes began grumbling at His disciples, saying, "Why do you eat and drink with the tax-gatherers and sinners?" (v. 30)

The Greek word for *grumbling* is gogguzō—the word sounds like someone grumbling, doesn't it? Do you ever gogguzō about what you see non-Christians doing? Pass a nightclub overflowing with partiers—gogguzō. The neighbors throw a big bash next door—gogguzō. A person nearby lights up a cigarette—gogguzō! It's not an issue of our convictions about these behaviors as much as our attitude toward the people. Jesus made sinners feel welcome in His presence. Consequently, He felt welcome in theirs. The Pharisees, of course, made everyone uncomfortable.

Overhearing them grumble to His disciples, Jesus stepped in to answer their accusation:

> "It is not those who are well who need a physician, but those who are sick. I have not come to call the righteous but sinners to repentance." (vv. 31–32)

Jesus nimbly wrapped His firm rebuke in a tongue-in-cheek compliment. His statement implied that the Pharisees were the healthy ones who didn't need to repent. But He knew their hearts. Their righteousness was really self-righteousness—a thin veneer of purity stretched across an ailing soul. As long as they refused to reveal their true condition, Jesus couldn't cure them. Sadly, hypocrites are the hardest to show grace to.

A Stimulating Defense: Jesus with the Grumblers

Having drawn the guest of honor away from His own party, the fretting Pharisees tried throwing a religious wet blanket on the whole affair.

A Criticism

> And they said to Him, "The disciples of John often fast and offer prayers; the disciples of the Pharisees also do the same; but Yours eat and drink." (v. 33)

Attached to their backhanded criticism was a tradition of fasting that defined their version of true spirituality. Each Monday and Thursday, from sunrise to sunset, they would sanctimoniously deny themselves food—having first whitened their faces so everyone could see what haggard martyrs they were.[3]

Jesus, of course, wasn't against fasting. But He was opposed to hypocrisy and to any tradition becoming set in concrete, for when that happens, hardened traditionalism is formed.

> By *traditionalism* we mean an attitude that resists change, adaptation, or alteration. It clutches tradition so tightly that the blood supply to our spiritual brain is cut off, distorting vision and blurring the distinction between custom and commandment. Traditionalism is suspicious and censorious of the new, the innovative, the different.[4]

Jesus told the Pharisees, "Loosen up your legalistic girdles!" Sure, there's a time to fast, but there's also a time to feast.

A Response

> And Jesus said to them, "You cannot make the attendants of the bridegroom fast while the bridegroom is with them, can you? But the days will come; and when the bridegroom is taken away from them, then they will fast in those days." (vv. 34–35)

In His response, Jesus gives us the first hint concerning His

---

3. See Barclay, *The Gospel of Luke*, p. 66.

4. This section is from the study guide *Living Above the Level of Mediocrity*, rev. ed., coauthored by Ken Gire, from the Bible-teaching ministry of Charles R. Swindoll (Anaheim, Calif.: Insight for Living, 1994), p. 91.

tragic destiny. The sorrowful days of the Cross would come, but now, it was time to celebrate.

The Pharisees, however, remained stuck in the mud of traditionalism. So Jesus tried pulling them free with a parable that illustrates the wisdom of letting go of the old when God is doing something new.

A Parable

> And He was also telling them a parable: "No one tears a piece from a new garment and puts it on an old garment; otherwise he will both tear the new, and the piece from the new will not match the old." (v. 36)

Anyone who grew up with unshrunk denim jeans and 100 percent cotton shirts can easily decipher this parable.[5] Patch an old, shrunken garment with a new, unwashed piece of cloth and the patch will pull away from the garment when it's washed.

Here, the old garments are the hand-me-downs of traditionalism. In an attempt to iron out the interpretation of God's Law, the Pharisees had added over six hundred new wrinkles. Like too much starch added to the wash, these rigid rules chafed the very people they sought to clothe.

To add even more punch to His message, Jesus draws a metaphor from the festive occasion.

> "And no one puts new wine into old wineskins; otherwise the new wine will burst the skins, and it will be spilled out, and the skins will be ruined. But new wine must be put into fresh wineskins. And no one, after drinking old wine wishes for new; for he says, 'The old is good enough.'" (vv. 37–39)

If you take freshly made wine and pour it into an old, worn, brittle wineskin, you're in for a leaky surprise. It won't be long, thanks to the fermentation process, before chemical changes in the wine will cause the bag to stretch like a balloon and finally burst.

The old, traditional skin of Judaism was simply too brittle for the new wine of God's kingdom that Jesus was offering. Judaism had become so inflexible that it was not a supple enough womb to give birth to this new era of God's grace. And so attached were the Jews to the wineskins of tradition that they actually preferred their

5. This section is adapted from Gire, *Living Above the Level of Mediocrity*, pp. 93–94.

stiff, empty wineskins to the full, festive truth of the gospel.

Two Challenges That Will Require Risking

It's easy for us to point our fingers at the crusty Pharisees and their binding traditions. But sometimes our encrusted ways of doing things can be just as rigid as theirs. Unless we learn to flex in the nonessentials, the ever fresh and relevant gospel will burst our old wineskin forms.

So how can we flex? Here are a couple of stretching challenges. First, *try moving closer to the unsaved.* Take some interest in their lives. Meet them on their turf. Enter their world. For many of us, it may require a deliberate effort to connect with neighbors or renew old friendships. Stepping outside the Christian bubble may feel uncomfortable at first, but don't be afraid; Christ is there.

Second, *try new ways of reaching and winning the lost.* If we are the hands of Jesus, the Great Physician who came to heal sinners, then we must not be afraid of adventurous thought. One writer pointedly asks, "How would medicine fare if doctors were restricted to drugs and methods and techniques three hundred years old?"[6] And we might ask ourselves: How might the gospel fare if we use irrelevant methods to communicate it? Be open to new, creative ideas. Soften up your wineskins for Christ's hearty and flavorful new wine.

 Living Insights STUDY ONE

The Pharisees perfected the holier-than-thou attitude. According to William Barclay, they "would not even let the skirt of their robe touch the like of Matthew."[7]

How's your attitude toward unbelievers? Do you ever gather up your skirts and turn away when someone comes near with a cigarette or a beer or a rough-edged demeanor?

Certainly, Jesus didn't approve of tax-gatherers' thieving lifestyles, but He was able to look past Levi's reputation and see Him as a potential disciple. If you were to look past your non-Christian neighbors' unsavory habits, what would you see? List a few names of unsaved people you know, and jot down the qualities that would

6. Harry Emerson Fosdick, as quoted by Barclay in *The Gospel of Luke*, p. 68.

7. Barclay, *The Gospel of Luke*, p. 65.

make them faithful disciples of Christ.

_____

_____

_____

_____

The next time you talk with these friends, picture them through Christ's eyes of grace. Perhaps they will be the next Matthews to hear the call and follow Him.

Living Insights   STUDY TWO

There must be more ways to communicate the good news of Christ than there are flavors of ice cream. Think of the various art mediums used by Christians today. Think of all the church service styles and witnessing strategies. How flexible are you when it comes to different ways of spreading the gospel, or are you a one-flavor Christian?

_____

_____

To Paul, what was the most important issue when he found out that some Christians were preaching Christ in a questionable manner (see Phil. 1:18)?

_____

_____

Do you share Paul's attitude? What can you do to become more open and flexible, while making sure that Christ is proclaimed?

_____

_____

_____

_____

Chapter 16

THE DEFIANT CHRIST
Luke 6:1–11

O ne thing to the credit of the Pharisees is that they knew the value of a good fence. Author William Coleman describes how they used fences to keep moral people away from immorality's ledge and safely within the green pasture of God's law.

> The Pharisees were desperately determined to not break the laws of God. Consequently they devised a system to keep them from even coming close to angering God. They contrived a "fence" of Pharisaic rules that, if man would keep them, would guarantee a safe distance between himself and the laws of God. Therefore, if God said we could not work on the Sabbath, then don't even pick grain to eat, just to play it safe. Don't even heal people because that might be a borderline case.[1]

Problems arise, however, when hedges like these start overshadowing the people and the laws they were built to protect. When that happens,

> we are no longer wrestling with the core problems of drunkenness and adultery. Rather we are fighting mock battles at the new fences we have erected. Now the new laws become the really important battlegrounds. Soon we will test a person's orthodoxy by his respect for the fences.[2]

In other words, we start erecting fences to keep us from the fences! Eventually, we feel like wild mustangs in a pigpen—so hemmed in that we can't run free in the open ranges of life that God in His grace has provided us.

When that happens, is it OK to push against the confines? Is it appropriate to defy some of the restrictions? Is it ever right to rebel?

---

1. William L. Coleman, *The Pharisees' Guide to Total Holiness* (Minneapolis, Minn.: Bethany House Publishers, 1977), p. 8.

2. Coleman, *Pharisees' Guide*, p. 9.

Is It Ever Right to Rebel?

If the apostles hadn't rebelled against the strictures of the high priests (see Acts 3–5), the light of Christ's hope might have been extinguished and all our centuries since left in darkness. But because they stood against false limits, their response has become a north star for generations of Christians looking for guidance in similar situations:

> But Peter and the apostles answered and said, "We must obey God rather than men." (5:29)

The principle is this: *When a man-made command contradicts a God-given truth, defiance is appropriate.*

Guided by this principle, William Wilberforce challenged the laws in England that sanctioned slavery and the barbaric slave trade. By it, Abraham Lincoln fought to rid the United States of the same blight. And by it, Jesus Christ defiantly stood toe-to-toe against an enslaving religious system.

Does it seem sacrilegious to say that Jesus was ever defiant? It certainly flies in the face of our modern images of a pale, meek Jesus. Yet think of the audacious things He did:

- He violently drove out the temple money changers (John 2:13–17).

- He fiercely denounced religious leaders as "hypocrites," "blind guides," and "fools" (Matt. 23:13–36).

- He unflinchingly stood up to powerful rulers (Luke 23:8–12).

What raised His righteous dander more than anything were the Pharisees' fastidious regulations, which they had constructed to dominate the people and elevate themselves. Jesus kicked against these repressive barriers, finding their weak points and knocking them down so people could escape to freedom in God's grace.

The highest and most guarded of the Pharisees' fences concerned the Sabbath. Upon this ground Jesus and His critics fought their most intense battles.

Two Sabbaths . . . When Christ Defied the Authorities

Our passage in Luke highlights two of Jesus' Sabbath confrontations. Because the issues may seem a little foreign to us, let's dig into some background information.

Sabbath roots go deep, all the way down to the bedrock of

Creation. After six days of fashioning stars and filling the earth with creatures, God rested on the seventh day as an example for us to follow.

> Then God blessed the seventh day and sanctified it, because in it He rested from all His work which God had created and made. (Gen. 2:3)

He *sanctified*—"set apart"—the seventh day of the week for us as a time of rest and refreshment.[3] Later, God etched this same principle into the tablets of the Ten Commandments:

> "Remember the sabbath day, to keep it holy. Six days you shall labor and do all your work, but the seventh day is a sabbath of the Lord your God; in it you shall not do any work, you or your son or your daughter, your male or your female servant or your cattle or your sojourner who stays with you." (Exod. 20:8–10)

Centuries passed. By the time the Pharisees in Jesus' day inherited this simple commandment, God's merciful principle of rest had grown into a merciless tangle of rules. The legalists had succeeded in squeezing the joy out of God's gift to His people.

Of the hundreds of Sabbath regulations that snared the Jews, four are particularly pertinent to our passage. On the Sabbath, Jews must refrain from all work, including reaping, threshing, winnowing, and preparing food. Unknowingly, the disciples would break all four regulations, and, of course, the patrolling morality police would be right there to catch them red-handed.

Rubbing and Eating Wheat

> Now it came about that on a certain Sabbath He was passing through some grainfields; and His disciples were picking and eating the heads of grain, rubbing them in their hands. But some of the Pharisees said, "Why do you do what is not lawful on the Sabbath?" (Luke 6:1–2)

---

3. The seventh day of the week is Saturday, the day Jews acknowledge as the Sabbath. Early in the history of the church, Christians started meeting on the first day of the week, Sunday, probably to honor the day of Christ's resurrection (see Acts 20:7; John 20:1–2).

On any other day, snacking on a neighbor's grain was lawful, as long as you picked the kernels and didn't use a sickle (see Deut. 23:25). But this was the Sabbath. William Barclay shows how they had crossed the Pharisees' line:

> By plucking the corn [the disciples] were guilty of reaping; by rubbing it in their hands of threshing; by flinging away the husks of winnowing; and the very fact that they ate it showed that they had prepared food on the Sabbath. To us the whole thing seems fantastic; but we must remember that to a strict Pharisee this was deadly sin.[4]

Of course, the disciples were well within the requirements of God's law, but the Pharisees' list of right and wrong stretched much longer than God's. Jesus' men had violated code 146b, section 42, paragraph 16, line 4, subclause 16d of the Sabbath Protection Act of A.D. 12! The Pharisees were just doing their duty to haul in these lawbreakers.

We marvel at the picky Pharisees, but we have to admit that sometimes we can be just as judgmental when someone violates our code of conduct. We all have our lists; we've all built our fences, based on personal convictions. Although they're vital to our own walk with God, we must remember that they are not God's law. We have no right to force them on others.

If anyone was an expert in God's law, Jesus was. His answer turned the legal tables on the Pharisees and at the same time taught them a lesson about who He was.

> And Jesus answering them said, "Have you not even read what David did when he was hungry, he and those who were with him, how he entered the house of God, and took and ate the consecrated bread which is not lawful for any to eat except the priests alone, and gave it to his companions?" And He was saying to them, "The Son of Man is Lord of the Sabbath." (vv. 3–5)

Jesus had created the Sabbath. How dare they question what

---

4. William Barclay, *The Gospel of Luke*, rev. ed., The Daily Study Bible Series (Philadelphia, Pa.: Westminster Press, 1975), pp. 69–70.

He could and could not do! Besides, if it was all right for David to eat holy bread because he was starving, surely His hungry disciples could glean a little food on the Sabbath.

According to Mark's gospel, Jesus added, "The Sabbath was made for man, and not man for the Sabbath" (Mark 2:27). God designed the Sabbath to serve the people's need for rest, but who could rest with all these regulations to follow? As often happens with legalists, the Pharisees couldn't see the forest of the principle for the trees of their rules.

Healing a Withered Hand

The battle between Jesus and the legalists escalated in a later incident. This time Jesus went out of His way to challenge their man-made traditions.

> And it came about on another Sabbath, that He entered the synagogue and was teaching; and there was a man there whose right hand was withered. And the scribes and the Pharisees were watching Him closely, to see if He healed on the Sabbath, in order that they might find reason to accuse Him. But He knew what they were thinking, and He said to the man with the withered hand, "Rise and come forward!" And he rose and came forward. (Luke 6:8)

By now, the lines had been clearly drawn. The hardened Pharisees would try with all their might to confine Jesus' new wine within the stiff wineskins of their traditions. Yet Jesus could not be contained. Knowing their hearts, He posed a question that said as much about their injurious motives as it did about His benevolent intentions.

> And Jesus said to them, "I ask you, is it lawful on the Sabbath to do good, or to do harm, to save a life, or to destroy it?" And after looking around at them all, He said to him, "Stretch out your hand!" And he did so; and his hand was restored. (vv. 9–10)

Like a lion being pelted with rocks, Jesus defiantly glared into the eyes of each of the Pharisees; then, without blinking, He roared—and the man was healed instantly.

Really, though, who was more defiant—Jesus or the Pharisees? They were more loyal to their system than to God. They gave more value to their rules than to people. And by their response, they were more determined to preserve their ways than to serve the living God.

Response of Opposition

In the next verse, Luke pulls back the Pharisees' curtain of piety and reveals their true, defiant nature.

> But they themselves were filled with rage, and discussed together what they might do to Jesus. (v. 11)

Here we've come upon a milestone. For the first time, Jesus' enemies started considering the unthinkable. Mark tells us more specifically that they began

> taking counsel with the Herodians against Him, as to how they might destroy Him. (Mark 3:6)

Remember Jesus' question? "I ask you, is it lawful . . . to save a life, or to destroy it?" It's amazing to us that the Pharisees didn't see their own hypocrisy as they walked away contemplating murder.

The Next Time You Wonder about Being Defiant

Jesus' example of defiance against legalism may be inviting you to break loose from some man-made restrictions and head for the open pastures of grace. But before you kick down the fences, temper your response by heeding a few words of wisdom.

Analyze the issue. This requires discernment. Is the issue worth fighting about or, perhaps, splitting a church over? Often, simply agreeing to disagree can settle things without a head-to-head confrontation.

Watch your motive. This takes honesty. Jesus' motive for defying the Sabbath codes was to clarify the difference between God's law and the Pharisee's traditions and between His authority and theirs. What is your purpose in challenging the restriction? Is it as pure?

Pray for wisdom. This takes courage. Just because you're doing the right thing in knocking down a long-standing fence doesn't mean you'll be protected from retaliation. Look what happened to Jesus. In prayer you'll gain the patience and fortitude to step into the fray. You'll also find the insight to separate the essentials from the nonessentials and the graciousness to defy the law while loving the legalist.

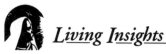 *Living Insights*

Fences can save your life. Anyone who has driven across a high bridge knows the value of those iron protectors lining the sides. In the same way, we all need moral protectors in our lives to keep us from weaving too close to the edge. But we must be careful not to force our fences on others. If it's not prohibited in Scripture, who are we to say that a certain activity is off-limits for someone else?

Have you been tempted to look down on others for stepping across the lines you've set for yourself? If so, in what ways?

_____

_____

_____

Does Matthew 7:1–5 take on new meaning for you in light of this study? How?

_____

_____

_____

Do you need to apologize to someone for your attitude toward them? What do you need to say to that person?

_____

_____

_____

 Living Insights

Usually, we don't recognize that we've been living under the roof of legalism until we breathe the fresh air of grace. We get used to others telling us what we should look like, who we should talk to, and how we should handle every situation. But one day we realize that God only gave ten commandments, not a hundred and ten—and we begin to understand that Christ's yoke really is easy and His load really is light (see Matt. 11:28–30).

Are you living under a burden of religious rules and expectations right now? What is it like to live that way?

_____

_____

_____

Paul's question to the Galatian Christians living under the thumb of legalism is a good one to ask yourself: "Am I striving to please men?" (see Gal. 1:10). What is your answer?

_____

_____

_____

How does 1 Corinthians 4:3–4 shift your focus?

_____

_____

_____

Breaking out of legalism's bondage may be frightening for you—living by grace feels risky. Just keep in mind who your Judge is, and seek to love Him "with all your heart, and with all your soul, and with all your mind, and with all your strength" (Mark 12:30).

Chapter 17

THE TWELVE . . . AND THEIR MARCHING ORDERS

Luke 6:12–26

W hen Napoleon set out to conquer the world, he amassed a vast army and razed a continent. When Marx and Engels conspired to create a new social order, they published *The Communist Manifesto* and altered the lives of millions. But when Christ answered the Father's call to change the course of history, He chose a different method. He didn't rally an army or publicize His theories. Nor did He run for office or seek the favor of kings. "His concern," wrote Robert Coleman, author of the pivotal book, *The Master Plan of Evangelism*,

> was not with programs to reach the multitudes, but with men whom the multitudes would follow.[1]

In short, His method was *discipleship*.

Building a Case for Discipleship

Jesus not only subscribed to this method personally, He advocated it for His followers: "Go therefore and make disciples of all the nations" (Matt. 28:19a). This verse may be familiar to us because of the missions banners that hang in our churches, but its meaning can be a bit mysterious. Exactly what does it mean to "make disciples"?

What It Is

Disciple-making, or discipleship, is a meaningful, hands-on relationship between a person who is qualified and willing to be a mentor and a few who desire to grow stronger in character and deeper in the Christian walk.

A qualified mentor would be any mature believer willing to invest the time to help a less mature Christian grow spiritually. Usually, men should mentor men and women should mentor women

---

1. Robert E. Coleman, *The Master Plan of Evangelism* (Grand Rapids, Mich.: Baker Book House, Fleming H. Revell Co., 1993), p. 27.

to allow for a deeper level of understanding. The goal of discipleship is godly character development, which is best accomplished through modeling. We learn patience, for example, by observing another person displaying that quality in the fray of everyday living. One life rubbing off on another life in an atmosphere of freedom, grace, acceptance, sharing, and discovery—that's discipleship.

What It Is Not

Now let's look at the flip side—what discipleship is not. First, it is not a short-term process. We grow slowly, like trees. It takes time for spiritual habits to take root and character qualities to blossom.

Second, discipleship cannot occur long-distance. It thrives on up-close, hands-on involvement.

Third, for that reason, discipleship is not formal, it's relational. There may be times when we learn more by setting aside the manuals and just talking about life.

Fourth, discipleship is not theoretical, it's practical. Knowing about God's grace is one thing, but being able to draw upon His grace daily is far more important.

Fifth, discipleship is not one person controlling another. At first, the concept of being discipled sounds threatening, like being brainwashed. But discipling is more like coaching; it does not involve control but encouragement.

Sixth, along those same lines, discipleship involves less teaching than it does training. Dispensing lectures is not discipling. Equipping others is more the idea—and that takes place best in an environment of interaction and dialogue.

Finally, discipleship is not completing a course. No one becomes a "certified disciple" by graduating from a program or finishing a workbook. You'll never receive a grade as a disciple—how can you measure maturity? But you will sense a higher degree of stability and discernment in your life. And, hopefully, you'll be growing more and more like Christ.

Observing Jesus' Method

Christ's own unlikely group of disciples set the world on fire with His gospel. Let's observe Jesus selecting and training His men so we can learn how it's done by the very best.

How He Prepared for It

While Jesus' ministry was still in its infancy, He determined to invest His life in others so they could carry on His work after Him. These individuals would be His most trusted friends, the ones into whom He would pour His life and vision. But whom should He select out of the sea of people awash around Him? It was a critical decision requiring the kind of wisdom that comes only through prayer. Luke writes that, "He went off to the mountain to pray, and He spent the whole night in prayer to God" (Luke 6:12).

Perhaps you once wrestled late into the night trying to make a decision. You prayed. You paced. You thought. You prayed some more. By morning's light, though, you knew what you needed to do, and you felt confident and decisive.

That's how Jesus felt the next day when the sun brightened the sky and skirted away any cloud of doubt as to the men the Father wanted Him to choose.

The Actual Selection of the Twelve

> And when day came, He called His disciples to Him; and chose twelve of them, whom He also named as apostles. (v. 13)

In a parallel passage, Mark tells us that Jesus chose certain men so that "they might be *with Him*" (Mark 3:14b, emphasis added). Their school would be the road Jesus traveled; their classroom, His campfire; and their guide, Jesus Himself. They would be His *mathētēs*—"disciples, learners." But learning was only the beginning. His goal was to "send them out" to carry on His ministry (v. 14c). Each would become an *apostolos*—"a messenger, one sent on a mission."[2]

The following chart shows the twelve men Jesus selected, as they appear in the four New Testament lists. Why did Jesus choose these twelve? What stands out about them? Well, from a human point of view . . . not a lot!

> For the most part they were common laboring men, probably having no professional training beyond the rudiments of knowledge necessary for their vocation. Perhaps a few of them came from families of some considerable means, such as the sons of Zebedee, but none of them could have been considered wealthy. They had no academic degrees in the arts and

2. G. Abbott-Smith, *A Manual Greek Lexicon of the New Testament*, 3d ed. (Edinburgh, Scotland: T. and T. Clark, 1937), p. 55.

The Twelve Disciples

The original twelve disciples of Jesus are mentioned in four lists in the New Testament. The lists could be divided into three groups each, with Peter heading the first group; Philip, the second; and James, the third. In all the lists each group has the same persons, but after the first name there is variety in the order. In all four lists, Peter is at the top and Judas Iscariot is at the bottom . . . except in the fourth list where he is omitted.

	Matthew 10:2–4	Mark 3:16–19	Luke 6:14–16	Acts 1:13
1.	SIMON PETER (elsewhere called Cephas)			
2.	Andrew	James	Andrew	John
3.	James	John	James	James
4.	John	Andrew	John	Andrew
5.	PHILIP			
6.	Bartholomew	Bartholomew	Bartholomew	Thomas
7.	Thomas	Matthew	Matthew	Bartholomew
8.	Matthew	Thomas	Thomas	Matthew
9.	JAMES, SON OF ALPHAEUS			
10.	Thaddaeus	Thaddaeus	Simon the Zealot	Simon the Zealot
11.	Simon the Cananaean	Simon the Cananaean	Judas, James' son	Judas, James' son
12.	Judas Iscariot	Judas Iscariot	Judas Iscariot	—

NOTE: Several disciples were called other names. For example, Thaddaeus and Judas, son of James, are one and the same. The same applies to Simon the Cananaean who is also called Simon the Zealot. Bartholomew is called Nathanael in John 1:45. Thomas is called Didymus ("twin") in John 11:16; 20:24, and 21:2. James is called "the Less" in Mark 15:40. Matthew is called Levi in Luke 5:27, 29. Judas is identified as Judas Iscariot, which probably means "man of Kerioth," a place ten miles from Hebron. If that is the meaning, Judas was from Judea . . . the only non-Galilean among the twelve original disciples.

Chart and copy adapted from W. Graham Scroggie, *A Guide to the Gospels* (London, England: Pickering Inglis, 1965), pp. 116–18.

philosophies of their day. . . . By any standard of sophisticated culture then and now they would surely be considered as a rather ragged aggregation of souls. One might wonder how Jesus could ever use them. They were impulsive, temperamental, easily offended, and had all the prejudices of their environment. . . . Not the kind of group one would expect to win the world for Christ.[3]

Yet, from the perspective of the One who sees the heart, they had the right stuff. They were available, flexible, teachable, and dependable.[4]

If you're thinking you could never make Christ's list, you might be surprised. Jesus sees beyond our faults and weaknesses to the person we can become. He finds the gemlike qualities inside us and polishes them until they shine for His glory. He's a master at doing the extraordinary with ordinary folks like us.

Vital Information for All Who Follow Christ

Right away, Jesus gave the Twelve their first taste of ministry as He descended to a "level place" on the side of the mountain (Luke 6:17). Standing by His side, they watched in amazement as He cured diseases and cast out demons. Many of His other disciples, as well as people from all over the nation, had flocked to this place and "were trying to touch Him, for power was coming from Him and healing them all" (v. 19).

Then, when all was silent, He delivered His greatest sermon, beginning with a series of beatitudes similar to those recorded in Matthew's gospel. His thesis was simple: Those who follow Him must operate under a set of values opposite that of the world. Those whom the world calls miserable, Jesus pronounces "blessed," or happy. The poor (v. 20)—or "poor in spirit" (see Matt. 5:3)—will receive the spiritual riches of God's kingdom. Those who hunger (Luke 6:21a)—or "hunger and thirst for righteousness" (see Matt. 5:6)—will be satisfied with God's truth. Those who weep

---

3. Coleman, *Master Plan of Evangelism*, pp. 28–29.

4. For further explanation of these four qualities, see "Beginning of Discipleship . . . Selection," from the study guide *Discipleship: Ministry Up Close and Personal*, coauthored by Lee Hough, from the Bible-teaching ministry of Charles R. Swindoll (Fullerton, Calif.: Insight for Living, 1990).

with compassion for the needy will laugh in the end (Luke 6:21b). Those who are hated and persecuted for His sake will "leap for joy, for behold, [their] reward is great in heaven" (v. 23).

Earthly sacrifices made for Christ pay rich dividends in heaven. But those who live selfishly receive their full reward in the present and set themselves up for future sorrow.

> "But woe to you who are rich, for you are receiving your comfort in full. Woe to you who are well-fed now, for you shall be hungry. Woe to you who laugh now, for you shall mourn and weep. Woe to you when all men speak well of you, for in the same way their fathers used to treat the false prophets." (vv. 24–26)

Jesus' sermon leads us to a crossroads. We must decide whether to pursue the wide path or the narrow path, the world's values or Christ's, immediate gratification or ultimate glorification. It's not an easy decision. Choosing Christ may open the door to insult and injury, and it may mean passing up some tantalizing, worldly delights. But however rocky the narrow trail gets, Jesus is there to satisfy our deepest hunger and bestow on us riches this world has never known. Which way will you choose?

Responding to These Things Today

In our passage, Luke showed us Jesus from three angles. We saw Him praying on the mountaintop, selecting His inner circle of disciples, and teaching the multitudes. Let's draw a line from each of these settings for corresponding areas of our lives today.

First, *when you feel unsure and indecisive, look up.* We sometimes use prayer as a last resort, to be tried only after human wisdom and efforts fail. Instead, *first* flee to the mountaintop, and only *then* face the decision.

Second, *when you need the right people, look within.* Perhaps you're pulling together a team for a particular purpose, or you're selecting someone for a close, spiritual relationship. Pay little attention to externals. Keep an eye out for inner qualities.

Third, *when you decide to follow Christ, look beyond.* The world places its highest value on what we see and touch. Look beyond those things to Christ's store of unseen riches. Remember Moses? Centuries before Jesus was born, he considered

> the reproach of Christ greater riches than the treasures

of Egypt; for he was looking to the reward. (Heb. 11:26)

May the same be said of us.

Living Insights

Most of us keep a list of our faults on hand for ready reference. If someone asks us for our strengths, though, we have to dig through the bottom drawer of our memories to come up with anything. So it's sometimes difficult to know why Jesus would want us as His disciples. We don't have the voice of a Billy Graham or the mind of a C. S. Lewis or the stirring testimony of a Corrie ten Boom.

But neither did the twelve disciples.

Do you feel unqualified to be Jesus' disciple? What reassurance do you gain from Jesus' selections for His inner circle?

_____

_____

_____

Can you imagine the thrill of being one of Jesus' disciples? What a privilege it was for them to be near Him day and night, watching Him do miracles, drinking in His teaching, and experiencing His grace firsthand. You *can* be His disciple if you want to. He said,

> "If you abide in My word, then you are truly disciples of Mine; and you shall know the truth, and the truth shall make you free." (John 8:31–32)

Would you like to be His disciple? Before answering too quickly, let's count the cost as we move into the next Living Insight.

Living Insights

In Jesus' mountainside sermon, Jesus tells us what a disciple can look forward to—trouble. You'll be richest when you're poor, fullest when you're hungry, happiest when you weep, and ecstatic when you're scorned.

Sounds like double-talk, doesn't it? The point is this: we are most fulfilled when we are depending upon Christ rather than ourselves or the things of this world. Trust in riches, and your spirit will go bankrupt. Trust in physical satisfaction, and your heart will go hungry. Trust in fun times, and your tears will flow when the party's over. Trust in people's opinions, and you'll fall prey to false teachers.

When you're poor, though, you're trusting Christ; when hungry, you're praying to Him; when mourning, you're leaning on Him like never before; when insulted, you're hoping in Him.

Is there anything you're depending on that is holding you back from trusting Christ no matter what happens?

Are you willing to transfer your complete trust to Him right now? What would you tell Him if you could talk to Him face-to-face? We've provided you some space to express your thoughts to the Lord.

We only covered the first part of Jesus' sermon in this chapter. Look at the next page for more compelling thoughts from our Lord!

Chapter 18

"ABSURD ADVICE" IN A SELFISH ERA

Luke 6:27–49

Bumper stickers say a lot about our philosophies of life—in ways we can all understand. You have to earn a college degree to untangle the meaning of "I exist, therefore I am." But everyone knows what the following sayings are talking about:

> Do unto Others *before* They Do unto You
> Don't Get Mad, Get Even
> Get All You Can, Can All You Get, Then Sit on
>   the Can!

One wonders if the chariots in Jesus' day sported slogans like these. People are people, then as now. Surely, our ancestors assented to the same philosophies of aggression, revenge, and greed.

Into our me-first world Jesus came to give us a telescopic view of another kingdom—an eternal place that turns our earthly system of values on its ear. Because this place is so foreign to us, Jesus' teaching about it sounds absurd . . . startling . . . extreme. But once we view life from His perspective, we begin to see that it's our way of thinking that's upside down, not His. He sets things aright.

Insightful Instruction for Jesus' Disciples

With the Beatitudes ("Blessed are you . . .") Jesus began His most famous sermon. He continues now with more radical counsel about how to respond to our enemies.

Radical Counsel

> "But I say to you who hear, love your enemies, do good to those who hate you, bless those who curse you, pray for those who mistreat you. Whoever hits you on the cheek, offer him the other also; and whoever takes away your coat, do not withhold your shirt from him either. Give to everyone who asks of you, and whoever takes away what is yours, do not demand it back." (Luke 6:27–30)

Can you imagine the hero in an action movie responding to his enemies with such kindness? The film would flop at the box office! We like to see him clobber those who curse him and return their slaps to his cheek with a right cross to their chops.

But if we'd think vertically instead of horizontally, our attitude toward real-life enemies would change. We would realize that they may face God's judgment some day for their misdeeds, and compassion would melt our revenge. Then we'd start doing the absurd, like praying for them.

Jesus isn't saying that we should throw out our justice system or allow others to strip away our dignity. Instead, He's saying, "Don't return verbal slap for verbal slap. Don't be quick to claim your rights and dial a lawyer. Don't become bitter. Don't be overly protective of your 'stuff.' Let things go. This world is passing away, and there are more important matters to dwell on, like learning how to treat others well."

Surprising Treatment

> "And just as you want people to treat you, treat them in the same way." (v. 31)

The Golden Rule knocks us off our couches of complacency and sends us into the world, offering others the same cup of kindness we would want them to offer us. And their antagonism, Jesus explains, is no excuse for us to stop giving.

> "And if you love those who love you, what credit is that to you? For even sinners love those who love them. And if you do good to those who do good to you, what credit is that to you? For even sinners do the same. And if you lend to those from whom you expect to receive, what credit is that to you? Even sinners lend to sinners, in order to receive back the same amount. But love your enemies, and do good, and lend, expecting nothing in return; and your reward will be great, and you will be sons of the Most High; for He Himself is kind to ungrateful and evil men." (vv. 32–35)

Our heavenly reward will outweigh any personal loss on earth, so we can afford to spill our love on our enemies, do good to them, and lend money to those in need.

Peter, who never forgot Jesus' sermon, taught this same principle years later with a slightly different twist:

> For what credit is there if, when you sin and are harshly treated, you endure it with patience? But if when you do what is right and suffer for it you patiently endure it, this finds favor with God. For you have been called for this purpose, since Christ also suffered for you, leaving you an example for you to follow in His steps. (1 Pet. 2:20–21)

Extraordinary Forgiveness

If following in Jesus' steps means anything, it means being able to forgive your enemies. And the basic building block of forgiveness is God's wonderful quality of mercy. "Be merciful," Jesus exhorts us, "just as your Father is merciful" (Luke 6:36). Be devoted children, and grow up just like your Father; show grace to those who least deserve it. Because, more often than not, they're the ones who most *need* it.

Jesus puts shoe leather on His point by giving some examples of mercy.

> "And do not judge and you will not be judged; and do not condemn, and you will not be condemned; pardon, and you will be pardoned. Give, and it will be given to you; good measure, pressed down, shaken together, running over, they will pour into your lap.[1] For by your standard of measure it will be measured to you in return." (vv. 37–38)

When we're merciful, we won't judge people, we won't condemn others, and we won't hold on to things. Jesus doesn't say, though, how or when the good deeds that we pour out will overflow into our laps. He just says they will. But if we're living by kingdom standards, we won't fret about what we get out of the deal. The Lord will repay us in His way and according to His timing.

---

1. "The picture is of grain poured into a container, pressed down and then shaken so that every little corner is filled and the grain is poured in until it runs over." In the same way, God will return to us our good favor toward others. Fritz Rienecker, *A Linguistic Key to the Greek New Testament*, ed. Cleon L. Rogers, Jr. (Grand Rapids, Mich.: Zondervan Publishing House, Regency Reference Library, 1980), p. 155.

Explanatory Parable

Jesus often colored His sermons with parables, or *parabolē*, which literally means something "thrown alongside." In this case, He strings together several images like pearls to form a parable necklace that He lays beside the truth He's been teaching.

> And He also spoke a parable to them: "A blind man cannot guide a blind man, can he? Will they not both fall into a pit? A pupil is not above his teacher; but everyone, after he has been fully trained, will be like his teacher." (vv. 39–40)

The point is this: if we wish to help others be virtuous, we must be virtuous ourselves. Otherwise, we'll be like the blind leading the blind. Jesus supports His point with a laughable exaggeration:

> "And why do you look at the speck that is in your brother's eye, but do not notice the log that is in your own eye? Or how can you say to your brother, 'Brother, let me take out the speck that is in your eye,' when you yourself do not see the log that is in your own eye? You hypocrite, first take the log out of your own eye, and then you will see clearly to take out the speck that is in your brother's eye." (vv. 41–42)

Jesus' sense of humor sparkles here. Imagine how ridiculous you would look with a log protruding out of your eye. People would have to duck every time you turned your head; you'd be knocking over lamps, bumping into doorjambs. But imagine that you are oblivious to the problem. Instead of getting rid of the log, you worry more about the next fellow with a tiny flake of a fault in his eye, a speck nobody notices but you.

That seems silly to us, but to Jesus, that's exactly what the hypocritical Pharisees were like. They were supposed to have been the nation's clear-eyed teachers of morality, respected men of the cloth. But all Jesus could see were logs of pride jutting from their faces. "First," Jesus was saying to them, "humbly deal with your own sin. Then you can help out a brother."

Unfortunately, all their religiosity was producing nothing but bad fruit. And there's only one reason for bad fruit: a bad tree.

> "For there is no good tree which produces bad fruit; nor, on the other hand, a bad tree which produces

good fruit. For each tree is known by its own fruit. For men do not gather figs from thorns, nor do they pick grapes from a briar bush. The good man out of the good treasure of his heart brings forth what is good; and the evil man out of the evil treasure brings forth what is evil; for his mouth speaks from that which fills his heart." (vv. 43–45)

The heart is the fountainhead of our lives. A pure heart, gushing with devotion to Christ, produces currents of goodwill; but a polluted heart, running over with selfishness, issues rivulets of jealousy that flow into streams of anger and bitterness.

Unusual Analogy

Jesus' sermon ends with a lightning bolt aimed right at the center of our lives.

"And why do you call Me, 'Lord, Lord,' and do not do what I say? Everyone who comes to Me, and hears My words, and acts upon them, I will show you whom he is like: he is like a man building a house, who dug deep and laid a foundation upon the rock; and when a flood rose, the torrent burst against that house and could not shake it, because it had been well built. But the one who has heard, and has not acted accordingly, is like a man who built a house upon the ground without any foundation; and the torrent burst against it and immediately it collapsed, and the ruin of that house was great." (vv. 46–49)

The secret to standing firm is not what's in our house nor in the quality of paint nor the elaborateness of the design. The secret is where we lay our foundation. There's no stronger bedrock than the truth Jesus preached. Wise people build their lives on it.

Personal Response from Jesus' Followers

What are you building your foundation on? Jesus' kingdom values? Or the bumper-sticker philosophies of this world?

The fact is, as much as we cherish our lives, many of the things we hold so dear will one day pass away. Those who spend their strength on the temporal are like children playing a board game. They roll the dice, collect the tokens, and try to beat out the other players. Eventually, though, the game ends, and the pieces are put away. It no longer matters who came in first or second or who wound up last. The only thing that really counts is what remains after the game is over.

What will remain after our game of life is through? Certainly not the revenge we thought would be so sweet; nor the toys we collected—they'll be sold to the highest bidder. Only the mercy we showed and the love we gave will last.

 Living Insights   STUDY ONE

Perspective is the difference between

a) riding in a roller coaster that is pitching and reeling like an out-of-control airplane and

b) riding in an out-of-control airplane that is pitching and reeling like a roller coaster.

The sensations may be similar, but in one case, you're screaming with delight, and in the other, you're screaming with terror. What's the difference? Perspective. You know that the surging roller coaster will return you safely to the platform. But you're not too sure where the airplane is taking you nor do you know if you'll be alive when you land there.

There's no doubt that life pitches us around. Trusted friends knock us for a loop. Competitors send us careening downward. Circumstances spin us at a dizzying speed.

Have things been topsy-turvy for you lately? Describe who or what has been making your life a whirling dervish.

_____

_____

_____

What has been your perspective? Have you been viewing these trials as an out-of-control plane ride with an uncertain future or a roller-coaster ride with a certain end?

_____

_____

Are you sure you know where your life is heading? If not, you can be. Read what Jesus says in John 5:24. How does His promise to deliver you safely to eternal life affect your perspective toward your present crises?

_____

_____

_____

Sure of your future, what specific things can you do this week to follow Christ's instructions in His sermon in Luke 6?

_____

_____

_____

Knowing where you're going can change your ups and downs from a frightening plane flight to a thrilling roller-coaster ride. It can free you to not take life's jostles so seriously. It can motivate you to give love to those you never thought you could. Perspective is everything.

 ## *Living Insights* STUDY TWO

Well, it's taken us eighteen chapters to study six chapters in the book of Luke. It may seem like we're "snailing" through the gospel, but look how far we've come.

We began by getting to know Luke as an author, then we followed Gabriel as he announced the coming of two special boys. We listened to Mary's beautiful song, we cheered when Zacharias named his boy John, and we knelt in wonder at the birth of Jesus. We marveled at the Boy when He confounded His professors. We repented when the Baptizer called us into account. We heard God's voice at Jesus' baptism. We felt His power in Jesus' miracles. We sensed His love in Jesus' words.

So far in His ministry, Jesus has managed to foil Satan, amass a huge following, call twelve devoted disciples, and stick a burr under the Pharisees' saddles. And this is just the beginning! We have three more study guides to cover eighteen more chapters of Luke's gospel.

Why don't you take this opportunity for a first-quarter break to review the principles you've learned so far. Thumb through the guide and pick the top five truths the Lord has been teaching you through your study of Christ's life. There may be many, but list just five. Then—in the spirit of Jesus' challenge for us not to simply call Him "Lord, Lord" and live as we please—write down what you plan to do about those principles. Don't say, "I'm going to get better at such-and-such"; try to be specific.

OK. Are you ready? Start thumbing!

Top Five Truths

1. _____

_____

2. _____

_____

3. _____

_____

4. _____

_____

5. _____

_____

My Plan of Action

_____

_____

_____

_____

_____

BOOKS FOR
PROBING FURTHER

Here are the symptoms: flabby faith muscles, weak heart for the less-fortunate, and joints a bit stiff with legalism.

Hmmm. Sounds like a case of the spiritual blahs. Luke's life of Christ is just what the doctor ordered to firm that faith, put a pounding passion in your heart, and free up those joints.

To supplement the doctor's prescription, we offer the following high-potency commentaries and devotionals that will enhance your understanding of Christ. Choose one or two and take small doses of them as often as you study Luke. You'll be recovering in no time!

Barclay, William. *The Gospel of Luke*. Revised edition. The Daily Study Bible Series. Philadelphia, Pa.: Westminster Press, 1975.

Gire, Ken. *Intimate Moments with the Savior: Learning to Love*. Grand Rapids, Mich.: Zondervan Publishing House, 1989.

Hendriksen, William. *Exposition of the Gospel according to Luke*. New Testament Commentary series. Grand Rapids, Mich.: Baker Book House, 1978.

Jesus: The Story Begins. Jesus and His Times series, vol. 1; 61 min. The Reader's Digest Association, 1991. Videocassette.

Lucado, Max. *God Came Near: Chronicles of the Christ*. Portland, Oreg.: Multnomah Press, 1987.

Some of these books may be out of print and available only through a library. For those currently available, please contact your local Christian bookstore. Books by Charles R. Swindoll may be obtained through Insight for Living. IFL also offers some books by other authors—please note the ordering information that follows and contact the office that serves you.

Ordering Information

The Origination of Something Glorious
Cassette Tapes and Study Guide

This Bible study guide was designed to be used independently or in conjunction with the broadcast of Chuck Swindoll's taped messages which are listed below. If you would like to order cassette tapes or further copies of this study guide, please see the information given below and the order form provided at the end of this guide.

		U.S.	Canada
OSG	Study guide	$ 4.95 ea.	$ 6.50 ea.
OSGCS	Cassette series, includes all individual tapes, album cover, and one complimentary study guide	62.20	73.50 ea.
OSG 1–9	Individual cassettes, includes messages A and B	6.30 ea.	8.00 ea.

The prices are subject to change without notice.

OSG 1-A: *The Doctor Gives a Second Opinion*—Survey of Luke
B: *Only the Best*—Luke 1:1–4

OSG 2-A: *A Baby? At Our Age? Get Serious!*—Luke 1:5–25
B: *The Day Mary Met Gabriel*—Luke 1:26–56

OSG 3-A: *The Prophet of the Most High*—Luke 1:57–80
B: *Nativity Revisited*—Luke 2:1–20

OSG 4-A: *A Sacrifice, a Savior, a Sword*—Luke 2:21–38
B: *The Day the Pupil Stumped the Profs*—Luke 2:39–52

OSG 5-A: *A Study in Contrasts*—Luke 3
B: *The Devil Never Made Him Do It*—Luke 4:1–13

OSG 6-A: *From the Frying Pan into the Fire*—Luke 4:14–30
B: *Ministry at the Grassroots Level*—Luke 4:31–44

OSG 7-A: *What It's Like to Fish with Jesus*—Luke 5:1–11
B: *Great Deeds, Strong Faith . . . Big God*—Luke 5:12–26

OSG 8-A: *Is It OK to Party with Sinners?*—Luke 5:27–39
B: *The Defiant Christ*—Luke 6:1–11

OSG 9-A: *The Twelve . . . and Their Marching Orders—*
Luke 6:12–26
B: *"Absurd Advice" in a Selfish Era—*Luke 6:27–49

How to Order by Phone or FAX
(Credit card orders only)

United States: 1-800-772-8888 from 7:00 A.M. to 4:30 P.M., Pacific time, Monday through Friday
FAX (714) 575-5496 anytime, day or night

Canada: 1-800-663-7639, Vancouver residents call (604) 596-2910 from 7:00 A.M. to 5:00 P.M., Pacific time, Monday through Friday
FAX (604) 596-2975 anytime, day or night

Australia: (03) 872-4606 or FAX (03) 874-8890 from 9:00 A.M. to 5:00 P.M., Monday through Friday

---

Other International Locations: call the Ordering Services Department in the United States at (714) 575-5000 during the hours listed above.

How to Order by Mail

United States
- Mail to: Ordering Services Department
  Insight for Living
  Post Office Box 69000
  Anaheim, CA 92817-0900
- Sales tax: California residents add 7.25%.
- Shipping: add 10% of the total order amount for first-class delivery. (Otherwise, allow four to six weeks for fourth-class delivery.)
- Payment: personal checks, money orders, credit cards (Visa, Master-Card, Discover Card, and American Express). No invoices or COD orders available.
- $10 fee for *any* returned check.

Canada
- Mail to: Insight for Living Ministries
  Post Office Box 2510
  Vancouver, BC V6B 3W7
- Sales tax: please add 7% GST. British Columbia residents also add 7% sales tax (on tapes or cassette series).
- Shipping: included in prices listed above.

- Payment: personal checks, money orders, credit cards (Visa, Master-Card). No invoices or COD orders available.
- Delivery: approximately four weeks.

Australia, New Zealand, or Papua New Guinea
- Mail to: Insight for Living, Inc.
  GPO Box 2823 EE
  Melbourne, Victoria 3001, Australia
- Shipping and delivery time: please see chart that follows.
- Payment: personal checks payable in U.S. funds, international money orders, or credit cards (Visa, MasterCard).

Other International Locations
- Mail to: Ordering Services Department
  Insight for Living
  Post Office Box 69000
  Anaheim, CA 92817-0900
- Shipping and delivery time: please see chart that follows.
- Payment: personal checks payable in U.S. funds, international money orders, or credit cards (Visa, MasterCard, and American Express).

Type of Shipping	Postage Cost	Delivery
Surface	10% of total order*	6 to 10 weeks
Airmail	25% of total order*	under 6 weeks

*Use U.S. price as a base.

Our Guarantee

Your complete satisfaction is our top priority here at Insight for Living. If you're not completely satisfied with anything you order, please return it for full credit, a refund, or a replacement, as *you* prefer.

Insight for Living Catalog

The Insight for Living catalog features study guides, tapes, and books by a variety of Christian authors. To obtain a free copy, call us at the numbers listed above.

Order Form
United States, Australia, and Other International Locations
(Canadian residents please use order form on reverse side.)

OSGCS represents the entire *Origination of Something Glorious* series in a special album cover, while OSG 1–9 are the individual tapes included in the series. OSG represents this study guide, should you desire to order additional copies.

OSG	Study guide	$ 4.95 ea.
OSGCS	Cassette series, includes all individual tapes, album cover, and one complimentary study guide	62.20
OSG 1–9	Individual cassettes, includes messages A and B	6.30 ea.

Product Code	Product Description	Quantity	Unit Price	Total
			$	$
	Subtotal			
	California Residents—Sales Tax *Add 7.25% of subtotal.*			
	U.S. First-Class Shipping *For faster delivery, add 10% for postage and handling.*			
	Non-United States Residents *U.S. price plus 10% surface postage or 25% airmail.*			
	Gift to Insight for Living *Tax-deductible in the United States.*			
	Total Amount Due *Please do not send cash.*		$	

Prices are subject to change without notice.

Payment by: ❏ Check or money order payable to Insight for Living   ❏ Credit card

(Circle one):   Visa   MasterCard   Discover Card   American Express

Number _____

Expiration Date _____   Signature _____
We cannot process your credit card purchase without your signature.

Name _____

Address _____

City _____   State _____

Zip Code _____   Country _____

Telephone (____) _____   Radio Station ____ ____ ____ ____
If questions arise concerning your order, we may need to contact you.

Mail this order form to the Ordering Services Department at one of these addresses:

Insight for Living
Post Office Box 69000, Anaheim, CA 92817-0900

Insight for Living, Inc.
GPO Box 2823 EE, Melbourne, VIC 3001, Australia

Order Form
Canadian Residents
(Residents of the United States, Australia, and other international locations,
please use order form on reverse side.)

OSGCS represents the entire *Origination of Something Glorious* series in a special album cover, while OSG 1–9 are the individual tapes included in the series. OSG represents this study guide, should you desire to order additional copies.

OSG	Study guide	$ 6.50 ea.
OSGCS	Cassette series,	73.50
	includes all individual tapes, album cover, and one complimentary study guide	
OSG 1–9	Individual cassettes,	8.00 ea.
	includes messages A and B	

Product Code	Product Description	Quantity	Unit Price	Total
			$	$
		Subtotal		
		Add 7% GST		
		British Columbia Residents *Add 7% sales tax on individual tapes or cassette series.*		
		Gift to Insight for Living Ministries *Tax-deductible in Canada.*		
		Total Amount Due *Please do not send cash.*	$	

Prices are subject to change without notice.

Payment by: ❑ Check or money order payable to Insight for Living Ministries
❑ Credit card

(Circle one): Visa   MasterCard   Number _____

Expiration Date _____ · Signature _____
We cannot process your credit card purchase without your signature.

Name _____

Address _____

City _____ Province _____

Postal Code _____ Country _____

Telephone (___) _____ Radio Station ____ ____ ____ ____
If questions arise concerning your order, we may need to contact you.

Mail this order form to the Ordering Services Department at the following address:

Insight for Living Ministries
Post Office Box 2510
Vancouver, BC, Canada V6B 3W7